VISUAL QUICKPRO GUIDE

UNIX ADVANCED

Chris Herborth

Peachpit Press

Visual QuickPro Guide
Unix Advanced
Chris Herborth

Peachpit Press
1249 Eighth Street
Berkeley, CA 94710
510/524-2178
800/283-9444
510/524-2221 (fax)

Find us on the Web at www.peachpit.com.
To report errors, please send a note to errata@peachpit.com.

Peachpit Press is a division of Pearson Education.
Copyright © 2005 by Chris Herborth
Editor: Whitney Walker
Production Editor: Becky Winter
Copy Editor: Elissa Rabellino
Technical Editors: David W. Aquilina and Martin Brown
Compositor: Kate Kaminski, Happenstance Type-O-Rama
Indexer: Julie Bess
Cover Design: The Visual Group

ISBN 0-321-20549-9

9 8 7 6 5 4 3 2 1

Printed and bound in the United States of America

Dedication

To my family, for all their love and for putting up with the way I vanished for a few months while writing this. Alex, thanks for being such a hilarious source of chaos. Lynette, you are my heart—thank you!

This Book Is Safari Enabled

The Safari® Enabled icon on the cover of your favorite technology book means the book is available through Safari Bookshelf. When you buy this book, you get free access to the online edition for 45 days.

Safari Bookshelf is an electronic reference library that lets you easily search thousands of technical books, find code samples, download chapters, and access technical information whenever and wherever you need it.

To gain 45-day Safari Enabled access to this book:

- Go to http://www.peachpit.com/safarienabled
- Complete the brief registration form
- Enter the coupon code KLQW-Y11Q-UMFB-L4P5-64BR

If you have difficulty registering on Safari Bookshelf or accessing the online edition, please e-mail customer-service@safaribooksonline.com.

Acknowledgments

There are quite a few people who need to be thanked. Without their help, I would never have finished this book with my sanity intact:

The tech editors, David W. Aquilina and Martin Brown, for catching my technical gaffes and omissions.

The folks at Peachpit: Cliff Colby (for tricking me into doing this), Elissa Rabellino (for her awesome editing powers and comprehensive double-checking), Rebecca Ross (for being patient with me and my Canada versus the IRS questions), and Whitney Walker (for shepherding the project and not yelling at me for being chronically late). I know I've left out the indexing and production crew, who also deserve some kudos for their excellent work.

The #beosghetto crew on Freenode's IRC network, for their free and timely technical support and random strangeness: Chris (Wyldfire), David (Mithrndir) and David (Beryllium), Geoff (DirtyWeaponry), Gord (Balatro), Ian (Xyverz), Kevin (Skorobeus), Mikael (tic), Thies (thies), and Wade (kurros). My apologies if I've left anyone out! Special thanks to Kevin's bot (Mamba) for randomly injecting surreal comments at inappropriate times.

The mighty Scot Hacker, for being the cause of all this when he declined Cliff's offer to write this book and sent him my way instead.

Finally, I'd like to thank my family for putting up with my erratic and stressed-out behavior for the past several months. Alex Woodward-Herborth, you're the best son anyone could wish for; thanks for reminding me to have fun. My lovely and talented wife, Lynette Woodward-Herborth, thanks for picking up my slack around the house and for letting me work insane hours to get things done (almost) on time.

TABLE OF CONTENTS

INTRODUCTION

With the explosion of home broadband connections to the Internet and the growing popularity of open-source software, Unix has become more common and popular among enthusiasts and people running home networks. Whether you're interested in a Unix operating system to run a home Web or file server, or you're considering using it at work, you're jumping in at a great time.

It used to be that only bearded, sandal-wearing gurus and computer-obsessed hermits knew anything about Unix, since it ran on expensive proprietary hardware and had a reputation for being inaccessible. But now anyone can run it on a desktop or laptop computer. And thanks to projects like Linux and FreeBSD, you won't have to pay a cent to give it a try.

By now you've been introduced to Unix as a user, possibly through the *Unix: Visual QuickStart Guide,* by Deborah S. Ray and Eric J. Ray, also published by Peachpit Press. The book you're holding now takes you to the next level, and it gets you up to speed on running things like Web, email, and database servers.

The Internet itself and all the major services it offers (such as email and the World Wide Web) were invented on Unix machines. Many other operating systems (such as Microsoft Windows XP) make use of Unix code to provide networking support. With the growth of home broadband and IT services at small companies, more people are interested in running Unix and in having their own servers.

Unix Defined

Possibly the only controversial thing in this book is my definition of Unix. Defining Unix has always been a bit of a challenge, something that true geeks will argue over for hours.

At one point, Unix ran only on exotic and expensive workstation and server hardware produced by an elite few companies. These days, you can run one or more flavors of free Unix on almost any kind of computer you can imagine.

Having worked for years at a company that makes a "Unix-like" microkernel operating system, I've been exposed to the POSIX standards that actually define, in excruciating detail, what a Unix system is and how it works.

My bold and controversial claim is that a "Unix" system is anything that implements these POSIX standards (specifically, POSIX 1003.1 and 1003.2), and I'll be covering four of these Unixen in this book.

Linux is a mishmash of features from other Unix systems, created because Linus Torvalds wanted a free operating system like Minix (a minimal Unix system used for teaching). Since then, Linux has been extended and expanded into one of the most popular Unix operating systems. Although it's never been officially tested or validated, it implements the POSIX APIs (application programming interfaces) and applications that define a Unix system.

FreeBSD is a direct descendant of the original BSD (Berkeley Software Distribution) Unix, and it has all of the POSIX programming APIs and command-line applications. Its "ports" system gives you access to almost every freely available Unix application in existence. FreeBSD is known for rock-hard stability and excellent network performance.

Many people view Microsoft Windows as the antithesis of Unix. Its DOS roots (and, with NT, 2000, and XP, its VMS roots) seem at odds with the power and elegance of a Unix system's command-line interface. Generally they're right, but there's still hope! Install Cygwin on Windows 2000 or Windows XP and you've suddenly got a very complete and capable Unix emulation layer implementing most if not all of the POSIX APIs and boasting a large collection of applications. Be careful about telling folks that you can run a Unix-like system on top of Windows, because pointing this out to some old-school Unix folks is a bit like telling kids about Santa.

When MacOS X was released, it suddenly became the world's most popular Unix desktop operating system. In fact, the GUI is so good, most Mac OS X users are never exposed to the BSD Unix layer lurking below. If Apple has somehow missed shipping a complete implementation of the POSIX applications, a third-party system called Fink makes it easy to add them to your Mac.

Any time I write "Unix," I mean any system that lets you write programs using the POSIX 1003.1 APIs, and that sports a command-line environment featuring a full suite of standard Unix applications (the POSIX 1003.2 commands). More specifically, I mean the four flavors of Unix we'll be looking at in this book: Fedora Core 3 Linux, FreeBSD 5.3, Cygwin, and Mac OS X.

Who Is This Book For?

This book was written with two kinds of readers in mind:

◆ Home users who want to set up a LAN server for their other computers, or for their friends and family to access over the Internet.

◆ IT professionals who are used to working with other operating systems and network services but want to learn more about Unix, either for personal growth or to help evaluate different technologies for the office.

In both cases, you've already gotten your feet wet as a Unix user (although we'll go through a quick overview in Chapter 1, "Unix Review") and want to know more.

You also need to be a little adventurous, because you'll be poking around in the unfamiliar guts of something new.

What's in a Name?

In 1994, the then-current owner of the "Unix" technology sold the trademark and certification rights to the X/Open Consortium, which then merged with the OSF/1 group to form the Open Group.

The Open Group works to define open standards for Unix, such as the Single Unix Specification, which is similar to (but not the same as) the POSIX 1003 specifications.

Before that was a dark time when people were sued for daring to use the name *Unix* without paying for a license. That's why you'll see some old-timers refer to *U*ix* or *ix* occasionally. Not only does this wild card "match" Unix-like operating systems (such as AIX, Ultrix, Xenix), but it also wards off the Unix trademark lawyers.

These days, being "Unix-like" is good enough for almost everybody.

If you want to know more about this, check out Wikipedia's excellent entry for *Unix*:

http://en.wikipedia.org/wiki/Unix

What's in This Book?

This book picks up where the *Unix: Visual QuickStart Guide* ends, by continuing your journey into the Unix world.

We start with Chapter 1, a quick review of Unix from a user's point of view, with information about using Unix, moving around the file system, mastering some of the more important commands, and working with two common text editors (vi and EMACS).

Next comes Chapter 2, "Configuring Unix," showing you how to determine which services start when the system boots. Chapter 3, "System Administration 101," covers the basics of—you guessed it!—system administration before we move on to Chapter 4, "Safety and Security," which includes backups and virus scanning.

Chapter 5, "Basic Services," runs through Telnet, FTP, and DHCP, along with sharing parts of your file system with NFS and Samba.

The next several chapters look at hosting a variety of services for the other systems on your network (Chapter 6, "Hosting a File Server"), printing with the traditional Unix lpd system and CUPS (Chapter 7, "Hosting a Print Server"), sending and receiving email with Sendmail and Postfix (Chapter 8, "Hosting an Email Server"), serving Web pages with Apache (Chapter 9, "Hosting a Web Server"), managing databases with MySQL (Chapter 10, "Hosting a Database Server"), and doing Web programming with PHP (Chapter 11, "Programming for the Web").

Finally, Chapter 12, "Advanced Services," looks at running your own caching DNS server, working with the firewall systems built into modern Unix systems, and using Squid to cache Web pages.

At the end of the book, you'll find a bunch of appendixes offering additional information and installation tips. The first appendix provides a laundry list of extra resources and a number of handy Web sites where you can learn more about Unix in general. Other appendixes tell you how to install and update Fedora Core 3, FreeBSD 5.3, Cygwin, and Fink. The last one explains how to find out about Webmin, a system-administrator interface you can use from your favorite Web browser.

How to Use This Book

This book has been designed to be used as a tutorial and as a reference. Each major topic stands by itself, so you can read each chapter back to back or hopscotch around. If you're not interested in a particular chapter now, feel free to skip it—you can always come back later when you need to set up something new.

Each chapter begins with an overview of a new topic, followed by specific step-by-step tasks accompanied by illustrations and examples of the code you're being asked to input and the resulting output from the computer. Commands you type appear as the text at the beginning of the numbered steps, with a description after. For example:

1. `This is a command, as you'd type it.`
   This is a description about this step, the options available to you, and the consequences of your actions.

`code text`

Used for Unix command-line text, including Unix commands and filenames. If you see something in **`code text`**, it is literally what would be typed into or would come out of the computer. If a line of text is too long for this book's margins, it wraps to the next line. Just continue typing without pressing the Enter key until you get to the end of the line.

`code highlight`

Used in code listings to distinguish the text you type in from text that comes from the computer.

`code italics`

These indicate text that you must type into the computer, but where you must substitute the appropriate value for the italicized text. For example, if you see

`ls -lF ` *`filename`*

A Note to Mac Users

For simplicity's sake, I'm going to refer to your Control key as Ctrl, and your Return key as Enter (even though some Mac applications might treat Return and Enter differently). Most of the keyboards out there will have those. (In fact, my iBook's keyboard has Ctrl instead of Control, and the Enter key also has Return printed on it.) Please don't feel slighted . . . remember, you're using the most popular desktop Unix in the world!

you would type the `ls -lF` part literally, and then the name of a file instead of *filename*.

body-text italics

Used for emphasis and also for unfamiliar words and phrases.

Code continuation

Wrapped lines begin with a continuation arrow that lets you know the line continues.

```
SET PASSWORD FOR 'user' @ 'host' =
→ PASSWORD('pass');
```

Case-sensitivity

In Unix, filenames and command names are case-sensitive. Mac OS X and Windows preserve the case when they store filenames, though they're case-insensitive. This means that there are some situations in which `COMMAND` and `command` are the same, but because those are exceptions and because case-sensitivity is the Unix standard, we assume that all commands and filenames are case-sensitive unless otherwise noted.

Keyboard combinations, such as Ctrl-C, mean you need to hold down the Control key, then press C while still holding down Control.

✔ Tip

- There are also handy tips, interesting (I hope!) tidbits, and more detailed information scattered throughout the chapters in notes. Look for these to increase your immersion in the land of Unix.

Requirements

This book assumes that you've got access to some sort of Unix system (such as a PC running Linux, or Windows with Cygwin; a Macintosh running Mac OS X; or a toaster running FreeBSD). And not just any access; to use some of the information in this book, you'll need **root** access.

If you don't have an existing Unix system or access to one where the owner trusts you enough to give you **root** access, we go over installing Fedora Core 3, FreeBSD 5.3, Cygwin, and Fink in the appendixes, so that you can set up your own Unix system.

Of course, not everything will require unrestricted access. You can almost always start a new service on a Unix system using either restricted functionality or a nonstandard configuration. It's a lot easier to learn some of these topics when you've got your own system to play with.

If you're using Mac OS X, you'll have to download and install the Mac OS X Developer Tools, which are available at http://developer.apple.com. (You'll have to sign up for a free Apple Developer Connection membership if you don't already have one.) Some old-timers might tell you that it's not a real Unix system if it doesn't have development tools!

REQUIREMENTS

Which Unix Is Right for You?

If you've already got full access to a working Unix system, that Unix is probably the right one for you. Unless, of course, you want to learn how to install a new one or start from a fresh system.

Even though this book focuses on the freely available Unixes that run on desktop (or even laptop) hardware, most of the information here will work with commercial Unixes such as Solaris, because it's focused on the applications.

If you're using a modern Apple computer, you're already using Unix when you boot into Mac OS X. If you wanted to use a Unix terminal instead of the normal Mac desktop, you could install Yellow Dog Linux or one of the BSDs, but then you'd lose the wonderful Quartz user interface. More power to you if you go down that path, but keep your Mac OS X CDs handy in case you don't like where it leads.

Users of x86 PCs have the most options available. If you need to keep Windows XP on your system (say, you need to access the office VPN or Microsoft Word to write a book, or, like me, you can't live without video games), Cygwin will give you a complete Unix environment without affecting Windows in any way. Cygwin applications can run alongside traditional Windows applications without any trouble or performance problems.

If you don't need to keep Windows on your system, you could start fresh with Linux (we'll be covering the Fedora Core 3 distribution) or FreeBSD.

Choosing Linux or FreeBSD depends on several things. FreeBSD is a good choice for stability, but Linux has a bigger development and user community, where things move faster and change more. Both support a vast range of hardware and offer similar capabilities. Ask a few friends if they use one or the other and go with what they're using . . . if you run into any trouble, they might be able to lend a hand.

Other Linux Distributions

I've chosen to cover Fedora Core 3 here because Red Hat's offerings have been very popular for home users as well as business users.

There are a few other, interesting distributions, though. My favorites include Mandrake, which is said to be the most "user-friendly" Linux for desktop use (although SuSE might be giving it a run for its money), and Gentoo.

Gentoo Linux is a bit of an oddball because during the install, you compile everything yourself. This is great if you have lots of time and if you want the absolute best binaries for your system. Everything is optimized specifically for your CPU.

If you're wondering which Linux is "right" for you (there are literally more than a thousand different Linux distributions out there!), you could try out the Linux Distribution Chooser (www.tuxs.org/chooser).

I've gone through it a couple of times and it keeps giving me Mandrake or Gentoo. As always, use these sorts of things as a springboard for your own research, and do some reading before you format your hard drive and start installing.

Or just use Fedora Core 3, because that's what this book covers!

Another option would be to run a computer emulator or virtualizer like Microsoft's Virtual PC or VMware Workstation. These programs behave like complete virtual computers running on your system, letting you install another OS from scratch while keeping your original system intact and available . . . you'll be running, for example, Linux in a window on your XP desktop. This emulation layer generally gives you a bit of a performance hit, however.

Dig in and enjoy!

WHICH UNIX IS RIGHT FOR YOU?

UNIX REVIEW

Unix's power, flexibility, and stability have kept it running the Internet for the past 30 or so years. Its features, ability to scale with almost any application, strong security, and support for multiple users have made it a benchmark that other operating systems are held against. Unix is one of the most popular operating systems in the world for servers, workstations, ridiculously powerful mainframes, and even desktop (or laptop!) computers.

In Unix, everything is a file. You must be able to navigate the file system in order to find what you want. Almost every Unix application has text-based configuration files, so all you need is a basic editor to reconfigure the system.

Assuming that you've got access to a running system, this chapter will provide a quick review of some essential Unix survival skills. If you're already adept at using Unix, you can skim through this information for anything that catches your interest.

If you're not already a Unix user, you'll want to start with *Unix: Visual QuickStart Guide, 2nd Edition,* by Deborah S. Ray and Eric J. Ray, also published by Peachpit Press. Follow along, try things out, explore, and experiment until you're comfortable moving through the file system and manipulating files. Once you're familiar with Unix basics, then you can come back to this book.

The information in this chapter applies to all flavors of Unix—Linux, FreeBSD, Solaris, the Mac OS X command-line environment, and Cygwin under Windows— even though the responses and prompts might be slightly different.

Using the Shell

The shell is your most powerful window into the world of a Unix system. Whether you're running it in an X Window System window or through a text-based dumb terminal, the shell gives you full access to a Unix system's many powerful command-line tools, configuration files, and devices.

Moving around and seeing what's there

When you first log in to a Unix system, whether it's via GUI, Telnet, or SSH connection, your current directory will be your account's home directory.

To find your current directory:

Do either of the following:

◆ pwd

When you first log in, type the **pwd** (*present working directory*) command. Unless you've got a strange shell startup script that changes your directory, your home directory will be displayed (**Code Listing 1.1**):

bender:~ chrish$ **pwd**

/Users/chrish

◆ echo $PWD

The $PWD environment variable displays the current working directory:

bender:~ chrish$ **echo $PWD**

/Users/chrish

Environment variables are easier to use in complex command sequences, as well as in shell scripts, because you can use **$PWD** anywhere in a command without any extra work.

From your current directory, you can get back to your home directory.

Code Listing 1.1 Using the pwd command and PWD environment variable to find your current directory.

```
bender:~ chrish$ pwd
/Users/chrish


bender:~ chrish$ echo $PWD
/Users/chrish
```

Code Listing 1.2 Getting back to your home directory using the HOME environment variable or the ~ shortcut.

```
bender:/tmp chrish$ pwd
/tmp
bender:/tmp chrish$ cd $HOME
bender:~ chrish$ pwd
/Users/chrish
bender:~ chrish$ cd /etc
bender:/etc chrish$ pwd
/etc
bender:/etc chrish$ cd ~
bender:~ chrish$ pwd
/Users/chrish
```

To get back home:

Do either of the following:

◆ cd $HOME

Just as the PWD environment variable always contains your current directory, the HOME environment variable always has your home directory inside.

◆ cd ~

Want to get home with the least amount of typing? The ~ (tilde) shortcut also refers to your home directory. Unix developers love shortcuts (**Code Listing 1.2**)!

✔ Tips

■ In some shells, typing **cd** without an argument will also return you to your home directory.

■ You can use the HOME environment variable or the ~ shortcut in any argument that uses a path or filename:

cat ~/*my-file*.txt

cp $HOME/*my-file*.txt
→ $HOME/*my-file*-backup.txt

■ The ~ shortcut also lets you refer to other people's home directories by including their login name immediately after the tilde. For example, this command copies *my-file*.txt to the user **david**'s home directory:

cp ~/*my-file*.txt
→ ~david/*your-file*.txt

USING THE SHELL

So now that we know where we are, what files are there? The `ls` command holds the answer. You have several options.

To list the files in a directory:

Do any of the following:

◆ `ls`

The `ls` command will show you which files are in your current directory (**Code Listing 1.3**):

```
bender:~ chrish$ ls
Default   Documents  Movies  Pictures
Sites     emacs-lisp
Desktop   Library    Music   Public
daily-urls.html
```

◆ `ls -F`

The `-F` option adds / to the end of directory names, * to executables, and @ to symbolic links. This makes it easier to find specific things in the file system.

```
bender:~ chrish$ ls -F
Default    Documents/  Movies/
Pictures/  Sites/      emacs-lisp/
Desktop/   Library/    Music/
Public/    daily-urls.html
```

◆ `ls -a`

Unix hides configuration files and directories by starting them with a . (period) character. These *dotfiles* are hidden by convention; Unix applications ignore them and usually only show them if you specifically ask them to. The `ls` command's *-a* option tells it to show all files, including the "hidden" dotfiles.

Code Listing 1.3 Listing files with the ls command and its -F (add file-type decorations) and -a (show all files) options.

```
bender:~ chrish$ ls
Default   Documents   Movies   Pictures   Sites     emacs-lisp
Desktop   Library     Music    Public     daily-urls.html

bender:~ chrish$ ls -F
Default    Documents/   Movies/   Pictures/   Sites/      emacs-lisp/
Desktop/   Library/     Music/    Public/     daily-urls.html

bender:~ chrish$ ls -a
.                  .bash_history   .lpoptions   Desktop     Public
..                 .cvspass        .ncftp       Documents   Sites
.CFUserTextEncoding                .emacs        .profile   Library      daily-urls.html
.DS_Store          .emacs.d        .ssh         Movies      emacs-lisp
.MacOSX            .irssi          .viminfo     Music
.Trash             .lftp           Default      Pictures

bender:~ chrish$ ls -aF
./                 .bash_history   .lpoptions   Desktop/    Public/
../                .cvspass        .ncftp/      Documents/  Sites/
.CFUserTextEncoding                .emacs        .profile   Library/     daily-urls.html
.DS_Store          .emacs.d/       .ssh/        Movies/     emacs-lisp/
.MacOSX/           .irssi/         .viminfo     Music/
.Trash/            .lftp/          Default      Pictures/
```

USING THE SHELL

Now that we've found some files, we probably want to see what's in them. Again, there are several options.

To look at a file's contents:

Do any of the following:

◆ `cat` *filename*

Now that you've used your **cd** and **ls** expertise to find a file you're interested in, **cat** will print the contents of a file to the terminal (**Code Listing 1.4**).

◆ `head` *filename*

Only want to see the beginning of the file? Use the **head** command instead (see Code Listing 1.4).

◆ `tail` *filename*

You can also use the **tail** command (see Code Listing 1.4) to see just the end of a file.

◆ `less` *filename*

Usually you'll want to use the **less** command (**Figure 1.1**) so that you can interactively page through or search the file.

◆ `more` *filename*

If **less** isn't available for some reason, its older, utilitarian brother **more** can help you out.

✔ Tip

■ Sometimes if you **cat** a binary file (such as a program, an image, or a sound file), it'll screw up your terminal's settings. This could result in strange keyboard behavior, invisible text, and so on. To fix it, carefully type this command and press Enter:

`stty sane`

Figure 1.1 The `less` command lets you view a file one screen at a time.

Code Listing 1.4 Looking at a file's contents with cat, head, and tail.

```
chrish@taffer [508]: cat unix-advanced-outline.txt
UNIX Advanced Visual QuickPro Guide - Outline

Introduction
- who this is for
- what's in this book
- how to use this book
- requirements
. . .
- Apache forums, etc.
- MySQL forums, etc.
- PHP forums, etc.


chrish@taffer [509]: head unix-advanced-outline.txt
UNIX Advanced Visual QuickPro Guide - Outline

Introduction
- who this is for
- what's in this book
- how to use this book
- requirements

Chapter 1 - Installing UNIX
- Which "UNIX"? - Fedora Core, FreeBSD, cygwin, MacOS X

chrish@taffer [510]: tail unix-advanced-outline.txt
Appendix A - Finding out more
- how to find out more - man, info (and pinfo), Google, mailing lists, RFCs
- Fedora Core forums, mailing lists, etc.
- FreeBSD forums, mailing lists, etc.
- cygwin forums, mailing lists, etc.
- fink forums, mailing lists, etc.
- system administration mailing lists (risks-l, CERT, etc.)
- Apache forums, etc.
- MySQL forums, etc.
- PHP forums, etc.
```

Redirecting input and output

Because so many Unix utilities operate on text files, it can be very useful to redirect a program's output to a file for later processing by another application. You can even use a file as input to a program.

To send a command's output to a file:

◆ command > *filename*

You can redirect a program's output to the specified file using the > character (**Code Listing 1.5**):

chrish@taffer [508]: **ps > ps.txt**

chrish@taffer [509]: **ls**

ps.txt

The ps.txt file now contains the output of the ps command.

To append a command's output to a file:

◆ command >> *filename*

Use the >> redirection (**Code Listing 1.6**) to append a program's output to an existing file instead of just overwriting it:

chrish@taffer [520]: **echo hello > hello-there.txt**

chrish@taffer [521]: **echo there >> hello-there.txt**

chrish@taffer [522]: **cat hello-there.txt**

hello

there

Code Listing 1.5 Redirecting output to a file with > and input from a file with <.

```
chrish@taffer [506]: ls


chrish@taffer [507]: ps > ps.txt
chrish@taffer [508]: ls
ps.txt


chrish@taffer [509]: sort < ps.txt
⇢ > ps-sorted.txt
chrish@taffer [510]: ls
ps-sorted.txt   ps.txt
```

Code Listing 1.6 Using >> to append to an existing file.

```
chrish@taffer [513]: echo "hello"
⇢ > hello-there.txt
chrish@taffer [514]: ls
hello-there.txt


chrish@taffer [515]: echo "there"
⇢ > hello-there.txt
chrish@taffer [516]: cat
⇢ hello-there.txt
there


chrish@taffer [517]: echo "hello"
⇢ > hello-there.txt
chrish@taffer [518]: echo "there"
⇢ >> hello-there.txt
chrish@taffer [519]: cat
⇢ hello-there.txt
hello
there
```

Streams

Unix has three standard text streams automatically associated with every program: stdin (*standard input*), stdout (*standard output*), and stderr (*standard error*).

While programmers can refer to these streams by name, shell users have to refer to them by number:

- 0—stdin
- 1—stdout
- 2—stderr

As we've seen, < redirects from stdin and > redirects the stdout stream, but what about stderr? That's an output stream for errors, but we can't redirect it with > because it's already taken by stdout.

By specifying the stream with the redirection, we can send stderr to a file as well:

```
chrish@taffer [511]: sort <
→ ps.txt
→ > ps-sorted.txt
→ 2> sort-errors.txt
```

This sorts the contents of ps.txt and saves the output to ps-sorted.txt. Any error messages will go to sort-errors.txt.

What if you wanted stdout and stderr in the same file? There's another special redirection for just such an occasion:

```
chrish@taffer [523]: sort
→ < ps.txt
→ > ps-sorted.txt 2>&1
```

You can think of the & as tying the error stream to the output stream for this command.

To get a command's input from a file:

- command < *filename*

  Use the < character to redirect a program's input from the specified file (Code Listing 1.5):

  ```
  chrish@taffer [510]: sort < ps.txt
  → > ps-sorted.txt
  ```

  As you can see, you can also combine the two redirections on one command line. In the example above, the output of the sort command, which is operating on the data in ps.txt, is stored in ps-sorted.txt.

Plumbing

Being able to chain together a series of commands without having to use intermediate files is a very powerful feature. It goes hand-in-hand with another Unix design philosophy: providing a set of small, well-defined tools that work together.

To use a program's output as input:

◆ *command | command*

Instead of redirecting the output from ps to a file and then sorting it, we could combine the two commands (**Code Listing 1.7**) using |, the pipe:

```
chrish@taffer [524]: ps | sort
→ > ps-sorted.txt
```

That's exactly the same as this sequence, but without the temporary file:

```
chrish@taffer [525]: ps > ps.txt
chrish@taffer [526]: sort < ps.txt
→ > ps-sorted.txt
```

This gets more powerful as you chain together more and more commands.

Code Listing 1.7 Piping the output of one command into another lets you create your own powerful chain of tools.

```
bender:~ chrish$ ps
  PID  TT  STAT     TIME COMMAND
 1853  p1  S     0:00.42 -bash
 2168  p1  S+    0:00.65 ssh taffer
 1875 std  S     0:00.51 -bash

bender:~ chrish$ ps | sort
  PID  TT  STAT     TIME COMMAND
 1853  p1  S     0:00.42 -bash
 1875 std  S     0:00.51 -bash
 2168  p1  S+    0:00.65 ssh taffer
 2175 std  R+    0:00.00 sort
```

tee for Two

If you're nosy like me, you'd probably prefer that commands show progress while redirecting their output, especially when they take a long time to finish.

Luckily, the tee command takes its input, saves it to a file, and then prints it to the terminal.

For example, the following command,

```
chrish@taffer [530]: ps |
→ tee ps.txt
```

will write the output of ps to ps.txt and also display it onscreen.

This gets really handy when you're using tee to watch something that runs forever (like a Web server) or that might take a long time (like a program compile).

Using Common Editors

If you've ever had to edit text for any length of time, you've probably got a favorite text editor that you know inside and out.

Unless you're a longtime Unix user, your favorite editor probably isn't from the vi or EMACS families, the two most common types of Unix editors.

There's probably a great Unix GUI text editor that closely matches your favorite, but what if you need to edit a file on a system with no display? Or over a slow remote connection? Or (horror!) what if your favorite text editor isn't installed yet and you need to change its Makefile?

Knowing how to use vi on a Unix system is similar to knowing how to start a fire by rubbing two sticks together. Even if you don't do it very often, it can really save you in a pinch.

We'll also take a quick look at EMACS, a friendlier editor installed on most Unix systems.

Even though EMACS is far superior to vi, we don't waste any time on the eternal "my editor is better than yours" debate. If you're interested, check the Wikipedia (http://en.wikipedia.org/wiki/Editor_war) entry!

✔ Tips

- If for some reason vi isn't available on your system, you can try one of the vi clones, such as vim or elvis. In fact, on most Linux systems, vi is just a link to vim.

- vim sports some other modern features, like syntax highlighting. Even if vi is available, you might want to try typing *vim* to see if something better is available.

- vim has extensive built-in help that you can access using the :help command.

vi

The vi editor is one of the first screen-oriented text editors; before vi, most text editors were line oriented, displaying only one line at a time for editing. Bill Joy created vi in 1976; he's done a little work for Sun since then on a minor project called Java.

To edit files with vi:

◆ vi *filename*

  To edit one or more files with vi, just include their names on the command line:

  bender:~ chrish$ **vi *file1 file2*** ...

  If you specify a filename that doesn't already exist, you'll be creating a new file with that name:

  bender:~ chrish$ **vi *a-new-file.txt***

  When vi starts up with a new file, you can see just how minimal its interface is (**Figure 1.2**).

To exit vi:

Do any of the following:

◆ :q

  Quit.

◆ :q!

  Quit even if the file has been edited.

◆ :x

  Save the current file and exit.

◆ :x!

  Save the current file even if it's read-only, and then exit.

To switch to vi's command mode:

◆ Press the Esc key to switch to vi's command mode.

  The vi editor is modal, meaning that you can be entering text or entering commands. You need to switch between input mode and command mode manually. When you first start vi, you're automatically in command mode.

Figure 1.2 vi with a new (empty) file.

✔ Tips

■ To signal the end of a multiple-character command, press Enter.

■ If you're already in command mode when you press Esc, you'll stay in command mode.

■ You must be in command mode to use any of the commands listed here.

To switch to vi's input mode:

Do any of the following:

- i

  Enter input mode at the current cursor position.

- o (lowercase *o*)

  Insert a blank line below the current cursor position, and enter input mode at the beginning of that new line.

- O (uppercase *O*)

  Insert a blank line above the current cursor position, and enter input mode at the beginning of that new line.

To move around in vi:

Do any of the following:

- j

  Move the cursor down one line.

- k

  Move the cursor up one line.

- l

  Move the cursor left one character.

- h

  Move the cursor right one character.

- :<digits>

  Move the cursor to the start of the line specified by <digits>. For example, entering :1 will move you to the first line of a file, and :99 will move you to line 99 (or the end of the file if it doesn't have more than 99 lines).

- [[

  Move the cursor to the start of the first line of the current buffer.

-]]

  Move the cursor to the start of the last line of the current buffer.

- ^

  Move the cursor to the start of the current line.

- $

  Move the cursor to the end of the current line.

To change buffers in vi:

Do either of the following:

- :n

  Switch to the next file.

- :N

  Switch to the previous file.

To search in vi:

Do any of the following:

- /*<pattern>*

  Search forward for *<pattern>* and move the cursor to the start of the matched text. For example, /*abc* will move the cursor to the *a* in the next instance of *abc* within the text.

- /

  Search forward for the next instance of the last pattern you searched for. This is a multiple-character command, with the search pattern omitted, so you have to press Enter right after entering the / character.

- ?*<pattern>*

  Search backward for *<pattern>* and move the cursor to the start of the matched text. For example, /*abc* will move the cursor to the *a* in the previous instance of *abc* within the text.

- ?

  Search backward for the previous instance of the last pattern you searched for. This is a multiple-character command, with the search pattern omitted, so you have to press Enter right after entering the ? character.

EMACS

EMACS started life as a set of macros for another ancient text editor before evolving into a full-blown text editor with extensions for almost anything you can think of. It's practically an operating system disguised as a text editor. Its name stands for *Editor MACroS*.

EMACS isn't a modal editor like vi, meaning that you can be entering text or commands without having to switch between modes. EMACS commands involve one or more keys used with one of the modifier keys on your keyboard, the most common being Ctrl and Meta.

Wait—you've never seen a keyboard with a Meta key, right? Neither have I; they seem to have disappeared into the mists of time. In EMACS, the Meta key is either the Esc key (when running the text-mode version) or the Alt key (when running a GUI version). If the Alt key works as Meta, the Esc key will also work, so if you've learned to use the text-only EMACS, you can keep using your EMACS skills when running a GUI version.

In EMACS documentation, the Ctrl key is referred to as C-, so C-G would be the same as Ctrl-G. The Meta key is referred to as M-, so M-X would be the same as Esc-X (or Alt-X). Note that using the Esc key as Meta works a little differently. It's not a "special"

key like Ctrl or Shift, so you don't hold it down. Press Esc once, let go, then press the next character in the command sequence. Commands that need uppercase characters are shown using the actual character instead of specifying the Shift key.

Some commands require a sequence of keys, such as Ctrl-H t, which starts the interactive EMACS tutorial. When you see C-H t, it means to press Ctrl-H, let go, then press T (which gives you a lowercase t because you haven't pressed Shift).

I'm going to refer to EMACS commands using this notation so that it matches up with what you'll see in the actual EMACS documentation and built-in online help.

✔ Tips

■ You can press Tab any time EMACS asks you for a filename, buffer name, command name, and so on, and it will provide a list of possible entries.

■ If you enter some text before pressing Tab, the completion list will only include things that matched the text you entered. For example, if you press C-X b to switch buffers, and then type *hel* Tab, only buffers starting with *hel* will show up in the list, such as `hello_world.c` or `helen-of-troy`.

■ EMACS has a built-in tutorial that you can pull up from the Help menu, or by pressing C-H t.

Figure 1.3 EMACS with a new (empty) file.

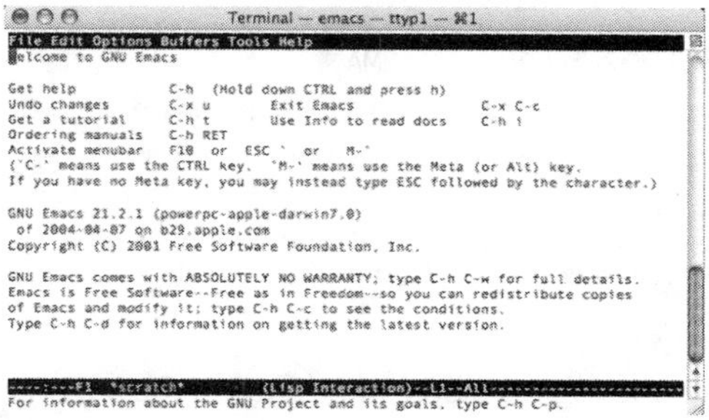

Figure 1.4 Starting EMACS without a file.

To edit files with EMACS:

Do any of the following:

◆ emacs *filename*

To edit one or more files with EMACS, just include their names on the command line:

bender:~ chrish$ **emacs file1 file2**
→ **...**

If you start EMACS with two files, you'll get a split-screen view of both files. You can press C-X o to switch between the buffers.

If you start EMACS with more than two files, you'll get a split-screen view of the first file, and a list of available buffers. Use the arrow keys to move around this list, then press Enter to display the file currently under the cursor.

If you specify a filename that doesn't already exist, you'll be creating a new file with that name:

bender:~ chrish$ **emacs**
→ **a-new-file.txt**

When EMACS starts up with a new file, you can see that there's a little more to its interface (**Figure 1.3**). Like traditional GUI editors, it has a menu bar at the top, a status bar, and one line at the bottom for entering commands.

◆ If you start EMACS without any files specified, you'll get a quick help summary, some information about the current build, and a quick overview of the license (**Figure 1.4**).

To exit EMACS:

- C-X C-C (Ctrl-X and then Ctrl-C)

  Exit EMACS. If you've made changes to a buffer without saving it, EMACS will prompt you to save it first by pressing Y or N. If you don't save (by pressing N), you will have to type *yes* (the entire word) to exit without saving your changes, or *no* to stay in EMACS.

To save files with EMACS:

Do either of the following:

- C-X C-S

  Save the current buffer to its default filename.

- C-X C-W

  Write the current buffer to a file; EMACS will prompt you for the filename in the mini-buffer at the bottom of the screen. Type a filename and press Enter to save the file.

To move around in EMACS:

Do any of the following:

- C-N

  Down (next line).

- C-P

  Up (previous line).

- C-B

  Left (back).

- C-F

  Right (forward).

- M-X `goto-line` *<digits>* Enter

  Move the cursor to the start of the line specified by *<digits>*. For example, pressing M-X, typing *goto-line 1*, and then pressing Enter will move you to the first line of a file.

- M-<

  Move the cursor to the start of the first line of the current buffer.

- M->

  Move the cursor to the start of the last line of the current buffer.

- C-V

  Move down one screen.

- C-A

  Move the cursor to the start of the current line.

- C-E

  Move the cursor to the end of the current line.

- M-V

  Move up one screen.

✔ Tip

- The cursor keys, Page Up, Page Down, and so on, will also work as expected, if your terminal maps them to something EMACS can understand.

USING COMMON EDITORS

To change buffers in EMACS:

Do any of the following:

◆ C-X b Enter

Switch to the default buffer. If you haven't switched buffers yet, this will be the next file or buffer. If you've already switched buffers, the default will be the previous buffer.

◆ C-X b Tab

List the names of all of the current buffers. A buffer's name is the same as its filename. EMACS's own temporary buffers have names like ***scratch*** so that you can easily identify them.

◆ C-X b *<name>* Enter

Switch to the buffer named *<name>*. For example, C-X b ***scratch*** Enter will switch to the **scratch** buffer.

To search in EMACS:

Do either of the following:

◆ C-S

Interactively search forward for the next characters you type. To search again for the same character sequence, press C-S again.

◆ C-R

Interactively search backward for the next characters you type. To search backward again, press C-R again.

Where Are the Important Files?

Being able to find, view, and edit files isn't that useful if you can't find what you're looking for.

Even though there are minor differences between the filesystem layouts on different Unix systems (**Figures 1.5–1.8**), the general layout is pretty similar. If there's an important difference that affects one of the topics we'll be looking at later, I'll describe each platform specifically so that you'll always be able to find what you need.

◆ /

The root of the filesystem tree; all other directories and files are created at some point under the root.

◆ /bin

Standard system programs (binaries in Unix speak).

◆ /boot

Files used during boot, such as the kernel image.

◆ /dev

System devices. Every piece of hardware in the system has an entry here, but there will also be many entries that don't correspond to actual hardware, such as /dev/random.

◆ /etc

System-configuration files. On Mac OS X, much of the information traditionally stored in /etc is actually maintained by the NetInfo database.

◆ /home

Home directories for user accounts. This is replaced by /Users on Mac OS X systems.

◆ /lib

Shared libraries and data files for standard system binaries.

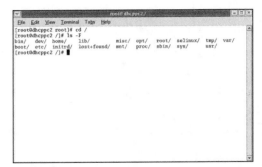

Figure 1.5 Fedora Core 3's / directory.

Figure 1.6 FreeBSD 5.3's / directory.

Figure 1.7 Cygwin's / directory.

Figure 1.8 Fink's / directory.

- **/lost+found**

  A directory created by the filesystem checker (**fsck**). If any files or directories are "lost" during a system crash, **fsck** will move them here.

- **/mnt**

  Mount points for network filesystems and removable devices, such as CD-ROMs. The Mac OS X equivalent is the **/Volumes** directory.

- **/opt**

  Commercial applications and optional software that could also be installed in **/usr/local**.

- **/proc**

  Process filesystem. The entries in here represent the running programs on the system, shared memory blocks, and so on.

- **/root**

  The home directory for the root account.

- **/sbin**

  Important system binaries that are necessary for system-administration tasks.

- **/tmp**

  A garbage dump for temporary files and directories. On some systems, **/tmp** is removed and created fresh during every system reboot.

- **/usr**

  Additional binaries and its own **/bin**, **/etc**, and **/lib** directories to support the additional binaries stored here.

- **/usr/local**

  An area for local system applications (useful things that weren't included in the main operating-system distribution) and data. Like **/usr**, it usually has its own **/bin**, **/etc**, and **/lib** directories.

- **/var**

  System logs, printer spools, and other files that tend to change a lot.

WHERE ARE THE IMPORTANT FILES?

Important Commands

Here's a short list of handy Unix commands that you'll use all the time. The **apropos** and **man** commands may be the most important to remember, because those are your gateways into the **man** pages, Unix's standard online help files. Please note that the italicized letters below are just placeholders. You will, of course, use your own file name instead. I used *x* to represent one file, *a* and *b* to represent two different files, and *d* to indicate a directory.

- **apropos** *x*
  Search for commands whose keywords match the specified keyword, x.

- **cat** *x*
  Print the contents of the specified file(s) to the terminal.

- **cd** *d*
  Change to the specified directory, *d*.

- **cp** *a b*
  Copy file *a* to *b*. If *b* is a directory, the new file will be named *b/a*.

- **echo** *x*
  Print *x* to the terminal. If x is surrounded by double quotes (**echo** "*x*"), the text is printed with any environment variables or other shortcuts expanded. If x is surrounded by single quotes (**echo** '*x*'), the text is printed without any special processing, *exactly* as it appears in the **echo** command.

- **emacs** *x*
  Start the EMACS text editor and load the specified file.

- **head** *x*
  Display the first ten lines of the specified file.

- **less** *x*
  Display the specified file(s) one screen at a time. Press the spacebar to advance to the next screen. Press Q to quit. This is like the **more** command but better. On some systems, **less** and **more** actually point to the same file ("less is more").

- **ls**
  List the files in the current directory.

- **man** *x*
  Look up the specified command in the online manual.

- **more** *x*
  Like the **less** command, but not as nice. Use this if **less** isn't available.

- **ps**
  Display information about your running programs.

- **pwd**
  Print the current working directory.

- **sort**
  Sort its input lines and print them.

- **stty sane**
  The **stty** command configures your terminal settings; its **sane** option resets everything to reasonable defaults.

- **tail** *x*
  Display the last ten lines of the specified file.

- **tee** *x*
  Copy its input to the specified file, and then print it onscreen.

- **vi** *x*
  Start the **vi** text editor and load the specified file(s).

2

Configuring Unix

Although you may have heard of people recompiling their kernels (the lowest-level "core" of a Unix system), Unix's extreme configurability is accessible with just a text editor and an understanding of the files used to start the system's resident programs (the *daemons*).

After the kernel is finished initializing your system's hardware, it starts the `init` program. `init` is one of the few programs started directly by the kernel (it always gets process ID 1), and it launches the scripts that start the daemons during the normal boot process and then begins the system's normal multiuser operations.

Although we're considering Cygwin a Unix system for this book, it doesn't depend on the `init` system because the Windows host OS is already up and running before Cygwin processes can start.

When users log in to a Unix system, their preferred shell (listed in the /etc/passwd file) starts up and loads several scripts. These global shell-configuration scripts let the administrator specify application locations and other general settings, and give users a way of personalizing their shells with custom environment variables, shell functions, and command aliases.

Startup Scripts

When a Unix system boots, it launches several startup scripts to initialize the system services. Note that this section applies mostly to Fedora Core and FreeBSD.

To find the startup scripts:

1. `cd /etc`

   System-configuration files live in the `/etc` directory, and the startup scripts are no exception to this rule.

2. `ls -lF | grep rc`

   List all of the files and directories, and search for the ones that have **rc** in them. This turns up a few extra files, but you'll be able to see the various **rc** files, directories, and (in the case of Linux) symbolic links.

   As you can see, Fedora Core 3 (**Code Listing 2.1**), FreeBSD 5.3 (**Code Listing 2.2**), and Mac OS X (**Code Listing 2.3**) all have slightly different **rc** files available.

Now that you know where to find these files, you might want to know how to add your own startup commands to the system boot process.

Code Listing 2.1 Fedora Core 3's rc files.

```
[root@dhcppc2 root]# cd /etc
[root@dhcppc2 etc]# ls -F | grep rc
bashrc
csh.cshrc
imrc
inputrc
mail.rc
Muttrc
pinforc
rc@
rc0.d@
rc1.d@
rc2.d@
rc3.d@
rc4.d@
rc5.d@
rc6.d@
rc.d/
rc.local@
rc.sysinit@
slrn.rc
vimrc
wgetrc
```

Code Listing 2.2 FreeBSD's rc files.

```
bsd# cd /etc

bsd# ls -F | grep rc

csh.cshrc
locate.rc
mail.rc
rc
rc.conf
rc.d/
rc.firewall
rc.firewall6
rc.resume*
rc.sendmail
rc.shutdown
rc.subr
rc.suspend*
```

Code Listing 2.3 Mac OS X's rc files.

```
bender:~ chrish$ cd /etc
bender:/etc chrish$ ls -F | grep rc
bashrc
csh.cshrc
efax.rc
mail.rc
rc
rc.boot
rc.cleanup
rc.common
rc.netboot
```

Code Listing 2.4 A skeleton startup script.

```
#!/bin/sh
#
# FreeBSD keywords used to control when
# this startup script is started on
# a FreeBSD system (these are ignored
# on other OSes):
#
# PROVIDE: insert-name-here
# REQUIRE: list-prerequisite-services
# BEFORE: launch-before-this
# KEYWORD: FreeBSD

# Include OS-specific code.
#
# You might want to read these scripts
# to see what standard startup script
# functions are provided for you.
case "$(uname -s)" in
    Linux)
        # Linux
        . /etc/init.d/functions
        ;;
    FreeBSD)
        # FreeBSD
        . /etc/rc.subr
        ;;
    CYGWIN*)
        # Cygwin
        ;;
    Darwin)
        # Mac OS X
        . /etc/rc.common
        ;;
esac

# Handle the command-line options.
case "$1" in
    start)
        # INSERT START HANDLING HERE
        ;;
    stop)
        # INSERT STOP HANDLING HERE
        ;;
    restart)
        # INSERT RESTART HANDLING HERE
        ;;
    *)
        # Ignore other commands.  Note
        # that FreeBSD also supports
        # "status", "poll", and "rcvar"
        # commands.  See the rc manpage
        # for more information.
        exit 0
        ;;
esac
```

To add startup commands:

1. Create your startup script using your favorite text editor. Startup scripts must respond appropriately to start, stop, and restart arguments. **Code Listing 2.4** shows you a skeleton script that you can start with; just add your own code at the **INSERT** points.

   If you're using FreeBSD, you need to add several comments that indicate the name of the service your script is providing (the **PROVIDE** comment in Code Listing 2.4), which services are required before your script can start (the **REQUIRE** list in Code Listing 2.4), the service that your script needs to start before (this is usually login in the **BEFORE** comment, Code Listing 2.4), and the FreeBSD **KEYWORD** line (Code Listing 2.4).

continues on next page

STARTUP SCRIPTS

If you're using Mac OS X, you'll also need to create a StartupParameters.plist file (**Code Listing 2.5**). Fill in the *short-description* and *service-name* with a description of your script and its name. The *prerequisites* are a list of other service names in quotes; if you don't require anything specific, use `Resolver`. The `order-value` can be `Early`, `Late`, or `None`.

2. `chmod +x` *scriptname*

Be sure to set the executable bit on your script, or it won't run.

Remember to test your script, too!

3. `cd /etc/rc.d`

Or, if you're using Fedora Core Linux (other Linux distributions may differ slightly; there are no standards for different run levels, so check the documentation):

`cd /etc/rc.d/rc5.d`

Or, if you're using Mac OS X:

`cd /Library/StartupItems`

Obviously you'll need to be in the same directory as the startup scripts to add your own command to the launch sequence.

4. `cp` *scriptname* `.`

Copy your new startup script to the current directory.

If you're using Linux, the *name* of the script will control when it starts. The scripts in the various `rc.d` directories are started in lexicographical order, so you'll need to rename your script with the `mv` command to fit it into the existing sequence.

If you're using Mac OS X, each startup script goes into its own directory (with a name that matches your script) with the StartupParameters.plist file.

Code Listing 2.5 A sample StartupParameters.plist file for Mac OS X.

```
{
    Description = "short-description";
    Provides = ("service-name");
    Requires = ("prerequisites");
    OrderPreference = "order-value";
    Messages =
    {
        start = "Starting service-name";
        stop = "Stopping service-name";
        restart = "Restarting service-name";
    };
}
```

✔ Tips

- To follow the standard form for startup scripts in Fedora Core, copy your script into `/etc/init.d` and then create a symbolic link to the script in the appropriate `/etc/rc.d` directory. For example, if you're logged in as `root`, you'd create `999myscript`:

```
cp 999myscript /etc/init.d
ln -s /etc/init.d/999myscript
→ /etc/rc5.d/999myscript
```

- To add a Unix daemon as a Windows service, use the `cygrunsrv` program. For example, you could use this command to install a Service that starts the Cygwin `inetd` (Internet daemon) every time the system boots:

```
cygrunsrv -I inetd -d "Cygwin inetd"
→ -p /usr/sbin/inetd -a -d
→ -e CYGWIN=ntsec
```

This installs (`-I`) a service named `inetd` with a description (`-d`) of `"Cygwin inetd"`. The service launches (`-p`) `/usr/sbin/inetd` with the `-d` argument (`-a`) and the `CYGWIN` environment variable (`-e`) set to `ntsec`.

We'll look at specific uses for `cygrunsrv` later in the book, but you can also run it with `help` to see a help message.

- If your Mac OS X system doesn't already have a /Library/StartupItems directory, you can create one and give it the correct permissions with these commands:

```
mkdir -p /Library/StartupItems
chmod 0755 /Library/StartupItems
sudo chown root:admin /Library/
→ StartupItems
```

- Scripts run from /Library/StartupItems on Mac OS X will have `root` permissions unless the script calls `sudo` to run its commands as another user.

- Windows systems use their own, mostly hidden startup procedures. It's better to let Windows start itself normally, and add Cygwin daemons as "native" services using the `cygrunsrv` command.

- Although Mac OS X systems have `/etc/rc` files (but not an `/etc/rc.d` directory because of its BSD heritage), their startup process is handled differently from that used by standard Unix systems. We'll show you how to start services on Mac OS X without disrupting the normal boot process. If you want to know more about Mac OS X's boot process, take a look at "SystemStarter and the Mac OS X Startup Process" (www.opendarwin.org/~kevin/ SystemStarter/SystemStarter.html).

STARTUP SCRIPTS

Shell Configuration

Like almost every other part of a Unix system, the shell is highly configurable. As it's the place where you type your commands and do a lot of complex work, you're going to want to tweak it until it feels comfortable.

Every Unix shell, be it the Bourne Again shell (bash) used on Fedora Core, Mac OS X, and Cygwin systems, or the C shell (csh) used on FreeBSD, supports global configuration files for sitewide changes, and local, user-specific configuration files.

To find the global shell-configuration files:

As you might have noticed earlier, the global shell-configuration files live in the same directory as the system-startup files.

1. cd /etc

   Change to the system-configuration-files directory.

2. echo $SHELL

   Find out which shell you're currently using. If you already know, you can skip this step.

   This detail is important, because each shell uses different configuration files.

3. If your shell is sh (usually /bin/sh), it will use the /etc/profile file.

   If your shell is bash (usually /usr/local/bash or /bin/bash), it will also use the /etc/profile file.

   If your shell is csh (usually /bin/csh or /bin/tcsh), it will use /etc/csh.cshrc and then /etc/csh.login.

   Even though the shell loads these files first, the local shell-configuration files can change anything set up by the global configuration files.

To find the local shell-configuration files:

Your local shell-configuration file also depends on which shell you're using, but they're always in your HOME directory.

1. `echo $SHELL`

   Find out which shell you're using. You can skip this step if you already know.

2. If your shell is sh, it will use the following local configuration files:

   ▲ `.profile`, if any

   ▲ The file specified in the ENV environment variable, if any

   If your shell is bash, it will use the following local configuration files:

   ▲ `.bash_profile`, if any, if bash was invoked as a login shell (or with the `--login` option)

   ▲ `.bash_login`, if any, if bash was invoked as a login shell (or with the `--login` option)

   ▲ `.profile`, if any, if bash was invoked as a login shell (or with the `--login` option)

   ▲ `.bashrc`, if any, if bash was invoked as a non-login shell

   ▲ The file specified in the BASH_ENV environment variable, if any

   ▲ `.bash_logout`, if any (only when exiting the shell)

   If your shell is csh, it will use the following local configuration files:

   ▲ `.cshrc`, if any

   ▲ `.login`, if any

To customize your shell:

1. Edit the appropriate configuration file using your favorite text editor. If you want these changes to apply to all users, edit the global files; otherwise, edit your local files.

2. Add useful directories to your PATH environment variable.

   In sh or bash:

   `export PATH=`*`new-path`*`:$PATH`

   In csh:

   `setenv PATH `*`new-path`*`:$PATH`

   new-path can be `/usr/local/bin` or any other directory with binaries in it; I usually add `~/bin` to my PATH and put my own programs in there.

3. Add any other environment variables you might need. These will be specific to the programs you use, so you'll have to consult the documentation for details.

4. Add aliases or shell functions. For example, I like to add this one, since I'm used to having `lc` because of an old Unix system I used in school:

   `alias lc="ls -F"`

SYSTEM ADMINISTRATION 101

System administration is the art and science of keeping your system running well, and being ready to deal with emergencies if and when they pop up. To look after your new Unix system, you're going to need to know how to keep the system secure, and how to make and restore backups of your precious data, among other things.

This chapter introduces you to the basics of system administration, giving you some simple, practical advice and some useful techniques for maintaining a healthy system.

Logging In as root

As you probably already know, the **root** account on a Unix system can do literally anything. This is the administrator's special account, and you had to set a password for it during the system install.

When you're modifying system-configuration files, mounting new file systems, or backing up the home directories of your users, you're going to need to be logged in as **root**.

Unfortunately, being logged in as **root** is a security problem. If you leave a **root** shell open on your desktop, anyone stopping by your desk can destroy your machine in seconds, or install software that captures login names and passwords. It's also easy to accidentally delete important files or directories.

To start a root shell with su:

1. su -

   The su command (*substitute user*) lets you quickly switch to another account, usually **root** (**Code Listing 3.1**), without logging out of your current account. This is handy if you have several tasks that need to be completed as **root**, because it starts a new **root** shell that exists until you exit.

2. Type the **root** password at the Password prompt, then press Enter.

   Being able to just pop into the **root** account by typing two characters wouldn't be good for system security, so you also need to know **root**'s password.

3. Do the work that needs to be done as **root**, such as editing files in /etc.

4. Type *exit*, then press Enter.

   Since the **root** shell created by **su** remains until you exit, it's important to remember this step. Without it, you're leaving a **root** shell open on your desktop.

Code Listing 3.1 Using su to become root.

```
[chrish@dhcppc2 chrish]$ id
uid=500(chrish) gid=500(chrish)
→ groups=500(chrish)


[chrish@dhcppc2 chrish]$ su -
Password:


[root@dhcppc2 root]# id
uid=0(root) gid=0(root)
→ groups=0(root),1(bin),2(daemon),3(sys),
→ 4(adm),6(disk),10(wheel)


[root@dhcppc2 root]# exit
logout


[chrish@dhcppc2 chrish]$ id
uid=500(chrish) gid=500(chrish)
→ groups=500(chrish)
```

Code Listing 3.2 Using su to become a specific user.

```
[root@dhcppc2 root]# id
uid=0(root) gid=0(root)
→ groups=0(root),1(bin),2(daemon),3(sys),
→ 4(adm),6(disk),10(wheel)


[root@dhcppc2 root]# su - chrish


[chrish@dhcppc2 chrish]$ id
uid=500(chrish) gid=500(chrish)
→ groups=500(chrish)


[chrish@dhcppc2 chrish]$ exit
logout


[root@dhcppc2 root]#
```

✔ Tips

- Instead of using the exit command to end a shell session, you can almost always press Ctrl-D.

- You can specify a user name on the su command line (**Code Listing 3.2**) to act as that user instead of **root**. If you're logged in as **root**, you don't need to enter a password.

- Use the id command to see your current user ID and group ID, as well as the list of groups you belong to (Code Listing 3.1).

LOGGING IN AS ROOT

To run a single command as root with sudo:

1. sudo *command*

The sudo command ("su do," but usually pronounced like "pseudo") runs a single command as the root user (**Code Listing 3.3**).

2. Type *your* password at the Password prompt, then press Enter.

Why is typing your own password enough security to give you access to root's powers? Because root had to add you to the /etc/sudoers file with appropriate permissions. If you're not in this file, you can't use sudo.

✔ Tips

■ You can specify a user name on the sudo command line with the -u option (**Code Listing 3.4**) to run the command as that user instead of root.

■ To add a user to the /etc/sudoers file, log in as root, then use your favorite text editor to add a line like this to the file (replace *userid* with the user's login name):

userid ALL=(ALL) ALL

■ To add an entire group to the /etc/sudoers file, log in as root, then use your favorite text editor to add a line like this to the file (replace *groupid* with the group's name):

%*groupid* ALL=(ALL) ALL

Code Listing 3.3 Using sudo to run a command as root.

```
[chrish@dhcppc2 chrish]$ id
uid=500(chrish) gid=500(chrish)
⇢ groups=500(chrish)


[chrish@dhcppc2 chrish]$ sudo id
Password:
uid=0(root) gid=0(root)
⇢ groups=0(root),1(bin),2(daemon),3(sys),
⇢ 4(adm),6(disk),10(wheel)


[chrish@dhcppc2 chrish]$ id
uid=500(chrish) gid=500(chrish)
⇢ groups=500(chrish)
```

Code Listing 3.4 Using sudo to run a command as a specific user.

```
[root@dhcppc2 root]# id
uid=0(root) gid=0(root)
⇢ groups=0(root),1(bin),2(daemon),3(sys),
⇢ 4(adm),6(disk),10(wheel)


[root@dhcppc2 root]# sudo -u chrish id
uid=500(chrish) gid=500(chrish)
⇢ groups=500(chrish)


[root@dhcppc2 root]# id
uid=0(root) gid=0(root)
⇢ groups=0(root),1(bin),2(daemon),3(sys),
⇢ 4(adm),6(disk),10(wheel)
```

```
[root@dhcppc2 root]# who
root      tty1      Oct 26 22:16
[root@dhcppc2 root]# telinit 1
INIT: Switching to runlevel: 1
INIT: Sending processes the TERM signal
Stopping system message bus:                    [  OK  ]
Stopping atd:                                   [  OK  ]
Stopping cups:                                  [  OK  ]
Shutting down xfs:                              [  OK  ]
Shutting down console mouse services:           [  OK  ]
Stopping sshd:                                  [  OK  ]
Shutting down sendmail:                         [  OK  ]
Shutting down sm-client:                        [  OK  ]
Shutting down smartd: _
```

Figure 3.1 Switching Fedora Core to single-user mode.

```
bsd# who
root          ttyv0     Oct 26 21:51
bsd# shutdown now
Shutdown NOW!
shutdown: [pid 559]
bsd#

*** FINAL System shutdown message from root@bsd ***
System going down IMMEDIATELY


Oct 26 21:51:41 bsd shutdown: shutdown by root:

System shutdown time has arrived
Stopping inetd.
Shutting down daemon processes:.
Stopping cron.
Shutting down local daemons:.
Writing entropy file:.
Terminated
Oct 26 21:51:45 bsd syslogd: exiting on signal 15
Enter full pathname of shell or RETURN for /bin/sh: █
```

Figure 3.2 Switching FreeBSD to single-user mode.

```
Telling INIT to go to single user mode.
INIT: Going single user
INIT: Sending processes the TERM signal
INIT: Sending processes the KILL signal
sh-2.05b# _
```

Figure 3.3 Single-user mode (Fedora Core).

To switch to single-user mode:

Single-user mode shuts down most services and prevents other users from logging in to the system. This is great for doing system maintenance without worrying about destroying other people's work or corrupting the file system.

Watch out, though. If you switch to single-user mode from a remote session (telnet or ssh, for example), you'll be kicked off the system, too, because the Internet services will be shut down.

1. Tell the system to switch to single-user mode by doing one of the following:
   ▲ If you're using Fedora Core (**Figure 3.1**):
   `telinit 1`
   ▲ If you're using FreeBSD (**Figure 3.2**):
   `shutdown now`

   The system shuts down everything except for the basic services, kicks off any users, and leaves you with a basic shell session (**Figure 3.3**).

2. Perform your system maintenance, such as running file-system checks or updating the kernel.

3. Reboot the system by doing one of the following:
   ▲ If you're using Fedora Core:
   `telinit 6`
   ▲ If you're using FreeBSD:
   `shutdown -r now`

The system reboots in all of its normal multi-user glory.

LOGGING IN AS ROOT

Administering Users and Groups

Unless you're using your Unix system as a personal workstation, you're going to want to give other people access to the system by creating user accounts and grouping them.

If your users are consuming disk space at an unreasonable pace, you can also consider turning on disk quotas to limit their disk usage before they fill your hard drive. Refer to your OS documentation for more information about activating and controlling quotas.

To add a new group (Fedora Core):

Fedora Core's graphical User Manager can be used to add, delete, and edit groups.

1. Launch the User Manager by clicking the red hat icon in the top left of the Fedora desktop to display the menu, the System Settings item in the menu to display the settings submenu, and then the Users and Groups item in the settings menu.

   The system displays a Query dialog asking for the **root** password (**Figure 3.4**).

2. Enter the **root** password and click OK to continue, or click Cancel to stop loading the User Manager.

   The system loads the User Manager (**Figure 3.5**).

3. Click the Add Group toolbar icon.

   The User Manager displays the Create New Group dialog (**Figure 3.6**).

4. Enter a name for the new group in the Group Name field.

5. If you need to specify an ID for the group, check the "Specify group ID manually" box and enter the group's ID (GID) in the GID field. If you don't specify a GID, an unused one will be assigned.

6. Click OK to create the new group.

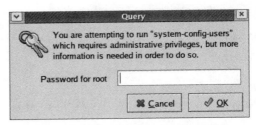

Figure 3.4 In the Query dialog, Fedora Core asks for authentication with the **root** password.

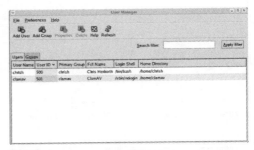

Figure 3.5 Fedora Core's User Manager application.

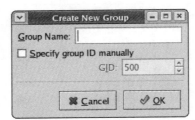

Figure 3.6 Creating a new group with the User Manager.

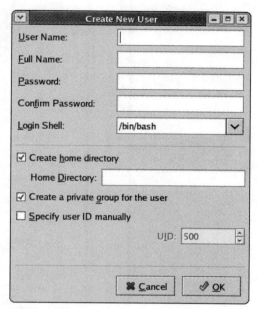

Figure 3.7 Creating a new user with the User Manager.

To add a new user (Fedora Core):

With a name like the User Manager, you'd expect it to also be able to add users.

1. Launch the User Manager by clicking the red hat icon, the System Settings menu item, and then the Users and Groups item.

   The system displays a Query dialog asking for the **root** password (Figure 3.4).

2. Enter the **root** password and click OK to continue, or click Cancel to stop loading the User Manager.

   The system loads the User Manager (Figure 3.5).

3. Click the Add User toolbar icon.

   The User Manager displays the Create New User dialog (**Figure 3.7**).

4. Enter a name for the new user in the User Name field.

5. Enter the user's full name in the Full Name field.

   continues on next page

ADMINISTERING USERS AND GROUPS

6. Enter the user's password in the Password field. Enter it again in the Confirm Password field to make sure you've entered it properly.

7. Select a default shell for the user from the Login Shell pop-up menu. This lists all of the shells available on the system. The default, /bin/bash, is an excellent choice, although some people will have other preferences.

8. To create the user's home directory automatically, check the "Create home directory" box; otherwise you will have to create the directory by hand or use an existing directory. Enter the path to the user's home directory in the Home Directory field.

9. Check the "Create a private group for the user" box if you want each user to have his or her own private group. This is a security measure.

10. To specify a user ID (UID) for the new user, check the "Specify user ID manually" box and enter the user ID in the UID field. If you don't specify a UID, an unused one will be assigned to the new user.

11. Click OK to create the new user.

Figure 3.8 The sysinstall tool lets you change much of FreeBSD's configuration, including adding new users and groups.

Figure 3.9 The FreeBSD Configuration Menu in sysinstall.

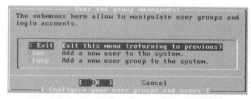

Figure 3.10 The "User and group management" dialog lets you create new users and groups.

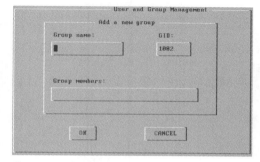

Figure 3.11 Adding a new group.

To add a new group (FreeBSD):

Like most configuration changes in FreeBSD, adding a new group is done through the sysinstall interface.

1. Log in as root.

2. sysinstall

   Launch the sysinstall tool (**Figure 3.8**). You'll recognize this from when you installed FreeBSD.

3. Use the down arrow key to select Configure, then press Enter to continue. The sysinstall tool displays the FreeBSD Configuration Menu (**Figure 3.9**).

4. Use the down arrow key to select User Management, then press Enter to continue. The sysinstall tool displays the "User and group management" dialog (**Figure 3.10**).

5. Press the down arrow key to select Group, then press Enter.

6. The installer displays the "Add a new group" pane (**Figure 3.11**).

7. Enter the new group's information:

   Group name—The name of the new group.

   GID—Group ID (GID); you can leave the default alone unless you need to create a group with a specific GID.

   Group members—A list of users that belong to this new group; you can leave this blank.

   Press Tab to select OK, and press Enter to return to the "User and group management" dialog (Figure 3.10).

8. Press the up arrow key to select Exit, then press Enter to return to the FreeBSD Configuration Menu screen.

9. Press the up arrow key to select Exit, then press Enter to return to the sysinstall main menu.

10. Press X to exit sysinstall.

To add a new user (FreeBSD):

The sysinstall tool's "User and group management" dialog is also used to create new users.

1. Log in as root.

2. sysinstall

   Launch the sysinstall tool (Figure 3.8). You'll recognize this from when you installed FreeBSD.

3. Use the down arrow key to select Configure, then press Enter to continue.

   The sysinstall tool displays the FreeBSD Configuration Menu (Figure 3.9).

4. Use the down arrow key to select User Management, then press Enter to continue.

   The sysinstall tool displays the "User and group management" dialog (Figure 3.10).

5. Select User, then press Enter.

   The installer displays the "Add a new user" pane (**Figure 3.12**).

6. Enter the new user's information:

   Login ID—The account's login name.

   UID—User ID; you can leave the default alone. Figure 3.12 shows a new user getting a UID of 1001, the same as the ID of the group we made in the previous task, "To add a new group (FreeBSD)". That's OK, if a little confusing, because the user IDs and group IDs come from different pools and can overlap without causing problems.

   Group—Group ID; enter *1001* here, for the users group we just created.

   Password—The user's initial password.

   Full name—The user's full name; you can include other useful information (phone extension, and so on) here as well, if there's room (63 characters will fit).

   Member groups—Other groups this user will belong to; you can leave this blank.

   Home directory—The user's home directory; you can use the default unless you need the user's home to be somewhere else.

   Login shell—The shell this user will use by default; use the default.

7. Select OK and press Enter to return to the "User and group management" dialog (Figure 3.10).

8. Select Exit, then press Enter.

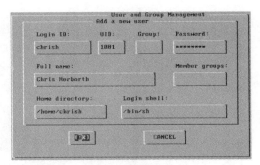

Figure 3.12 Adding a new user.

To add a new group (Windows with Cygwin):

◆ To add a new group to Cygwin, you need to create it first using the Windows User Accounts control panel or the Computer Management administrative tool. Refer to your Windows documentation for more information about how to use those tools.

mkgroup -l -g *name* >> /etc/group

Adds information about the group specified by *name* to the /etc/group file, for use with Cygwin.

The -l option means local groups only (if you're on a domain, use -d instead), and -g is to display information for the specified group only. Without the -g option, mkgroup would print information about all known groups.

To add a new user (Windows with Cygwin):

◆ To add a new user to Cygwin, you create it with the User Accounts control panel or the Computer Management administrative tool. Then open a Cygwin window and use the mkpasswd command to add the new user *name* to the /etc/passwd file:

mkpasswd -l -u *name* >> /etc/passwd

The -l option means local users only (if you're on a domain, use -d instead), and -u is to display information for the specified user only. Without the -u option, mkpasswd would print information about all known users.

ADMINISTERING USERS AND GROUPS

To add a new group (Mac OS X):

The NetInfo Manager handles groups on Mac OS X, providing a graphical interface for creating, deleting, and modifying groups.

1. Launch the NetInfo Manager, found in /Applications/Utilities on your boot volume.

   The system starts the NetInfo Manager, with a view of your local information tree (**Figure 3.13**).

2. Click the lock icon in the lower-left corner; this lets you make changes to the NetInfo database.

   NetInfo displays a dialog asking you for the user ID and password for an administrator's account (**Figure 3.14**).

Figure 3.13 Apple's NetInfo Manager handles a database of information that other Unix variants store in text files in /etc.

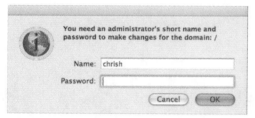

Figure 3.14 Logging in as an administrator to modify NetInfo's database.

Figure 3.15 NetInfo shows you the existing groups.

Figure 3.16 Creating a new group in NetInfo.

3. Enter the user ID and password for an administrator's account, then click OK or press Enter to continue.

4. Click the groups entry in NetInfo's second column.

NetInfo displays the available groups (**Figure 3.15**).

5. Click the New icon in the toolbar.

NetInfo creates a new entry in the groups list named new_directory (**Figure 3.16**).

6. Double-click the name property's value (currently new_directory) to change it to an editable field. Enter the name of your new group.

7. Choose New Property from NetInfo's Directory menu to create a new property.

continues on next page

8. Double-click new_property in the property list and change it to password. Now do the same to change new_value to * (an asterisk).

9. Create another new property, named gid, and set its value to an unused group ID. You may need to look at /etc/group or the existing group entries to see which IDs are already used. Starting with 1001 seems like a safe bet.

10. Choose Save Changes from the Domain menu to create your new group.

    NetInfo displays a confirmation dialog (**Figure 3.17**).

11. Click the "Update this copy" button in the confirmation dialog to save your changes.

Figure 3.17 Confirming your changes to NetInfo's database.

To add a new user (Mac OS X):

◆ In Mac OS X, you use the Accounts pane of System Preferences to create new users.

No additional intervention is required. Please refer to your Mac OS X documentation for information about using the Accounts pane.

Figure 3.18 Webmin's System page gives you access to several handy system tools.

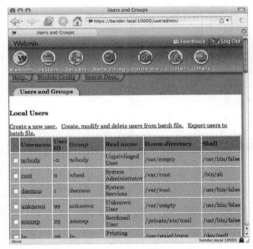

Figure 3.19 The Users and Groups page lets you manipulate users and groups on your system.

Using Webmin

Webmin is a powerful tool that handles every aspect of system administration. And if it doesn't do something you need it to do, you can create (or download) an add-on module to expand its capabilities.

To cover all of Webmin's features would take an entire book, so we'll take a quick look at how Webmin can simplify a couple of tasks from the previous section. (For more on installing and securing Webmin, see Appendix F, "Installing Webmin.")

To add a new group:

Adding groups is easy if you have a nice graphical interface.

1. Bring up Webmin in your favorite Web browser and log in.

2. Click the System icon in the toolbar at the top of the page. This displays the System tools page (**Figure 3.18**).

3. Click the Users and Groups icon to display the Users and Groups page (**Figure 3.19**).

continues on next page

USING WEBMIN

4. Scroll down to the Local Groups table (below the Local Users table) and click the "Create a new group" link to display the Create Group page (**Figure 3.20**).

5. Enter the details for your new group, then click the Create button.

Webmin creates the new group and returns you to the Users and Groups page.

To add a new user:

Being able to add users by going to your Web browser makes this process much less painful.

1. Bring up Webmin in your favorite Web browser and log in.

2. Click the System icon in the toolbar at the top of the page. This displays the System tools page (Figure 3.18).

3. Click the Users and Groups icon to display the Users and Groups page (Figure 3.19).

4. Click the "Create a new user" link to display the Create User page (**Figure 3.21**).

5. Enter the details for your new user, then click the Create button.

Webmin creates the new user and returns you to the Users and Groups page.

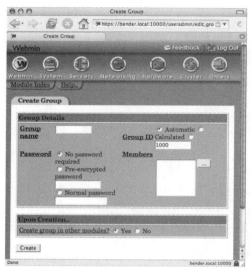

Figure 3.20 Creating a new group with Webmin.

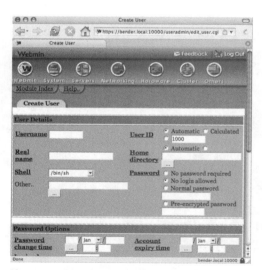

Figure 3.21 Creating new users with Webmin.

Understanding Logs

Unix systems traditionally record interesting events, such as services' starting or stopping, errors encountered while reading configuration files, or anything else that strikes the program author's fancy. These logs can contain important information about failing services.

To find system logs:

◆ The system logs are usually stored as regular files, although there are a couple (such as /var/adm and /var/log/wtmp) that contain binary data and aren't meant for human consumption.

cd /var/log

The files and directories in /var/log, the standard log file directory, make up the system log. Various application log files are also stored there.

To read log entries:

◆ Entries in the system log files almost always follow the same pattern:

date time [*process*] *message*

The *date* and *time* should be self-explanatory, and the *process* is the name of the program that made the log entry (it might also contain the name of the host that sent this log message). The *message* could be literally anything, but it should tell you what the programmer was recording in the log.

To write log entries:

◆ You can create your own log entries, which might be useful in a shell script.

logger *message*

Write *message* to the system log (/var/log/ messages on Fedora Core and FreeBSD, the system Event Viewer on Cygwin, and /var/log/system.log on Mac OS X).

To view system logs with Webmin:

Finding the right log can be frustrating, but Webmin gives you a handy list to choose from.

1. Bring up Webmin in your favorite Web browser and log in.

2. Click the System icon in the toolbar at the top of the page. This displays the System tools page (Figure 3.18).

3. Click the System Logs icon to display the System Logs page (**Figure 3.22**).

4. Click the View link for the log you're interested in to display the View Logfile page (**Figure 3.23**).

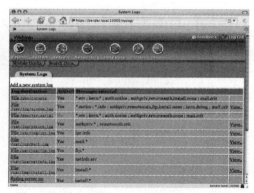

Figure 3.22 Webmin's System Logs page lists all of the system logs and tells you whether each log is active or not.

Figure 3.23 Viewing a log file with Webmin.

```
root@dhcppc2:~
File  Edit  View  Terminal  Tabs  Help
[root@dhcppc2 root]# mount
/dev/hda2 on / type ext3 (rw)
none on /proc type proc (rw)
none on /sys type sysfs (rw)
none on /dev/pts type devpts (rw,gid=5,mode=620)
usbdevfs on /proc/bus/usb type usbdevfs (rw)
/dev/hda1 on /boot type ext3 (rw)
none on /dev/shm type tmpfs (rw)
sunrpc on /var/lib/nfs/rpc_pipefs type rpc_pipefs (rw)
[root@dhcppc2 root]#
```

Figure 3.24 The mount command lists your devices and where they're mounted in the file system.

Checking Your File System

Normally you should be able to trust that your OS's file system will keep your data safe, but what about circumstances beyond your control? Maybe your power went out and you couldn't shut down the machine properly, for example.

You're going to need to be able to check your file systems for errors. Windows and Mac OS X both have operating-system-specific tools for checking the file system (although Mac OS X's is called fsck behind the scenes). Please refer to your operating system documentation for more information.

To check your file system with fsck:

1. Switch to single-user mode (see "To switch to single-user mode," earlier in the chapter).

   This will let fsck do its job without your having to worry about other users poking around while it's working.

2. mount

   Using the mount command without any arguments prints a list of the mounted file systems and the devices they reside on (**Figure 3.24**).

3. fsck *filesystem*

   Use the fsck command to check the specified file system. You can specify a file system by giving its device (the cryptic /dev path) or by giving its mount point (such as /tmp).

Spying On Your File System

Sometimes it can be handy to keep track of changes in your file system. For example, you may have a stable system, with nothing changing except for the user data in /home and the usual logs and temporary files in /var and /tmp.

Or so you think. If someone compromised your system, he or she might replace scripts and programs anywhere in the system with ones that log passwords or provide back doors.

It might be helpful to have a couple of scripts on hand that will help you find changed files.

✔ Tip

■ Mac OS X users will need to install the GNU **textutils** package to use these scripts, using the following Fink command in a Terminal window:

```
sudo fink install textutils
```

Code Listing 3.5 The spygen script creates file signatures for the directories you specify.

```
#!/bin/sh
#
# Record file signatures for future
# comparison.

# Edit the following lines to customize
# this script for your needs.

# Destination location for the file
# signatures.
DEST_DIR=/var/spy

# Directories to take the signatures
# from:
SOURCE_DIRS="/bin /etc /lib /sbin /usr"

# End of customization... ready to go!

# Figure out which tool to use for
# signatures, based on our OS.
case $(uname) in
    Linux | CYGWIN* | Darwin)
        SIG_TOOL=sha1sum
        ;;

    FreeBSD)
        SIG_TOOL="sha1 -r"
        ;;

    *)
        echo Unknown system: $(uname)
        exit 1
esac
```

(code continues on next page)

Code Listing 3.5 *continued*

```
# Check to see if the DEST_DIR exists; if
# not, create it.
if [ ! -d $DEST_DIR ] ; then
    echo Creating $DEST_DIR
    mkdir -p $DEST_DIR
fi


# Loop through the SOURCE_DIRS and create
# a duplicate directory structure, with
# files containing signatures.
for d in $SOURCE_DIRS ; do
    if [ ! -d $d ] ; then
        echo WARNING: skipping $d
        continue
    fi

    for s in $(find $d -type d) ; do
        if [ ! -d $DEST_DIR$s ] ; then
            echo Creating $DEST_DIR$s
            mkdir -p $DEST_DIR$s
        fi
    done

    echo Creating signatures for $d
    for f in $(find $d -type f) ; do
        if [ -e $DEST_DIR$f ] ; then
            rm -f $DEST_DIR$f
        fi
        $SIG_TOOL $f > $DEST_DIR$f
    done
done
```

To record file signatures:

1. Log in as **root**, use **su** to become **root**, or use **sudo** to edit and run this script.

2. Using your favorite text editor, edit the **spygen** script (**Code Listing 3.5**) to customize the following values:

   ▲ DEST_DIR—This directory (which will be created if it doesn't exist already) will contain the file signatures. The signatures are created in a mirror of the source directories and stored in files with names matching the original file. For example, if signatures are made for /bin, $DEST_DIR/bin will end up with a file named **sh** containing the signature for /bin/sh.

   ▲ SOURCE_DIRS—A list of directories (note that you *must* enclose this list in double quotes) that will be included while creating signatures. If one of the SOURCE_DIRS doesn't exist during the scan, a warning is displayed.

3. Save **spygen** and make it executable by adding the executable mode:

   chmod 700 spygen

   Mode **700** is "readable, writable, and executable by owner," which will keep other users from reading, modifying, or running the script.

4. ./spygen

   Run the script to create (or update) your file signatures.

To check file signatures:

1. Log in as **root**, use su to become **root**, or use **sudo** to edit and run this script.

2. Using your favorite text editor, edit the spycheck script (**Code Listing 3.6**) to customize the following value:

   ▲ DEST_DIR—The file signature directory. Set this to the same value as DEST_DIR in the **spygen** script.

3. Save spycheck and make it executable by adding the executable mode:

   chmod 700 spycheck

4. ./spycheck

   Run the script to check the file signatures. If none of the files have been tampered with, no messages will be printed. If changes are detected, the file's full path and the word FAILED will be displayed.

Code Listing 3.6 The spycheck script checks the signatures created by spygen against the files on your system.

```
#!/bin/sh
#
# Check previously recorded file
# signatures to help detect tampering.

# Edit the following lines to customize
# this script for your needs.

# Destination location for the file
# signatures.
DEST_DIR=/var/spy


# End of customization... ready to go!

# Fake sha1 checking tool for FreeBSD,
# which doesn't have a built-in method
# for checking signatures.
sha1checker() {
    # Load existing signature.
    sig="$(cat $1)"

    # Extract the file name.
    f=$(echo $sig | awk '{ print $2 }')

    # Generate a sha1 signature for
    # the existing file.
    curr=$(sha1 -r $f)
```

(code continues on next page)

Code Listing 3.6 *continued*

```
    if [ "$sig" = "$curr" ] ; then
        echo $f: OK
    else
        echo $f: FAILED
    fi
}


# Figure out which tool to use for
# signatures, based on our OS.
case $(uname) in
    Linux | CYGWIN* | Darwin)
        SIG_TOOL=sha1sum —check
        ;;

    FreeBSD)
        SIG_TOOL=sha1checker
        ;;

    *)
        echo Unknown system: $(uname)
        exit 1
esac


# Go through the signatures in DEST_DIR
# and compare them to the files on your
# disk.
for f in $(find $DEST_DIR -type f) ; do
    $SIG_TOOL $f | egrep FAILED
done
```

Testing Your LAN

Even though you configured your Internet connection while installing your operating system, you might need to test it to help diagnose network problems.

To test your connection with ping:

◆ ping *hostname*

Use the ping command (**Code Listing 3.7**) to test your connection to the specified *hostname*. ping sends out small network packets and waits for a response from the remote system, keeping track of how much time it takes.

✔ Tips

■ If you're using ping on Linux, FreeBSD, or Mac OS X, you'll have to press Ctrl-C to stop the pinging and get the summary. By default, the Windows ping command stops after four packets.

■ As you can see from the code listing, this will also tell you the "true" name of the system you're pinging. For example, the URL www.cbc.ca resolves to a Web host in the network of a big hosting company called Akami.

If your ping attempts fail, you can use **traceroute** to see where the problem might be.

Code Listing 3.7 Using the ping command to test your Internet connection.

```
chrish@taffer [501]: ping www.cbc.ca

Pinging a1849.gc.akamai.net [199.232.61.145] with 32 bytes of data:

Reply from 199.232.61.145: bytes=32 time=42ms TTL=52
Reply from 199.232.61.145: bytes=32 time=53ms TTL=52
Reply from 199.232.61.145: bytes=32 time=49ms TTL=52
Reply from 199.232.61.145: bytes=32 time=40ms TTL=52

Ping statistics for 199.232.61.145:
    Packets: Sent = 4, Received = 4, Lost = 0 (0% loss),
Approximate round trip times in milli-seconds:
    Minimum = 40ms, Maximum = 53ms, Average = 46ms
```

To test your connection with traceroute:

◆ traceroute *hostname*

Or, if you're using a Windows system, tracert *hostname*.

The traceroute command (**Code Listing 3.8**) does more work than a simple ping. It sends packets out to the specified system, but it also polls the systems between you and your target.

✔ Tips

■ The columns in the output are the network *hop* number, the response times for three packets, and the name of the host at that hop.

■ If a host doesn't respond, times of * are displayed, and the host's name is Request timed out. When your destination can't be reached, traceroute will print these lines several times as it tries to reach the end point.

Code Listing 3.8 Using the traceroute command to test your Internet connection.

```
chrish@taffer [503]: tracert www.cbc.ca

Tracing route to a1849.gc.akamai.net [65.161.97.143]
over a maximum of 30 hops:

  1    1 ms     1 ms     1 ms   router [192.168.0.1]
  2   21 ms     9 ms    11 ms   10.116.76.1
  3   11 ms    10 ms    11 ms   gw03.flfrd.phub.net.cable.rogers.com [66.185.90.241]
  4    *         *         *     Request timed out.
  5   13 ms    13 ms    14 ms   gw02.mtnk.phub.net.cable.rogers.com [66.185.82.125]
  6   35 ms    39 ms    35 ms   igw01.ny8th.phub.net.cable.rogers.com [66.185.81.13]
  7   35 ms   114 ms    35 ms   dcr1-so-4-3-0.NewYork.savvis.net [206.24.207.101]
  8   31 ms    32 ms    31 ms   dcr2-loopback.NewYork.savvis.net [206.24.194.100]
  9   31 ms    43 ms    29 ms   144.232.9.117
 10   35 ms    35 ms    29 ms   sl-bb21-nyc-6-0.sprintlink.net [144.232.13.186]
 11   34 ms    42 ms    44 ms   sl-bb27-pen-12-0.sprintlink.net [144.232.20.97]
 12   52 ms    35 ms    51 ms   sl-bb22-pen-8-0.sprintlink.net [144.232.16.53]
 13   34 ms    37 ms    33 ms   sl-bb21-pen-15-0.sprintlink.net [144.232.16.29]
 14   66 ms    51 ms    48 ms   sl-bb23-rly-0-0.sprintlink.net [144.232.20.32]
 15   45 ms    42 ms    41 ms   sl-st20-ash-10-0.sprintlink.net [144.232.20.152]
 16   42 ms    42 ms    43 ms   65.161.97.143

Trace complete.
```

TESTING YOUR LAN

SAFETY AND SECURITY

Keeping systems secure is a hot topic these days, with mainstream media reporting on viruses and security flaws affecting popular (and, unfortunately, widespread) software. As the administrator of a system, you are responsible for making sure that your system is as safe and secure as possible.

While a part of this entails keeping your software up-to-date to incorporate security fixes, you also need to disable dangerous services that might be active by default on your system. You'll need to make sure that you and your users have a good password that can't be easily broken.

Making regular backups improves the safety of your system. Even if your system is never cracked by nefarious people, you'll still probably suffer from a failed hard disk or a user accident ("I just deleted my home directory!") at some point. It's also a good idea to install a virus scanner to prevent viruses on other operating systems from passing through your email server to attack the machines pulling their email from your Unix system. This chapter will show you how to keep your network safe and secure.

About Security

Seems like you hear about a new hacking exploit or security flaw almost every week. Making your system secure isn't a single task you can perform once, it's an ongoing series of small tasks.

Luckily, there are several things anyone can do to make sure their system is reasonably secure. Keeping your passwords secure, disabling any unnecessary and potentially dangerous services, paying attention to security advisories, and keeping your system up-to-date (which we cover in the appendixes) are good ways to keep your system secure.

To change your password:

1. `passwd`

   The `passwd` command will lead you through the process of changing your password.

   If you're using Windows or Mac OS X, use the standard operating-system control panels for changing your password.

2. Unless you're logged in as **root**, you'll be prompted to enter your old password. Type it and press Enter. Your existing password won't show up onscreen, so type carefully.

   If you're changing **root**'s password, skip this step and go straight to step 3.

3. Enter your new password, then press Enter.

   Your new password doesn't show up onscreen, so type carefully.

4. To ensure that you typed it correctly, you will be asked to retype your password; do so and then press Enter again.

Securing a Password

Your password should be easy for you to remember but impossible for someone else to guess.

- ◆ Pick a short word, phrase, or sequence of letters and/or numbers at least eight characters long.

- ◆ Don't pick family names, birth dates, or terms that others might trace back to you. On the other hand, passwords are useless if you can't remember them, so keep it simple. You don't want to end up locked out of your system, and if you have to write your password down, then anyone can break into your computer.

- ◆ Switch at least one of the letters to uppercase or to a similar number. For example, you could use 0 (zero) instead of o, or 3 instead of E.

- ◆ Substitute at least one symbol for a character.

Now you should have a password that's a minimum of eight characters long, with letters, numbers, case changes, and symbols in it.

✔ Tip

- ■ Change your password using the `passwd` command (**Code Listing 4.1**) periodically. Some corporate IT groups suggest doing so every three months, but every six months to a year is probably often enough, and you'll be less likely to forget your current password.

Code Listing 4.1 Changing your password with the passwd command.

```
$ passwd

Changing local password for chrish
Old Password:
New Password:
Retype New Password:
```

Code Listing 4.2 Disabling xinetd services.

```
[root@dhcppc2 xinetd.d]# ps aux | grep
→ xinetd | awk '{ print $2; }'
1880
2573
[root@dhcppc2 xinetd.d]# kill -HUP 1880
```

To disable dangerous services (xinetd):

If you're using Fedora Core or Mac OS X, the xinetd service controls all of the standard Internet services, such as telnet and ftp.

1. **cd /etc/xinetd.d**

   If your system uses xinetd (Fedora Core or Mac OS X) to control Internet services, the configuration information is stored in the xinetd.d subdirectory of /etc.

2. Edit the various files, each named after the service it configures, in the xinetd.d directory using your favorite text editor.

   Lines beginning with the # character are comments. Each file lists the service name and several keyword/value pairs, one per line.

   Disabled services will have a disabled = yes line in the configuration file.

3. Make sure that any unnecessary services are disabled by adding a disabled = yes line to their configuration files, if one isn't already there.

   Services you'll want to disable (if they aren't already) include telnet, ftp, shell, login, exec, talk, ntalk, and tftp. You probably don't require any of these.

4. **ps aux | grep xinetd |**
   → awk '{ print $2; }'

   Find the process ID (PID) of xinetd (**Code Listing 4.2**).

   You'll see two entries here; the second is for the grep command you just entered.

5. **kill -HUP *pid***

   Send the "hang up" signal to xinetd. By convention, this signal tells servers to reload their configuration files.

To disable dangerous services (inetd):

1. `cd /etc`

If your system uses `inetd` (FreeBSD or Cygwin with the `inetd` package installed) to control Internet services, the configuration information is stored in the usual directory.

2. Edit the inetd.conf file using your favorite text editor.

Lines beginning with the # character are comments. Each line lists the service name, information about the service's connections, the program that supports the service, and any program arguments.

3. Make sure that any unnecessary services are commented out by adding a # character at the start of the line.

Services you'll want to disable (if they aren't already) include `telnet`, `ftp`, `shell`, `login`, `exec`, `talk`, `ntalk`, and `tftp`. You probably don't require any of these.

4. `ps aux | grep /usr/sbin/inetd |`
`→ awk '{ print $2; }'`

Find the process ID (PID) of `inetd` (**Code Listing 4.3**).

5. `kill -HUP pid`

Send the "hang up" signal to `inetd`. By convention, this signal tells servers to reload their configuration files.

Code Listing 4.3 Disabling `inetd` services.

```
bsd# ps aux | egrep /usr/sbin/inetd | awk '{
→ print $2; }'

437
bsd# kill -HUP 437
```

Figure 4.1 The US-CERT Web site tracks network-security issues worldwide.

Backing Up and Restoring Data

If you've worked with computers for any length of time, you've probably discovered why making regular backups is important. Specifically, if you haven't backed up your data, you're going to lose it.

To back up data using tar:

◆ `tar -czvf` *`archive.tar.gz`* *`filesordirs`*

Where *`archive.tar.gz`* is the name of the archive you'll be creating, and *`filesordirs`* is a list of one or more files or directories to include in the archive.

The `-czvf` options are, in order: create an archive, compress the archive, be verbose, and store the archive data in the file specified by the next argument.

To restore data using tar:

◆ `tar -xpzvf` *`archive.tar.gz`*

Where *`archive.tar.gz`* is the name of an existing archive created with `tar`. This extracts the files and directories in *`archive.tar.gz`* into the current directory.

The `-xpzvf` options are, in order: extract the contents of an archive, preserve ownership and permissions, read compressed archives, be verbose, and read the archive data from the file specified by the next argument.

Tracking Security Advisories

US-CERT (U.S. Computer Emergency Readiness Team) tracks the spread of security exploits (including viruses, worms, Trojans, **root** compromises, and so on) around the Internet, their danger level, and the response, if any, of vendors, such as a patch or work-around. As a system administrator, you would be wise to pay attention to US-CERT in case any of the many new and exciting problems discovered almost weekly affect the software you're running.

At the US-CERT Web site (www.us-cert. gov), you can find major announcements, notification of current security exploit activity, and information on how to prepare for and respond to problems (**Figure 4.1**).

If you join the US-CERT mailing list through the Cyber Security Alert System (www.us-cert.gov/cas/signup.html), you'll get emails about new exploits and security patches. You'll also want to install any security patches for your operating system, servers (including Web, email, and FTP if you have them installed), and other software. The CERT advisories will almost always point you toward an appropriate patch.

To back up data using dd:

◆ `dd bs=1M if=`*`in-path`* `|`
 `⇥ gzip >` *`out-path`*`.gz`

This dumps *in-path* (which can be a file or a device) through `gzip`, one megabyte at a time. The `gzip` command compresses the data, which is then stored in *out-path*`.gz`.

Using **dd** this way, you can make an exact backup of a device, such as a disk partition.

To restore data using dd:

◆ `gzcat` *`in-path`*`.gz |`
 `⇥ dd bs=1M of=`*`out-path`*

This decompresses *in-path*`.gz` and sends it through **dd**. The **dd** command writes the data to *out-path*, one megabyte at a time.

✔ Tip

■ Be very careful with **dd**; you can easily destroy the contents of your hard drive by feeding it the wrong arguments. For example, accidentally swapping the `of=` and `if=` arguments could overwrite your file, the contents of a device, or your backup data.

Scanning for Viruses

Even though Windows systems get the most attention from virus writers, other platforms can still act as sources of infections. Compromised Web sites and email servers could send viruses on to unsuspecting client systems.

ClamAV (www.clamav.net) is a free high-quality virus-scanning tool for Unix systems; you can use it to make sure your system isn't storing any known viruses, worms, or Trojans. Because Unix viruses are rare enough to be almost nonexistent, ClamAV is usually used on Unix mail servers to ensure that Windows viruses don't make it through to the Windows client systems receiving their email from the Unix server.

✔ Tip

■ As of this writing (shortly after the release of Fedora Core 3), ClamAV couldn't be built on Fedora Core, and there wasn't a binary package available. Keep on eye on the ClamAV Web site (www.clamav.net) and your favorite Fedora package sites for more information.

To install ClamAV (FreeBSD):

1. Log in as root.

   You could also use the su command to become root if you're already logged in.

2. cd /usr/ports/security/clamav

   ClamAV is included in the ports collection.

3. make install clean

   The "Options for clamav" dialog is displayed (**Figure 4.2**).

4. Press Enter to select the MILTER option (it adds email-filtering capabilities) in the "Options for clamav" dialog.

5. Press Tab, then Enter to dismiss the "Options for clamav" dialog and continue with the installation.

   The installer downloads the source code, then builds and installs ClamAV and its dependencies.

Figure 4.2 Sometimes optional packages are included with FreeBSD's ports; this version of ClamAV can work with the Milter email interface.

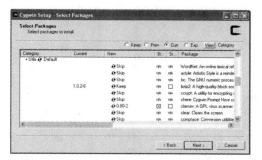

Figure 4.3 Finding ClamAV in the Cygwin Setup program.

To install ClamAV (Cygwin):

1. Launch the Cygwin installer (setup.exe); if you didn't keep this handy, refer to Appendix D for download instructions.

2. In the installer, click the Next button until you reach the package list.

3. Expand the Utils category by clicking the + (plus) sign next to the category name.

4. Drag the Cygwin Setup window's lower-right corner to expand the window so that you can find the `clamav` entry.

5. Click the circle-arrow icon in the `clamav` row so that Skip changes to a version number (**Figure 4.3**). This is the version that will be installed.

6. Click the installer's Next button. Cygwin Setup downloads and installs `clamav` and any updated versions of packages you've already installed.

7. Click Finish to exit the installer.

To install ClamAV (Mac OS X):

1. Open a Mac OS X Terminal window.

2. `sudo fink install clamav`

   Tell Fink to download, build, and install ClamAV.

3. At the Password prompt, type your password, and then press Enter to continue.

4. If prompted to download the latest virus definitions, press Enter.

To update the ClamAV signature database:

1. Log in as **root**, or use the **su** command to become **root** if you're already logged in.

2. `freshclam`

   The `freshclam` command examines your current ClamAV databases and downloads new virus signatures if there are any available.

To scan your system for viruses with ClamAV:

1. Log in as **root**, or use the **su** command to become **root** if you're already logged in.

2. `clamscan -r -i path`

   Scan the specified *path* (which can be a file, or can be a directory if you also use the -r option) for viruses. The -i option tells `clamscan` to list only infected files instead of every file that gets scanned.

BASIC SERVICES

One of the reasons why Unix systems have always been popular is that they provide services to other computers on the network, as well as to any users who might be logged in to the machine. Back in the days when memory and disk space were expensive, it made a lot of sense for businesses and universities to have centralized computers handling things like email, file distribution, and backup storage. In a lot of cases, the "computers" on people's desks were simple *dumb terminals,* basically composed of a keyboard and a monitor with some way of communicating (such as a network card) with the Unix system where the users ran all of their programs.

Even though almost nobody uses dumb terminals on today's networks, it still makes a lot of sense to have at least one machine on your network providing useful services to the other computers. In this chapter, you'll learn how to start and stop your servers without rebooting, install a daemon to provide a service for everyone on the local machine or the network, install and configure a DHCP server for a small LAN, log in to a remote Unix system with Telnet and SSH, and transfer files with FTP, rsync, and Open SSH.

Controlling Services

To live with services that run all the time (as opposed to the ones that are started when necessary by a super-server that monitors network ports (such as inetd and xinetd), you'll need to know how to start and stop them without rebooting the system. Reboots mean downtime, and that's not a good thing in the server world.

To find a service's control script:

If a service has a control script, it will be installed in the standard startup-script directory, along with the service's configuration scripts, or with the service's program itself.

1. Log in as root, or use su (or sudo) to get a root shell.

   Unless you've started the service from your normal user account, you'll need root's power to stop or start the service.

2. cd *path_to_startup_scripts*

   On Fedora Core Linux (and other Unixes that follow the lead of AT&T's System V), the *path_to_startup_scripts* is /etc/rc.d/init.d (**Code Listing 5.1**), with symbolic links made into each of the rc.d directories for specific run levels.

   On FreeBSD, the *path_to_startup_scripts* is /etc/rc.d (**Code Listing 5.2**).

   On Cygwin, daemons are usually started as Windows services (see the "Tips" section below), or from inetd or xinetd.

   On Mac OS X, the *path_to_startup_scripts* is /System/Library/StartupItems or /Library/StartupItems (**Code Listing 5.3**). Look in both directories, but keep in mind that /Library/StartupItems takes precedence over the /System directory.

Code Listing 5.1 Using the find command to look for xinetd's startup script.

```
[chrish@dhcppc0 ~]$ cd /etc/rc.d/init.d
[chrish@dhcppc0 init.d]$ find . -name
→ \*inetd\*
./xinetd
```

Code Listing 5.2 Searching for inetd's startup script on FreeBSD.

```
freebsd# cd /etc/rc.d

freebsd# find . -name     \*inetd\*

./inetd
```

CONTROLLING SERVICES

3. `find . -name \*service\*`

Use the `find` command to search the startup-script directory and any sub-directories for a script named after the *service* you're interested in.

Note that a simple `ls` might also do the job, unless there are a huge number of services on your system.

Mac OS X systems might use different names (such as `SystemLog` instead of `syslogd`) for the startup scripts.

4. `man service`

If you haven't found anything in the startup-script directory, use the service's `man` pages to find out where its control scripts are, if any exist.

Code Listing 5.3 Looking for startup scripts on Mac OS X can be more of a challenge, because the names have changed slightly.

```
bender:~ chrish$ cd /System/Library/StartupItems
bender:/System/Library/StartupItems chrish$ ls
AMD             CoreGraphics        LoginWindow         Postfix
Accounting      CrashReporter       NFS                 PrintingServices
Apache          Cron                NIS                 RemoteDesktopAgent
AppServices     DirectoryServices   NetInfo             SNMP
AppleShare      Disks               Network             SecurityServer
AuthServer      IPServices          NetworkExtensions   SystemLog
BIND            KernelEventAgent    NetworkTime         SystemTuning
ConfigServer    LDAP                Portmap             DNSResponder
bender:/System/Library/StartupItems chrish$ find . -name \*Log\*
./LoginWindow
./LoginWindow/LoginWindow
./SystemLog
./SystemLog/SystemLog
```

To stop a running service:

Stopping a running service depends on how it was started.

◆ If the service has a startup script, run the script with the **stop** argument:

/path/to/startup_script stop

◆ If the service uses its own control script (you'll find out about this in the service's *man* pages), follow the instructions in the service's *man* pages. They usually have a **stop** script, or a script that accepts a **stop** or **exit** argument.

◆ If you can't find any information about cleanly stopping a service and you really need it to stop, use the kill command to send it a terminate signal:

kill -TERM *pid*

How do you find the process ID, *pid*? Using ps and grep (**Code Listing 5.4**):

ps -ax | grep *service_name*

The first column of the output is the PID, and you can ignore the line with your grep command in it.

◆ Some systems (including Fedora Core and FreeBSD) have a pkill command that will kill a process by name:

pkill -TERM ntpd

◆ Fedora Core and Mac OS X have a **service** command, which will send a command to the named service:

service ntpd stop

Code Listing 5.4 Using the ps command and grep to find the process ID of the NTP daemon.

```
bender:~ chrish$ ps ax | grep ntpd
  321  ??  Ss     0:00.14 ntpd -f
→ /var/run/ntp.drift -p /var/run/ntpd.pid
  647 std  R+     0:00.00 grep ntpd
bender:~ chrish$
```

To start a service:

Starting a service depends on whether it has a startup script.

- If the service has a startup script, run the script with the **start** argument:

  `/path/to/startup_script start`

- If the service uses its own control script (you'll find out about this in the service's man pages), follow the instructions in the service's man pages. They usually have a **start** script, or a script that accepts a **start** or **run** argument.

- If you can't find any information about properly starting a service, you can probably run it directly from the command line:

  `/path/to/service &`

  Check the service's man pages for a **-d** or **-D** option (usually marked "run as daemon" in the documents) and any other useful arguments you might need to include.

To restart a running service:

There are two ways to restart a running service.

- `kill -HUP service_pid`

  Sending the HUP signal to a service usually tells it to reload its configuration and restart. I say "usually" because this is only a convention, not a requirement. Check the man page for your service to be sure.

  You can generally find the `service_pid` using the **ps** command and **less** or **grep**. You might also find the service's program ID in `/var/run/service.pid`.

- `/path/to/startup`
  `→ scripts/service_script restart`

  Modern Unix systems all use scripts to launch services during system startup (see Chapter 2), and the **restart** option will restart a running service. If **restart** isn't supported on your system, use **stop** and then **start** to have the same effect.

  continues on next page

CONTROLLING SERVICES

✔ Tips

- Fedora Core has a nice graphical service editing tool created by Red Hat, the Service Configuration tool (**Figure 5.1**). You can start this by going to the Applications menu in the top left of the screen and choosing System Settings > Server Settings > Services.

- If you've installed a Cygwin daemon as a Windows service (using the `cygrunsrv` command), you can use the Services item in the Administrative Tools folder of Control Panel (**Figure 5.2**). Scroll down the list until you find the service you're interested in, then right-click it and choose your desired action from the contextual pop-up menu.

- Mac OS X services can mostly be controlled through the Sharing pane of System Preferences (**Figure 5.3**). Simply select the desired service, and then click the Start/Stop button.

- Need to kill multiple copies of a process? Try this:

  ```
  ps ax | grep process_name |
  → awk -e '{ print $1; }' |
  → xargs -n 1 kill -TERM
  ```

  This `ps` command lists all of the processes currently running on your system. `grep` then picks out the ones that match *process_name*, and `awk` takes those and prints only the process IDs. The `xargs` command takes those PIDs and fires off one `kill -TERM` command per PID to tell each instance of the service to exit.

- For a pesky service that won't exit with the `TERM` signal, use `KILL` instead. The advantage of using `TERM` is that it gives the program a chance to clean up after itself. With `KILL`, it just exits immediately.

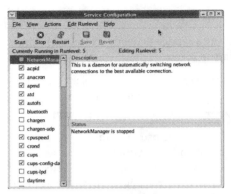

Figure 5.1 Red Hat's Service Configuration tool lets you modify the running services using a graphical interface.

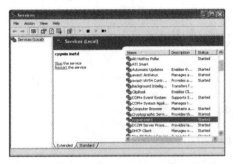

Figure 5.2 The Services control panel application under Windows lets you control the myriad services installed on a modern Windows system.

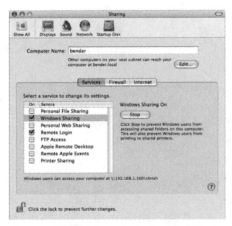

Figure 5.3 The Sharing pane in the Mac OS X System Preferences controls several standard Internet services.

Installing an Internet Daemon on Cygwin

In Unix-speak, a *daemon* is a specialized program that exists only to provide a service for users (including other programs) on the local machine or the network. Daemons can be started when necessary by a super-server that monitors network ports (such as inetd and xinetd), or they can start at boot time and sit around waiting for requests (such as cupsd, which handles printing on a number of modern Unix systems). By convention, daemons have names that end in *d,* such as inetd, cupsd, ntpd, and named.

When you install Cygwin (see Appendix D), you don't automatically get one of the Internet daemons, inetd or xinetd. Generally, you'd want to use native Windows services to handle things like file transfer and Web serving to maximize performance.

If you want to use inetd or xinetd with Cygwin, you can install them, but you'll probably want to disable the Telnet service in the Services control panel if it isn't already disabled.

To install an Internet daemon (Cygwin):

We're going to install `inetd` because it's more integrated with the Windows notion of services.

1. Launch the Cygwin setup.exe, then click the Next button until you get to the package-selection screen.

2. Expand the Net category by clicking the plus sign next to it (**Figure 5.4**).

3. Click the circle-arrow icon for the `inetutils` package, so that the Skip entry changes to a version number.

4. Click Next in the Cygwin Setup window to install the new package and any updates to packages you already have installed.

5. Click Finish to exit the Cygwin Setup program.

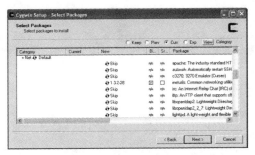

Figure 5.4 Expanding the Net category in the Cygwin Setup application to find the `inetutils` package.

Figure 5.5 Setting environment variables in Windows.

Figure 5.6 Adding a new systemwide environment variable.

To activate inetd (Cygwin):

The `inetd` server is installed as part of the `inetutils` package, but it's not active as a service until you set it up.

1. Open a Cygwin window.

2. `inetd --install-as-service`

   This installs a Windows service, controllable through the standard Services control panel, for the Cygwin `inetd`.

3. Use your favorite text editor to edit `/etc/inetd.conf` and add a # character to the start of every line that doesn't already have one.

   This disables all of the services; it's a good idea to disable everything, and then go back to enable the services you actually want.

4. Click the Windows Start menu, then open Control Panel.

5. Double-click the System control panel.

6. Click the Advanced tab, then the Environment Variables button.

   The Environment Variables dialog is displayed (**Figure 5.5**).

7. Click the New button in the "System variables" section.

8. In the New System Variable dialog (**Figure 5.6**), type *CYGWIN* in the "Variable name" field. Type *ntsec* in the "Variable value" field.

   This tells Cygwin to use Windows users and groups for authentication, which lets you add users and groups through the standard graphical tools.

continues on next page

9. Click OK to close the New System Variable dialog.

10. Select the Path variable in the "System variables" section of the Environment Variables dialog, then click the Edit button.

11. Add *c:\cygwin\bin* to the start of the "Variable value" field in the Edit System Variable dialog (**Figure 5.7**).

12. Click OK to exit the dialog. Click OK in the Environment Variables dialog and System control panel to close them.

13. Reboot.

Yes, this isn't very Unix-like, but it's necessary. When your system finishes rebooting, the Cygwin inetd service is running.

Figure 5.7 Editing a systemwide environment variable.

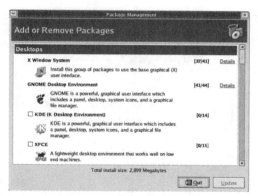

Figure 5.8 Fedora Core's Package Management application lets you install additional packages.

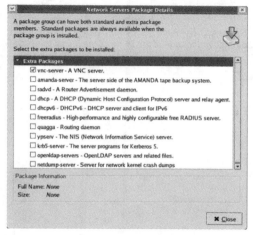

Figure 5.9 The Network Servers Package Details dialog lets you choose specific network servers.

Assigning Network Addresses Dynamically

Chances are that you've configured a personal computer or workstation to pick up its network information dynamically from a DHCP server. Most ISPs work this way, and more and more company LANs are being configured with DHCP.

In this section, you'll see how to install and configure a DHCP server for a small LAN.

To install a DHCP server (Fedora Core):

Fedora Core includes a DHCP server in its list of available packages; all we need to do is install it.

1. Launch the Package Management application (**Figure 5.8**) by opening the Applications menu in the top left of the screen and choosing System Tools > Add/Remove Programs.

2. If you're not logged in as **root**, you'll be prompted to enter the **root** password. Type the password, then press Enter.

3. Scroll down to the Servers section in the package category list and find the Network Servers category.

4. Click the Details link to display the Network Servers Package Details dialog (**Figure 5.9**).

continues on next page

5. Check the box next to dhcp, then click the Close button to return to the Package Management window.

6. Click Update. The Package Management window displays a dialog (**Figure 5.10**) showing details about the packages you're installing.

7. Click Continue to begin the installation. The Package Management window prompts you to put in the appropriate Fedora Core installation CD (**Figure 5.11**).

8. Insert the required CD, then click OK to continue.

9. The Package Manager installs the DHCP server and displays an Update Complete dialog. Click OK to close the dialog, and then close the Package Manager window.

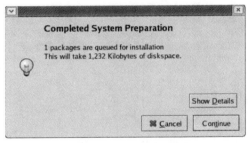

Figure 5.10 A dialog opens, showing details about the packages to be installed.

Figure 5.11 The Package Management application will prompt you for one of the Fedora Core installation CDs.

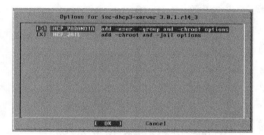

Figure 5.12 A couple of helpful additional packages can be installed on FreeBSD with the DHCP server.

To install a DHCP server (FreeBSD):

The DHCP server provided as part of the FreeBSD ports system is from the Internet Systems Consortium (www.isc.org), a non-profit corporation dedicated to supporting the public Internet.

1. Log in as `root`.

2. `cd /usr/ports/net/isc-dhcp3-server`
   Change to the DHCP server directory.

3. `make install clean`
   Build and install the DHCP server, then clean up.

   The ports system displays a dialog listing options for the DHCP server (**Figure 5.12**).

4. Press Tab, then Enter to go with the default options.

   The DHCP server software is downloaded and installed.

✔ Tips

■ Unfortunately, there is no supported DHCP server that you can run under Cygwin or Mac OS X. You might be able to get the ISC DHCP server (www.isc.org) to work with both systems, but you'd be entering uncharted territory. For Cygwin, it would probably be a better idea to find a native Windows DHCP server. And the Mac OS X Server operating system can act as a DHCP server, and includes graphical tools (the Server Admin application) for configuration and administration.

■ Cygwin users on Windows 2000 Professional or Windows XP Professional can support DHCP clients through their Internet sharing features. Please refer to your OS documentation for more information.

ASSIGNING NETWORK ADDRESSES DYNAMICALLY

To configure your DHCP server:

Although you don't need to tell client systems anything about the DHCP server (other than the fact that they should use DHCP), you do need to tell your DHCP server a few things about the network it's configuring.

1. Log in as **root** or use **su** to become **root** (or use **sudo**).

2. **cd /etc** (for Linux)

   or

   cd /usr/local/etc (for FreeBSD)

   Change to the configuration directory for the DHCP server.

3. **cp /usr/share/doc/dhcp-3.0.1/**
   → dhcp.conf.sample dhcp.conf (for Fedora Core)

   or

   cp dhcp.conf.sample dhcp.conf (for FreeBSD)

   Copy the sample configuration file to the DHCP server-configuration file, so that we can edit it to suit our network.

4. Use your favorite editor to edit the DHCP server-configuration file.

5. Change the following settings:

   ▲ **option domain-name**—Set this to your domain name (you can make one up if your LAN is behind a firewall).

   ▲ **option domain-name-servers**—The host names or IP addresses of one or more name servers.

   ▲ **authoritative**—Uncomment this (delete the # character at the start of the line) if this is the only DHCP server on this network.

6. Delete the rest of the file after the **log-facility** option's line.

7. Add a **subnet** configuration to control the dynamic IPs that this DHCP server will dish out:

   ```
   subnet 10.0.0.0 netmask
   255.255.255.0 {
       range 10.0.0.100 10.0.0.200;
       option routers router_name;
   }
   ```

   The IP address and **netmask** after the **subnet** option indicate the network for which this DHCP server provides addresses. In the example above, we're using the 255 addresses in the 10.0.0.* network.

   The IP addresses in the **range** option indicate the possible range for the dynamic IPs. In this case, we can serve as many as 100 client systems, with IPs from 10.0.0.100 to 10.0.0.200.

   The **option routers** line lets you provide the IP address or host name of one or more routers available to these client machines.

8. Save the file, then restart (or start) the DHCP server to activate your new settings.

Code Listing 5.5 Activating Telnet support under Fedora Core.

```
[chrish@dhcppc1 ~]$ cd /etc/xinetd.d
[chrish@dhcppc1 xinetd.d]$ sudo vi krb5-
→ telnet
. . .
[chrish@dhcppc1 xinetd.d]$ ps -ax | egrep
→ xinetd
Warning: bad syntax, perhaps a bogus '-'?
→ See /usr/share/doc/procps-3.2.3/FAQ
 2032 ?        Ss     0:00 xinetd -stayalive
→ -pidfile /var/run/xinetd.pid
20162 pts/2    S+     0:00 egrep xinetd
[chrish@dhcppc1 xinetd.d]$ sudo kill -HUP
→ 2032
```

Code Listing 5.6 Activating Telnet support under Mac OS X.

```
bender:~ chrish$ cd /etc/xinetd.d
bender:/etc/xinetd.d chrish$ sudo vi telnet
Password:
. . .
bender:/etc/xinetd.d chrish$ sudo kill -HUP
→ $(cat /var/run/xinetd.pid)
```

Serving Remote Shells With Telnet

The Telnet protocol is the default for insecure remote access. Using the `Telnet` command, users of almost any system can connect to Unix systems and run interactive shells.

However, Telnet is insecure because it's not encrypted. Everything you type in a Telnet session is sent across the wire exactly as you type it, including your password. Later we'll look at a secure replacement for Telnet.

When someone accesses a computer through Telnet, he or she logs in using his or her normal user ID and password *for that system*. If you don't have a user ID and password there, you can't log in.

To enable Telnet access (xinetd):

Fedora Core and Mac OS X use the `xinetd` super-server to control Telnet access.

1. `cd /etc/xinetd.d`

   Change to the `xinetd` configuration directory.

2. If you're using Fedora Core (**Code Listing 5.5**), Kerberos (a secure authentication service) is installed, and it handles normal Telnet connections. Edit the `krb5-telnet` file using your favorite editor.

   If you're using Mac OS X (**Code Listing 5.6**), the standard BSD Telnet daemon handles your Telnet connections. Edit the `telnet` file using your favorite text editor.

3. Change the `disable=yes` line to `disable=no`, then save the file.

4. `kill -HUP` *xinetd_pid*

   Restart `xinetd` by sending it the HUP signal.

SERVING REMOTE SHELLS WITH TELNET

To enable Telnet access (inetd):

FreeBSD and Cygwin use the `inetd` super-server to control Telnet access.

1. `cd /etc`

   Change to the `inetd` configuration directory.

2. Use your favorite text editor to edit the inetd.conf file.

3. Remove the # character(s) at the start of the `telnet` line, then save the file.

4. `kill -HUP` *inetd_pid*

   Restart `inetd` by sending it the HUP signal.

✔ Tip

■ You may have noticed that `xinetd` has a `-pidfile` option that takes a full path as an argument (specified as `/var/run/xinetd.pid` on both Fedora Core and Mac OS X). As a shortcut for doing `ps -ax | grep` to find the process ID, you could use the contents of the `xinetd.pid` file (Code Listing 5.6):

   ```
   sudo kill -HUP
   → $(cat /var/run/xinetd.pid)
   ```

Code Listing 5.7 Activating FTP support on Fedora Core.

```
[chrish@dhcppc1 ~]$ cd /etc/xinetd.d
[chrish@dhcppc1 xinetd.d]$ sudo vi gssftp
. . .
[chrish@dhcppc1 xinetd.d]$ ps ax | egrep
→ xinetd
 2032 ?        Ss      0:00 xinetd -stayalive
→ -pidfile /var/run/xinetd.pid
20162 pts/2    S+      0:00 egrep xinetd
[chrish@dhcppc1 xinetd.d]$ sudo kill —HUP
→ 2032
```

Code Listing 5.8 Activating FTP support on Mac OS X.

```
bender:~ chrish$ cd /etc/xinetd.d
bender:/etc/xinetd.d chrish$ sudo vi ftp
Password:
. . .
bender:/etc/xinetd.d chrish$ sudo kill -HUP
→ $(cat /var/run/xinetd.pid)
```

Serving Files with FTP

FTP was, until the advent of the World Wide Web, the most popular method of transferring files across the Internet.

Like Telnet, FTP is insecure; the user ID and password are sent across the network in plain text. We'll look at a secure replacement for FTP access when we talk about OpenSSH later in this chapter.

Also as with Telnet, the user ID and password you use to access the FTP server are the same user ID and password you use for logging in to the system.

To enable FTP access (xinetd):

Fedora Core and Mac OS X use the xinetd super-server to control FTP access.

1. cd /etc/xinetd.d

   Change to the xinetd configuration directory.

2. If you're using Fedora Core (**Code Listing 5.7**), Kerberos (a secure authentication service) is installed, and it handles normal FTP connections. Edit the gssftp file using your favorite editor.

   If you're using Mac OS X (**Code Listing 5.8**), the standard BSD FTP daemon handles your FTP connections. Edit the ftp file using your favorite text editor.

3. Change the disable=yes line to disable=no, then save the file.

4. kill -HUP *xinetd_pid*

   Restart xinetd by sending it a HUP signal.

To enable FTP access (inetd):

FreeBSD and Cygwin use the `inetd` super-server to control FTP access.

1. `cd /etc`

   Change to the `inetd` configuration directory.

2. Use your favorite text editor to edit the inetd.conf file.

3. Remove the # character(s) at the start of the `ftp` line (make sure you've got the `ftp` line and not the **tftp** line—that's something different), then save the file.

4. `kill -HUP inetd_pid`

   Restart `inetd` by sending it a HUP signal.

Code Listing 5.9 Installing rsync through FreeBSD's ports system.

```
bsd# cd /usr/ports/net/rsync

bsd# make install clean

rsync comes with an included version of
→ popt.
To build rsync with devel/popt instead,
→ hit Ctrl-C now and define WITH_POPT_PORT
===>   Vulnerability check disabled, database
→ not found
>> rsync-2.6.2.tar.gz doesn't seem to exist
→ in /usr/ports/distfiles/.
>> Attempting to fetch from
→ http://rsync.samba.org/ftp/rsync/.
. . .
```

Synchronizing Files with rsync

The rsync program is used for synchronizing files and directories between systems, and it can be used as a backup tool.

But again, it's an insecure method because none of the rsync traffic is encrypted in any way, so you should only allow rsync connections between trusted computers.

Since rsync is so insecure, we'll look at ways of making your system share file-system resources "the right way" in the next chapter.

Note that you can secure rsync transfers by combining it with SSH.

To install rsync (FreeBSD):

By default, rsync isn't installed under FreeBSD, so we'll have to install it from the ports collection (**Code Listing 5.9**).

1. cd /usr/ports/net/rsync

   Change to the rsync directory in the ports system.

2. make install clean

   Download, build, and install rsync, then clean up the build directory.

SYNCHRONIZING FILES WITH RSYNC

To install rsync (Cygwin):

Like FreeBSD, rsync isn't installed by default (or by the inetutils package) on Cygwin, so we'll have to install it.

1. Launch the Cygwin setup.exe, then click the Next button until you get to the package-selection screen.

2. Expand the Net category by clicking the plus sign beside it.

3. Click the circle-arrow icon for the rsync package, so that the Skip entry changes to a version number (**Figure 5.13**).

4. Click Next in the Cygwin Setup window to install the new package and any updates to packages you already have installed.

5. Click Finish in the Cygwin Setup window to exit the Cygwin Setup program.

To enable rsync access (xinetd):

Fedora Core and Mac OS X use the xinetd super-server to control rsync access.

1. cd /etc/xinetd.d

   Change to the xinetd configuration directory.

2. If you're using Fedora Core (**Code Listing 5.10**), edit the rsync file using your favorite editor.

   If you're using Mac OS X, you need to create the rsync file (**Code Listing 5.11**) using your favorite text editor.

3. Change the disable=yes line to disable=no, and then save the file.

4. kill -HUP *xinetd_pid*

   Restart xinetd by sending it a HUP signal.

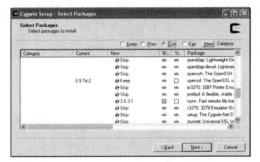

Figure 5.13 Installing rsync with the Cygwin Setup application.

Code Listing 5.10 Activating rsync support on Fedora Core.

```
[chrish@dhcppc1 ~]$ cd /etc/xinetd.d
[chrish@dhcppc1 xinetd.d]$ sudo vi rsync
. . .
[chrish@dhcppc1 xinetd.d]$ ps ax | egrep
→ xinetd
 2032 ?        Ss      0:00 xinetd -stayalive
→ -pidfile /var/run/xinetd.pid
20162 pts/2    S+      0:00 egrep xinetd
[chrish@dhcppc1 xinetd.d]$ sudo kill –HUP
→ 2032
```

Code Listing 5.11 Adding rsync support to xinetd on Mac OS X.

```
service rsync {
        disable = no
        socket_type = stream
        wait = no
        user = root
        server = /usr/bin/rsync
        server_args = --daemon
        log_on_failure += USERID
}
```

To enable rsync access (inetd):

FreeBSD and Cygwin use the `inetd` super-server to control `rsync` access.

1. `cd /etc`

   Change to the `inetd` configuration directory.

2. Use your favorite text editor to edit the inetd.conf file.

3. Remove the # character(s) at the start of the `rsync` line, then save the file.

4. `kill -HUP` *inetd_pid*

   Restart `inetd` by sending it a HUP signal.

To use rsync to back up a directory:

One use for `rsync` is to copy directories between systems, to duplicate them or just to make a backup.

◆ `rsync -PpogrtlHcz` *source destination*

   Use `rsync` to copy the *source* to the *destination*.

   The *source* is specified as a local directory path.

   The *destination* is specified as *hostname_or_IP:directory_path*.

   The options are -P (show progress and keep partial files), -p (preserve file permissions), -o (preserve ownership), -g (preserve group), -r (recursive; copy directories and their contents), -t (preserve times), -l (preserve symbolic links), -H (preserve hard links), -c (checksum the files to make sure they're transferred properly), and -z (use compression while transferring files).

✔ Tips

■ The `rsync man` page includes a lot of examples for copying things to and from remote machines.

■ There's a program called `rsnapshot` (www.rsnapshot.org) for making backups on local and remote systems. It's written in Perl and uses the `rsync` protocol for data transfers. Take a look—you might find it useful!

SYNCHRONIZING FILES WITH RSYNC

Securing Remote Shells and File Transfers with OpenSSH

OpenSSH is an open-source implementation of the SSH (Secure Shell) protocol, a popular method of providing secure shell access and secure file transfers. All of the data transmitted between systems through the SSH protocol is encrypted, making it a much safer option for systems accessible from the Internet.

One handy thing about SSH is that it's already installed on Fedora Core. Even the SSH server (sshd) is set up and ready to accept connections. So we'll move on to FreeBSD.

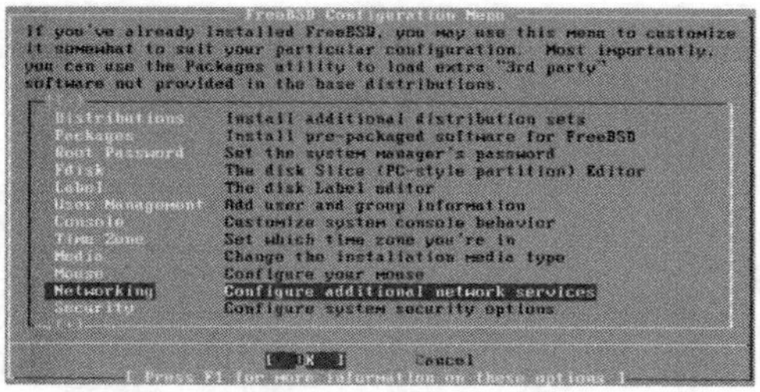

Figure 5.14 Configuring networking settings with the FreeBSD Configuration Menu.

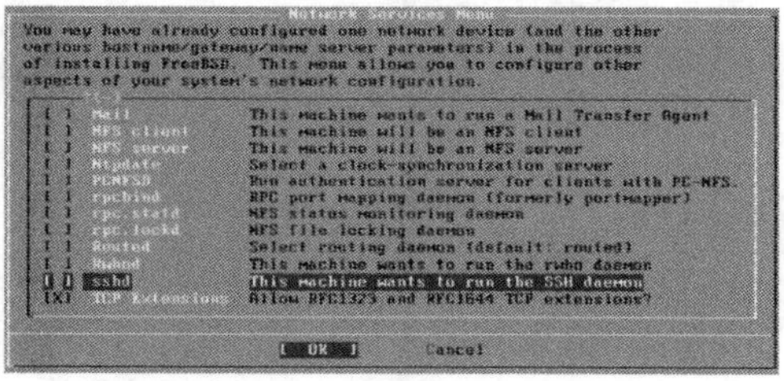

Figure 5.15 Adding sshd to the system with the Network Services menu.

To activate OpenSSH (FreeBSD):

OpenSSH is installed by default with FreeBSD, but you need to activate it.

1. Log in as **root**, or use **su** to become **root**.

2. **sysinstall**

   Launch the system installation and configuration tool.

3. Press *C* to choose the Configure option, and then press Enter.

4. Press the down arrow key several times until Networking is highlighted in the FreeBSD Configuration Menu (**Figure 5.14**), then press Enter.

5. Press the down arrow key several times until **sshd** is highlighted in the Network Services Menu (**Figure 5.15**), then press Enter to select it.

6. Press *X* to return to the Exit item, and then press Enter to return to the FreeBSD Configuration Menu.

7. Press *X* to return to the Exit item, then press Enter to return to the **sysinstall** Main Menu.

8. Press *X* to exit **sysinstall**.

   Restart to generate your SSH keys and activate the SSH daemon.

To install OpenSSH (Cygwin):

OpenSSH isn't installed by default with Cygwin, so we'll need to install and configure it.

1. Launch the Cygwin Setup program.

2. Click the Next button in the Cygwin Setup window several times until you get to the Select Packages screen.

3. Expand the Net category by clicking the plus sign beside it.

4. Scroll down to find the **openssh** package.

5. Click the circle-arrow icon to change its Skip entry to a version number (**Figure 5.16**).

6. Click Next to install the new package and updates to any packages you already have installed.

7. Click Finish to exit the Cygwin Setup program.

8. Open a Cygwin window.

9. `ssh-host-config`

    The `ssh-host-config` command creates the various cryptographic keys used by SSH.

10. When prompted, you can answer *yes* to all of the questions, except for the `CYGWIN` environment variable question. Type *ntsec* and press Enter.

11. `net start sshd`

    When the script is finished, you can start the SSH server with the `net start` command.

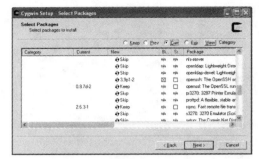

Figure 5.16 Installing the openssh package with the Cygwin Setup application.

Figure 5.17 Mac OS X's System Preferences application lets you control most aspects of the operating system's behavior.

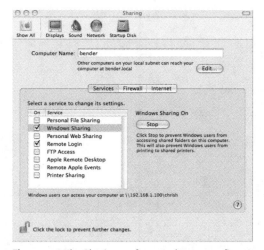

Figure 5.18 The Sharing preferences let you configure several standard Internet servers, such as the SSH (Remote Login) server.

To activate OpenSSH (Mac OS X):

Under the current version of Mac OS X (10.3, code-named Panther), OpenSSH is already installed, although it may not be activated.

1. Launch the System Preferences application (**Figure 5.17**) by choosing System Preferences from the Apple menu.

2. Click the Sharing icon in the Internet & Network section.

3. In the Sharing pane (**Figure 5.18**), if the Remote Login item is not checked, click the Start/Stop button.

SECURING REMOTE SHELLS

To log in through ssh:

Because Telnet sessions aren't secure, you should use ssh to open shells on remote computers.

◆ ssh *userid@hostname*

Connect through ssh to *hostname* as *userid*. If your current user ID is the same as your user ID on *hostname*, you can leave out the *userid@* part and just connect to *hostname*.

To transfer files through ssh:

The FTP component of OpenSSH is a drop-in replacement for the standard Unix ftp command, except it's secure.

◆ sftp *userid@hostname*

Create a file-transfer session to *hostname*, logging in as *userid*. As with ssh, you can leave off the *userid@* part if your current user ID matches your user ID on *hostname*.

Once you're connected, sftp works exactly like the ftp command; all of the same commands are there, and they all work the way you expect them to.

✔ Tips

■ Under Cygwin, Windows users without passwords cannot log in through the SSH server. You wanted to make them use a password anyway, didn't you?

■ lftp (http://lftp.yar.ru) is an excellent command-line FTP client that can also transfer through HTTP, HTTPS (if built with the OpenSSL libraries), and OpenSSH. Because it supports the SSH protocol, it makes an outstanding replacement for the sftp command.

HOSTING A FILE SERVER

One of the most popular things to do with a Unix system is to set it up as a file server so that computers across the network can access the same files from a central location. This holds true for corporate LANs serving hundreds of client systems and sharing important documents or software, as well as for small home LANs sharing pictures of the kids or the family's music collection.

In this chapter, you'll learn about two commonly used network file systems, Samba and NFS. Samba is often thought of as a Windows technology (it is technically the native network file system for Windows), but it's an excellent choice for sharing directories on a network with a variety of different systems. NFS is the original Unix network file system, so it can be handy when dealing with older systems that don't have a Samba client.

Serving Files with Samba

Samba (www.samba.org) is an open-source project designed to give Unix systems the ability to share directories and printers in a way that's compatible with Windows. Actually, it's also compatible with any system running Samba, OS/2, and LAN Manager; all of these implement the same basic protocol, which was later standardized as *CIFS* (for the *Common Internet File System,* formerly known as *SMB,* which is where the name *Samba* came from).

Besides being almost ubiquitous, Samba has the advantages of being secure, reliable, and fast. There's nothing stopping you from using it on networks that don't have any Windows machines.

Because Cygwin runs on top of Windows, it already supports CIFS natively; you use the standard Windows techniques for mounting a shared directory or for sharing part of your file system.

Mac OS X supports CIFS directly from the Finder's Go menu (although it's running Samba under the covers), making it easy to mount shared directories.

Fedora Core also comes with Samba *client* support, and you can access Windows networks from the desktop by double-clicking the Computer icon, double-clicking the Network icon, and then double-clicking the Windows network icon. It can't currently work as a Samba *server,* because of a conflict with the built-in firewall.

To install Samba:

FreeBSD systems need to install Samba through the ports system (**Code Listing 6.1**).

1. Log in as root, or use su to get a root shell.

2. cd /usr/ports/net/samba3

continues on next page

Code Listing 6.1 Using smbclient to list the shares on a server.

```
bsd# smbclient -U chrish -L taffer

Password:
Domain=[TAFFER] OS=[Windows 5.1] Server=[Windows 2000 LAN Manager]

    Sharename       Type        Comment
    ---------       ----        -------
    E$              Disk        Default share
    IPC$            IPC         Remote IPC
    D$              Disk        Default share
    print$          Disk        Printer Drivers
    SharedDocs      Disk
    scribe          Printer     Lexmark Z22-Z32 Color Jetprinter (Copy 1)
    home            Disk        Taffer's home
    Movies          Disk
    G$              Disk        Default share
    wallpaper       Disk        Desktop wallpaper galore
    tmp             Disk
    Music           Disk
    ADMIN$          Disk        Remote Admin
    C$              Disk        Default share
Domain=[TAFFER] OS=[Windows 5.1] Server=[Windows 2000 LAN Manager]

    Server          Comment
    ---------       -------


    Workgroup       Master
    ---------       -------
bsd#
```

3. `make install clean`

The ports system displays the "Options for samba" dialog (**Figure 6.1**).

4. Unless you need one of the disabled options, you can go with the defaults. To turn on an additional option, use the up and down arrow keys to move to the option's entry, then press the spacebar to select (or deselect) it.

The options include

LDAP—Add support for authenticating users stored in an LDAP server.

ADS—Add support for authenticating users stored in an Active Directory server.

CUPS—Add support for sharing CUPS-based printers.

WINBIND—Add support for adding the Samba server to an existing Active Directory or Windows domain.

ACL_SUPPORT—Add support for ACLs (Access Control Lists; detailed Windows-style file and directory permissions).

SYSLOG—Add support for standard sys-log error and diagnostic reporting (as opposed to writing log messages in a Samba-specific log file).

QUOTAS—Add support for per-user disk quotas.

Figure 6.1 FreeBSD offers to build Samba with quite a few options.

UTMP—Add support for checking for currently logged-in users through the `/var/log/utmp` file.

MSDFS—Add support for the Microsoft Distributed File System.

SAM_XML—Allow storing Samba passwords in an XML file.

SAM_MYSQL—Allow storing Samba passwords in a MySQL database.

SAM_PGSQL—Allow storing Samba passwords in a PostgreSQL database.

SAM_OLD_LDAP—Samba 2.x–compatible LDAP user-authentication support.

PAM_SMBPASS—Add support for authenticating users with PAM.

POPT—Build with Samba's built-in `popt()` function instead of trying to use the OS's. You should leave this one alone on the theory that the BSD folks knew what they were doing when they made it the default.

5. Press Tab and then Enter to dismiss the "Options for samba" dialog and continue the installation with your selected options.

6. Using your favorite text editor, add the following line to `/etc/rc.conf`:

   `samba_enable="YES"`

7. Restart the machine, or run the following command to start Samba:

   `/usr/local/etc/rc.d/samba.sh start`

SERVING FILES WITH SAMBA

To configure Samba:

Cygwin users need to share directories or printers through the standard Windows interfaces. Everyone else controls their shares through the /etc/smb.conf file.

1. Open a **root** shell, or use **su** (or **sudo**) to become **root**.

2. If you're using FreeBSD,

   cd /usr/local/etc

   or, if you're using Mac OS X,

   cd /etc

3. Use your favorite text editor to create or edit the smb.conf file.

   The smb.conf file consists of comments (lines starting with a semicolon or # character), section headings (lines enclosed in square brackets), and section data (anything after a section heading up to the next section heading).

4. Add or edit the [global] section so that it has at least the following entries:

   ```
   [global]
       workgroup = name
       security = user
       hosts allow = nets 127.
       log file = /var/log/samba/log.%m
       max log size = maxlog
       passdb backend = tdbsam
   ```

   Replace *name* with the name of the domain or workgroup. *nets* should be one or more networks (use 192.168.0. to allow 192.168.0.*, for example) that are allowed to attach to your Samba server; all others will be denied. Set *maxlog* to the maximum log file size, such as 50 for 50 Kbytes maximum.

```
bsd# testparm
Load smb config files from /usr/local/etc/smb.conf
Processing section "[homes]"
Processing section "[tmp]"
Loaded services file OK.
Server role: ROLE_STANDALONE
Press enter to see a dump of your service definitions
^C
bsd# █
```

Figure 6.2 Using testparm to test your Samba configuration.

Setting **security** to **user** means that users will be authenticated with the server using a user ID and password stored locally. Using the above value for **log file** will create one log file per machine (named log.*machine_name*) in the /var/log/samba directory. Finally, the **passdb backend** indicates which type of database to use for storing user IDs and passwords—in this case, a TDB file.

5. **testparm**

   Test your configuration (**Figure 6.2**) to see if you've made any syntax errors. If you have, fix them.

To add users to Samba:

If you've configured Samba with user-level security (as we have, above), you'll need to add users to the Samba-specific password database. This is separate from the OS password database found in /etc/passwd, allowing you to create users specifically for Samba without needing to muck with your machine configuration.

1. Log in as **root**, or use **su** (or **sudo**) to become **root**.

   Manipulating the Samba password database requires **root**'s privileges.

2. **pdbedit -a -u** *userid*

   Add (**-a**) the specified *userid* to the Samba password database. Note that **pdbedit** works transparently with whatever database back end is specified in the global smb.conf file (and you can force it to use another back end with the **-b** option).

3. Type the user's password at the "new password" prompt. Type it again at the "retype new password" prompt to make sure you've got it right.

SERVING FILES WITH SAMBA

To share a directory with Samba:

To share a directory with Samba, you add a new section to the smb.conf file giving details about what you're sharing.

1. Open a **root** shell, or use **su** (or **sudo**) to become **root**.

2. If you're using FreeBSD,

   cd /usr/local/etc

   or, if you're using Mac OS X,

   cd /etc

3. Use your favorite text editor to create or edit the smb.conf file.

4. Add one or more share sections similar to this:

   ```
   [sharename]
       path = /the/directory/to/share
       writable = yes
       guest ok = no
       browseable = yes
       comment = description
   ```

Each section like this creates one shared directory; in this case, it will be named *sharename* and map to */the/directory/to/share* on this system. Set **writable** to **no** if you want a read-only share, **guest ok** to **yes** if you want to let anonymous users access the share, and **browseable** to **no** if you want to hide the share from network browsing (as through the **smbclient** command or Windows' View Workgroup Computers). If you've set **browseable** to **no**, you can also leave off the **comment**, which is displayed next to the share name during network browsing.

5. Save the file, then run **testparm** to make sure you didn't accidentally include some syntax errors.

6. If you're using FreeBSD:

   /usr/local/etc/rc.d/samba.sh
   → restart

   or, if you're using Mac OS X:

   service smbd stop
   service smbd start

   Restart the Samba services to incorporate your changes in smb.conf.

To mount a shared directory:

For systems that don't sport a nice graphical interface for mounting remote shares, we'll need to know how to discover the shares, and mount them locally.

1. `smbclient -U` *userid* `-L` *server*

Use the `smbclient` command's `-L` option to list the shares available on the specified *server* (Code Listing 6.1), connecting as the user specified in *userid*. You'll be prompted for *userid*'s password.

Or, if you're using Cygwin:

`net view \\\\`*server*

This lists the available shares on *server* in a slightly different format (**Code Listing 6.2**) and leaves out the "hidden" administrative shares. The four backslash characters are required because the shell uses \ to escape "special" characters; \\ turns into one \ being passed to the command.

continues on next page

Code Listing 6.2 Using `net view` under Cygwin to list the shares on a server.

```
chrish@taffer [514]: net view \\\\taffer
Shared resources at \\taffer
Taffer (P4 2.53GHz)
Share name  Type    Used as  Comment
-------------------------------------------------------------------------------
home        Disk             Taffer's home
Movies      Disk
Music       Disk
scribe      Print            Lexmark Z22-Z32 Color Jetprinter
SharedDocs  Disk
tmp         Disk
wallpaper   Disk             Desktop wallpaper galore
The command completed successfully.
chrish@taffer [515]:
```

2. Use **su** to become **root**, or use **sudo** with the commands in the following steps. On most systems, only **root** can mount file systems.

3. mkdir /path/to/*mountpoint*

If you don't already have a directory to use as a mount point, create one. This can be anywhere in the file system, although it's usually under /mnt (or /Volumes on Mac OS X).

4. mount -t smbfs -o username=*userid*
→//server/share /path/to/*mountpoint*

on Fedora Core, or, if you're using FreeBSD:

mount -t smbfs
→ //*userid*@*server*/*share*
→ /path/to/*mountpoint*

or, if you're using Cygwin:

mount -f //*server*/*share*
→ /path/to/*mountpoint*

or, if you're using Mac OS X:

mount -t smbfs -o -U=*userid*
→ //*server*/*share* /path/to/*mountpoint*

Mount *share* on *server* as the directory at *mountpoint*, logging in to *server* as *userid*. You will be prompted for *userid*'s password.

✔ Tips

■ Samba comes with a Web-based configuration tool called *SWAT* (*Samba Web Administration Tool*). Check the Samba Web site (www.samba.org) for more information.

■ Cygwin can use network paths directly (for example, **cd //server/share**) if you're already authenticated with the server via a domain controller or if your user ID and password on the server are identical to your user ID and password on your Cygwin system.

■ If you've mounted a remote share as a local drive (for example, X:) on Windows, you can access it under Cygwin through /cygdrive/x as you would any other Windows drive.

■ If you're serving a large number of Mac client systems, check out the Netatalk server (http://netatalk.sourceforge.net) for Unix systems, including Linux and FreeBSD.

■ The smbclient command can also be used like an FTP client for shared directories. This can be useful if you're having trouble using the GUI front ends or if you need to do something that isn't supported by the GUI.

Serving Files with NFS

NFS was the most common network file system before Windows became popular, and it's definitely one of the oldest. Created by Sun back in the 1980s, NFS has a history of known security deficiencies and other shortcomings.

Don't use it over an insecure network, as it doesn't encrypt data, and it's possible for a **root** client to have **root** access to the server's file systems. NFS doesn't handle file locking reliably, and it doesn't support per-user restrictions.

File permissions on the NFS server are honored by the clients, which can cause confusion if the server doesn't have the same users and groups as the client machine.

NFS clients may not notice when a server fails or becomes unavailable, causing the client to hang indefinitely, waiting for the server to return data. Applications attempting to read data over NFS will also, therefore, hang forever.

Have I scared you off? NFS is still a good choice for simple file sharing on a local, trusted network, especially if you need to mount file systems from older Unix systems.

Cygwin has no support for NFS.

To start NFS (Fedora Core):

Use Fedora Core's Service Configuration window to start the NFS service.

1. Click the Applications menu at the top left of your desktop to open it.

2. Select System Settings > Server Settings > Services to open the Service Configuration window.

   If you're not currently logged in as **root**, you'll be prompted for the **root** password.

3. Scroll down the list of services until you find the "nfs" item (**Figure 6.3**).

4. Make sure the nfs box is checked, then click the Start button to launch the NFS services.

   The services start, and the Status area is updated to show the status of the daemons (**Figure 6.4**).

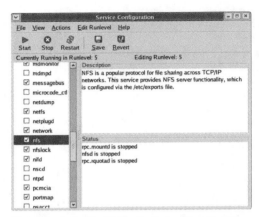

Figure 6.3 Activating NFS in the Fedora Core Service Configuration window.

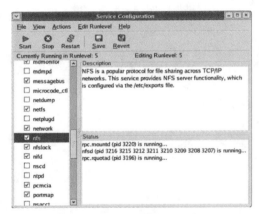

Figure 6.4 NFS uses several daemons, shown running here.

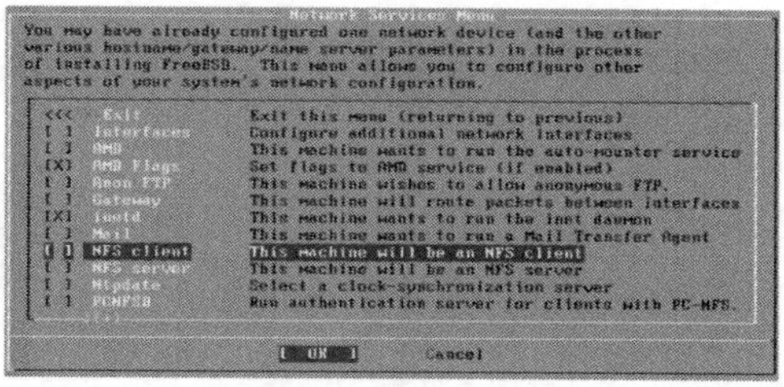

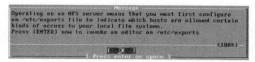

Figure 6.5 FreeBSD's Network Services Menu lets you configure various networking services.

Figure 6.6 NFS requires an /etc/exports file for configuration.

To install and start NFS (FreeBSD):

Use FreeBSD's `sysinstall` utility to activate NFS. Fedora Core and Mac OS X have active NFS support by default.

1. Log in as `root`.

2. `sysinstall`

   Launch the `sysinstall` utility.

3. Press the down arrow key several times to choose the Configuration entry. Press Enter to switch to the FreeBSD Configuration Menu.

4. Press the down arrow key until the Networking entry is selected, then press Enter to switch to the Network Services Menu (**Figure 6.5**).

5. Press the down arrow key until the "NFS client" entry is selected, then press Enter to mark it.

6. Press the down arrow key until the "NFS server" entry is selected, then press Enter to mark it.

   The Network Services Menu displays a Message dialog (**Figure 6.6**) telling you about the need for an /etc/exports file. Press Enter to create an /etc/exports file.

continues on next page

SERVING FILES WITH NFS

7. Use the supplied vi editor session to add a basic share of the /tmp directory:

```
/tmp -network 192.168.0.0
→ -mask 255.255.255.0
```

This shares /tmp with all machines on the 192.168.0.* network; replace this and the network mask with something reasonable for your network. We'll be editing this later, and explaining the syntax in more detail.

8. Save the file and exit the text editor to return to the Network Services Menu.

9. Press Tab to move to the OK button in the Network Services Menu, and then press Enter to return to the FreeBSD Configuration Menu.

10. Press X and then press Enter to return to the sysinstall Main Menu.

11. Press X to exit sysinstall.

12. ```
/etc/rc.d/rpcbind start;
→ /etc/rc.d/nfsserver start;
→ /etc/rc.d/nfsclient start
```

Start the servers that provide NFS support.
```

To share a directory with NFS:

The /etc/exports file controls which directories are shared through NFS, as well as how those directories are shared.

1. Log in as root, or use su (or sudo) to become root.

2. Using your favorite text editor, edit or create /etc/exports.

   Lines beginning with a # character are comments.

3. Add one line per directory you want to export.

   /path/to/export hosts(options)
   /path/to/export
   → *network/mask(options)*

   or, for FreeBSD:

   /path/to/export options hosts
   /path/to/export options -network
   → *network -mask mask*

   This exports */path/to/export* to users on the specified *hosts*. The *hosts* can be specified as one or more hostnames, or a *network* and *mask*.

   The options are different for each OS. Under Linux, use (ro,sync) for most of your shares (read-only, synchronized). For FreeBSD, use -ro (it's automatically synchronized).

4. Tell the system to update the directories it's exporting. On Fedora Core, use the exportfs command:

   exportfs -r

   On FreeBSD, restart the mountd daemon:

   kill -HUP
   → $(cat /var/run/mountd.pid)

✔ Tip

■ You can share directories through Mac OS X as well, but it requires editing the NetInfo database (using the NetInfo Manager application) or a third-party utility such as NFS Manager (www .bresink.de/osx/NFSManager.html).

To mount an exported directory:

Use the standard `mount` command to mount an exported NFS directory.

1. Use `su` to become `root`, or use `sudo` with the commands in the following steps. On most systems, only `root` can mount file systems.

2. `mkdir /path/to/mountpoint`

   If you don't already have a directory to use as a mount point, create one.

3. `mount -t nfs server:/export`
   `→ /path/to/mountpoint`

   Mount *export* on *server* as the directory at *mountpoint*.

✔ Tips

- Export only the most-needed data.

- Use read-only exports when writes aren't absolutely necessary.

- Under Fedora Core, use the `root_squash` option in `/etc/exports` to reduce (but not eliminate!) the risk of a `root` user on the client having `root` access on the server. FreeBSD automatically maps the `root` user to a user ID/group ID of -2/-2.

- Always use the `sync` option.

HOSTING A PRINT SERVER

Setting up printers and print queues on Unix systems has always been viewed as a sort of black art. From a user's point of view, sending a file off to a queue and having it appear on the printer at some point in the future (especially when the printer is on another floor or in another building) can seem almost magical.

Luckily for us, it's fairly straightforward, especially with *CUPS* (the *Common Unix Printing System*) taking over for the traditional lpd (*line printer daemon*) system of printing.

In this chapter, we'll take a quick look at the old way of printing through an lpd, and then we'll move on to CUPS. Finally, we'll see how to share our CUPS print queue through Samba so that other computers on the network can print to the shared printer.

Controlling Traditional Unix Print Services

What happens when a user sends a job to a printer using the standard `lp` command? The answer is, of course, "It depends."

Originally, the only kinds of printers available were plain-text printers. The more exotic and expensive models could bang out an entire line (or even an entire page) in one whack, but they were still limited to plain-text output.

Accordingly, the print services on Unix were designed to handle multiple users' sending plain-text files. The `lpd` would check the queued-up files and send them one after another to the printer, possibly sending a form feed between files.

Things got more exciting when printers capable of rendering complex graphics appeared, but as we'll see in this section, they can be handled behind the scenes.

Please note that if you'll be switching to CUPS (which is the default print engine on Fedora Core and Mac OS X), the `/etc/printcap` file will be controlled by the CUPS configuration tools, so you might want to skip this section.

Code Listing 7.1 Sample `/etc/printcap` entries for a local printer and a remote printer.

```
# The primary printer, located in
# location.
primary|secondary|description
  :sd=/var/spool/lpd/primary
  :lp=/dev/outputDevice
  :mx#0
  :lf=/var/log/lpd/primary.log


# The remote printer, located in
# location.
remote|description
  :sd=/var/spool/lpd/remote
  :rm=hostname
  :mx#0
  :lf=/var/log/lpd/remote.log
```

To configure a line printer:

Unix line printers are configured through the `/etc/printcap` file, which lists every known printer, its location, and its capabilities.

1. Log in as **root**, or use **su** (or **sudo**) to become **root**.

2. Using your favorite text editor, edit the `/etc/printcap` file.

3. The printer entries in `/etc/printcap` go over multiple lines, with the # character indicating a comment line (**Code Listing 7.1**). A printer entry follows this format:

   ```
   # The primary printer, located in
   # location.
   primary|secondary|description
     :sd=/var/spool/lpd/primary
     :lp=/dev/outputDevice
     :mx#0
     :lf=/var/log/lpd/primary.log
   ```

   ▲ The comment at the beginning should describe the printer and its location (and possibly other information) so that the administrator can keep things straight while editing the file.

   ▲ Change *primary* to the primary name for this printer; lp is the name of the default printer, unless you change it. The optional *secondary* name is one or more aliases for this printer, separated by | (pipe) characters. The *description* entry goes until the end of the line and should describe the printer in a useful way.

   ▲ Use the **sd=** property to specify a spool directory. This needs to be different for each printer, because print jobs will be stored here until **lpd** sends them to the printer. Naming the directory after the printer is a good idea.

   ▲ Use the **lp=** property to specify the port that the printer is connected to, usually `/dev/lpt0` or something similar (it's OS dependent, and it also depends on how you've got the printer connected). You can use **rm=**_hostname_ instead of the **lp=** property if you're printing to a remote printer located at *hostname*.

   ▲ The **mx#0** entry tells **lpd** to accept any size print job. Set it to a smaller value (it's described in the **man** pages as being in "**BLKSIZ** blocks," which isn't helpful; **BLKSIZ** is a programming constant and is usually 512 bytes) to limit the size of print jobs.

   ▲ The **lf=** property specifies the file for log entries related to this printer.

4. Save the file and exit your text editor.

✔ Tips

■ You don't need to restart **lpd** after editing the `/etc/printcap` file. The file is loaded every time someone sends a print job, so your changes are noticed right away.

■ Although Cygwin has an **lpr** command (**lpr** is the older, nonstandard version of **lp**), it's not quite the same as the Unix **lpr** command. It can, however, send *raw* (printer-formatted) data to a printer connected to your PC or to a shared printer on the Windows network.

Administering CUPS

A few years ago, folks finally noticed that Unix printing was getting a little old, and the original /etc/printcap-and-lpd-based system was being stretched to its limits by the new kinds of printers that were widely available.

Late in 1999, the OS-agnostic *Internet Printing Protocol* (*IPP*) was released. The first version of CUPS was also released in 1999 and quickly became the default print engine for Linux and other free operating systems.

To install CUPS (FreeBSD):

FreeBSD installs the traditional lp/lpd combination by default, but installing CUPS is easy, courtesy of the ports collection.

Warning: Installing CUPS will overwrite the existing lpd printer configuration.

1. Log in as **root**, or use **su** to become **root**.

2. cd /usr/ports/print/cups

   Change to the CUPS directory in the ports tree.

3. make install clean

   Install CUPS, then clean up.

   During the installation, the "GNU Ghostscript driver configuration" dialog (**Figure 7.1**) is displayed.

4. Press Tab and then Enter in the dialog to go with the default settings, which build a large number of drivers for different printers and output formats.

   The build continues and eventually finishes installing CUPS and its related software.

5. cd /usr/local/etc/rc.d

   Change to the rc.d directory for local software installations.

Figure 7.1 GNU Ghostscript options encountered while installing CUPS on FreeBSD.

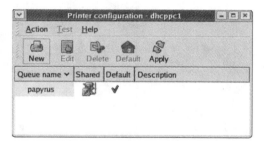

Figure 7.2 Fedora Core's graphical printer-management application.

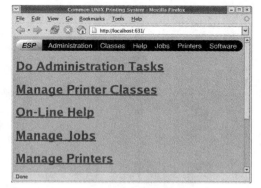

Figure 7.3 The Common UNIX Printing System page, the CUPS portal.

6. `mv cups.sh.sample cups.sh`

The `cups.sh.sample` script created during the CUPS installation process works fine under FreeBSD, so we can just rename it.

7. Using your favorite text editor, add this line anywhere in the `/etc/rc.conf` file:

`cups_enable="YES"`

This will automatically start the CUPS server when the machine restarts.

8. `/usr/local/etc/rc.d/cups.sh start`

Start the CUPS server.

✔ Tips

■ On Mac OS X, use the Print & Fax pane of System Preferences to manage your printers.

■ Fedora Core has a graphical interface for managing printers (**Figure 7.2**): Open the Applications menu at the top left of the screen, then choose System Settings > Printing.

To be sure CUPS is running:

You can interact with the CUPS server through an HTTP connection on any of the supported platforms (Fedora, FreeBSD, and Mac OS X). In fact, this is how you'll be configuring it.

◆ Using your favorite Web browser, visit port 631 on the server (use `localhost` for *hostname* if CUPS is running on the same machine):

http://*hostname*:631/

Your Web browser displays the Common UNIX Printing System page (**Figure 7.3**).

To add a printer to CUPS:

The Web interface integrated with CUPS provides you with an easy way to add and manage printers.

1. Using your favorite Web browser, connect to the CUPS server:

   http://*hostname*:631/

   Your Web browser displays the Common UNIX Printing System page (Figure 7.3).

2. On the CUPS main page, click the Printers button in the toolbar at the top.

   Your Web browser displays the Printer page (**Figure 7.4**).

3. On the Printer page, click the Add Printer button.

   Note: If your Web browser prompts you for authentication after clicking the Add Printer button, use root@*hostname* and the **root** password.

   Your Web browser displays the Add New Printer page (**Figure 7.5**).

4. Enter a name, the printer's location, and a description of the printer in the Name, Location, and Description fields, respectively, on the Add New Printer page.

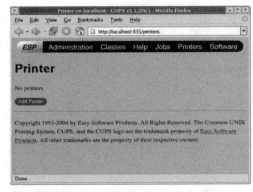

Figure 7.4 The Printer page lets you add and manage printers with CUPS.

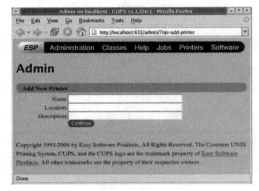

Figure 7.5 The CUPS Add New Printer page.

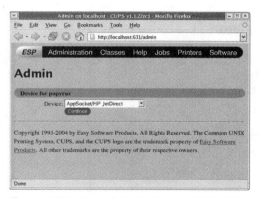

Figure 7.6 Selecting a device for the new printer in the "Device for *name*" page (here the name is "papyrus").

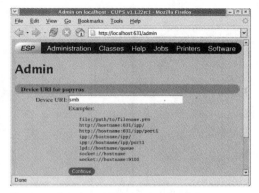

Figure 7.7 Entering a URI for a remote printer.

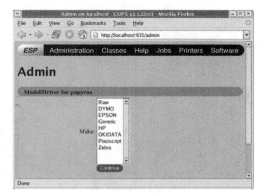

Figure 7.8 Selecting a printer make.

5. Click the Continue button.

Your Web browser displays the "Device for *name*" page (**Figure 7.6**).

6. In the Device pop-up menu, select the device that this printer is connected to, such as a parallel port or USB port. The Device menu also lists several network options.

7. Click the Continue button.

If you've selected a network device, your Web browser displays the "Device URI for *name*" page (**Figure 7.7**).

On the "Device URI for *name*" page, enter a URI (*Universal Resource Identifier*) that gives a path to the networked printer.

8. Click the Continue button.

Your Web browser displays the "Model/Driver for *name*" page (**Figure 7.8**).

continues on next page

ADMINISTERING CUPS

9. Select a printer make from the Make list. Click the Continue button.

Your Web browser displays the second screen of the "Model/Driver for *name*" page (**Figure 7.9**).

10. Select a printer model from the Model list. Click the Continue button.

CUPS finishes installing the printer and displays a success page (**Figure 7.10**).

If we visit the Printer page (http://hostname:631/printers) again, it shows your new printer (**Figure 7.11**).

✔ Tips

- CUPS supports a number of additional configuration options that aren't exposed through the Web interface. Your cupsd.conf file (located in **/etc/cups** on Fedora Core or **/usr/local/etc/cups** on FreeBSD) is filled with comments and can be edited with your favorite text editor. Remember to restart the CUPS service (**cupsd**) when you're done!

- Fedora Core's "Printer configuration" tool (in the Applications menu choose System Settings > Printing) supports more printers natively than the CUPS interface for adding new printers by using additional filters from the Gimp-Print package.

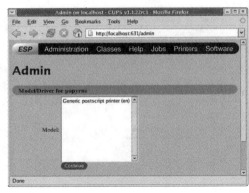

Figure 7.9 Selecting a printer model.

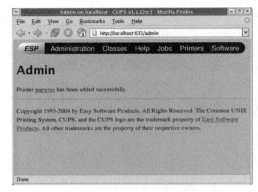

Figure 7.10 Now we've successfully created a new printer with CUPS.

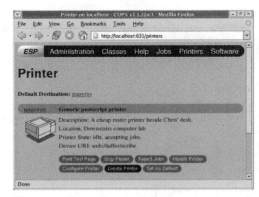

Figure 7.11 The populated Printer page.

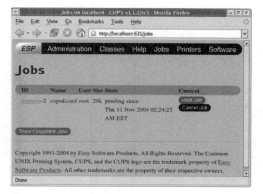

Figure 7.12 Viewing the CUPS Jobs page.

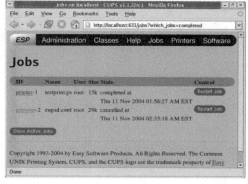

Figure 7.13 Viewing the CUPS Jobs page displaying completed jobs.

To manage print jobs with CUPS:

A Web interface for managing printers wouldn't be that helpful without a way of managing print jobs on those printers, and CUPS provides a nice one.

1. Using your favorite Web browser, connect to your CUPS server:

   http://*hostname*:631/

   Your Web browser displays the Common UNIX Printing System page (Figure 7.3).

2. On the CUPS main page, click the Jobs button in the toolbar at the top.

   Your Web browser displays the Jobs page (**Figure 7.12**).

   The Jobs page lists all of the currently active printing jobs, as well as the jobs waiting in the queue for their chance to become hard copy.

3. To put a job on hold, click the "Hold job" button next to the job's entry on the Jobs page.

   The print job will remain on hold until you release it by clicking the Release button.

4. To cancel a job, click the "Cancel job" button next to the job's entry on the Jobs page.

   Warning: There is no confirmation step; the job is deleted as soon as you click the "Cancel job" button!

5. To see print jobs that have finished printing or been canceled, click the Show Completed Jobs button at the bottom of the Jobs page.

   Your Web browser displays the Jobs page showing completed jobs (**Figure 7.13**).

continues on next page

ADMINISTERING CUPS

✔ Tips

- You can still use the lp command to send jobs to a CUPS printer from the command line.

- Use the lpstat command to get a list of your submitted print jobs displayed in the order in which they'll be printed. Use the -p option to find out which files and printers are currently active. Use -o with -p to view your jobs plus information on the active file and printer.

- Use the cancel or lprm command to cancel a print job. Pass the job ID (found with the lpstat command, or reported from lp when you sent the job for printing) as an argument to either command.

Sharing Printers with Samba

After you've added some printers to your CUPS configuration, you might want to give other users on your network access to them. Not everyone needs (or wants) a printer on their desk.

CUPS automatically shares all printers through *IPP*, its native protocol. If you've got a system that can't connect to IPP printers, it can probably connect to printers shared on a Windows network.

To share a CUPS printer with Samba:

By adding a few configuration changes to our Samba setup (**Code Listing 7.2**), we can share our CUPS printers on the Windows network.

Mac OS X users can use the Print & Fax pane of System Preferences to share printers.

1. Open a root shell, or use su (or sudo) to become root.

2. If you're using Fedora Core,

   cd /etc/samba

   or, if you're using FreeBSD,

   cd /usr/local/etc

3. Use your favorite text editor to edit the smb.conf file.

4. Locate the [global] section of the smb.conf file.

5. Add the following directives to the [global] section of smb.conf:

   ```
   printcap name = /etc/printcap
   load printers = yes
   cups options = raw
   ```

6. Add a [printers] section to smb.conf (or edit the current [printers] section):

   ```
   [printers]
       comment = Shared Printers
       path = /var/spool/samba
       browseable = yes
       guest ok = no
       writable = no
       printable = yes
   ```

7. Save the smb.conf file, exit your editor, and restart the Samba services (see Chapter 6, "Hosting a File Server," for details).

Code Listing 7.2 Adding CUPS printers to your Samba shares.

```
# Add these lines to the existing
# [global] section:
    printcap name = /etc/printcap
    load printers = yes
    cups options = raw


# Add a [printers] section, or edit an
# existing [printers] section to look
# like this:
[printers]
    comment = Shared Printers
    path = /var/spool/samba
    browseable = yes
    guest ok = no
    writable = no
    printable = yes
```

Hosting an Email Server

8

Until the advent of the World Wide Web, email was the Internet's killer application. The ability to exchange messages with friends and colleagues almost instantly, regardless of physical distance, was a huge boon for students, researchers, and office workers.

Unfortunately, with the rise of spam, email has become something we love and hate. One of the sources of spam continues to be improperly configured email servers around the world being used to send millions of spam messages every hour.

In this chapter, we'll learn how to configure Sendmail, the most common email server on the Internet today. We'll also look at Postfix, an outstanding replacement for Sendmail, designed for speed and security.

Configuring Sendmail

Although Fedora Core and FreeBSD already have Sendmail installed and configured for local delivery, you'll want to tweak the default configuration a bit to prevent abuse and to tell Sendmail what to do with mail destined for external systems.

Cygwin users don't have a Sendmail port to deal with, and Mac OS X users can skip ahead to the Postfix sections because Postfix is installed as part of their base operating system.

To configure Sendmail:

Sendmail configuration has a reputation for being painful and error-prone. You might want to pick up a cup of your favorite beverage before diving in.

1. Log in as **root** or use **su** to become **root**.

2. **cd /etc/mail**

   Sendmail's configuration files are collected in one standard location.

3. Use your favorite text editor to edit the sendmail.mc file.

   If you're using FreeBSD, you'll edit *hostname*.mc instead; the Sendmail configuration file on FreeBSD is named after the host.

4. Because Sendmail's main configuration file gets processed with the M4 macro processor, follow these rules when editing:

   ▲ Create comments, or end lines with the **dnl** command. This deletes the rest of the line (from **dnl** onward) from the output file.

   ▲ Quote strings with a backtick and single quote. For example, the **SMART_HOST** macro must appear as `SMART_HOST'` in the configuration file.

Sendmail or Postfix?

Choosing whether to use Sendmail or Postfix can be fairly straightforward. Your standard FreeBSD and Fedora Core installations include a configured Sendmail suitable for delivering messages locally. Similarly, Mac OS X comes with Postfix installed and ready. If you're content with the status quo, your work here is (almost) done. If you want to maximize the security of your system and minimize your administrative headaches, you should consider upgrading from Sendmail to Postfix.

If you're thinking of running Sendmail or Postfix on a Cygwin system, you might want to reconsider. Mixing Windows users, groups, and permissions with very Unix-specific applications that make lots of assumptions about their operating environment is going to be more work than setting up a small Fedora Core or FreeBSD system.

Of course, you should take a look at the documentation for both and pick the one that makes the most sense to you.

---

5. If your system can't send mail directly to other hosts on the Internet (it should be able to, unless you're part of a residential ISP network, don't have a valid reverse DNS record, or have other configuration problems) and/or you want to use your ISP's system to send your mail, uncomment (remove the `dnl` command at the beginning of the line) the `define(`SMART_HOST',...)` line and change *hostname* to the fully qualified domain name of your ISP's SMTP relay:

```
define(`SMART_HOST',`hostname')dnl
```

6. If Sendmail should reject connections from other systems, find the `DAEMON_OPTIONS` macros and add this after the existing `DAEMON_OPTIONS` macros:

```
DAEMON_OPTIONS(`Port=smtp
→ ,Addr=127.0.0.1, Name=MTA')dnl
```

To allow connections from any system on your local network, comment out this line (Fedora Core includes this setting by default). Allowing connections from the LAN lets other systems use this machine as a relay.

Warning: To prevent connections from external systems, remember to block the SMTP port (25) at the firewall between your LAN and the Internet.

7. To prevent access from systems with unresolvable domains (this is a spam risk!), comment out the `accept_unresolvable_domains FEATURE` macro, if one exists:

```
dnl FEATURE
→ (`accept_unresolvable_domains')
```

continues on next page

CONFIGURING SENDMAIL

8. If your system doesn't have a proper domain associated with it (for example, a small LAN in your basement probably doesn't have its own domain), uncomment or add (after the `DAEMON_OPTIONS` macros) the `MASQUERADE_AS` macro:

`MASQUERADE_AS(`yourisp`')dnl`

Replace *yourisp* with the domain name of your ISP; all email coming from this system will appear to have been sent from *yourisp* instead of whatever internal domain name you've been using on the LAN.

9. Save the Sendmail configuration file, and exit your editor.

10. `make`

In the `/etc/mail` directory, running the `make` command (**Code Listing 8.1**) will rebuild the Sendmail databases and other files.

11. `make restart`

Restart the Sendmail daemon so that it picks up the configuration changes.

✔ Tip

■ Fedora Core users will need to install the sendmail-cf package before rebuilding Sendmail's configuration files. Use `up2date` to do this:

`up2date -i sendmail-cf`

Code Listing 8.1 Using the `make` command to rebuild sendmail.cf from the sendmail.mc file.

```
bsd# cd /etc/mail
bsd# vi bsd.chrish.local.mc
...
bsd# make
/usr/bin/m4 -D_CF_DIR_=/usr/share/sendmail/cf/   /usr/share/sendmail/cf/m4/cf.m4
→ bsd.chrish.local.mc > bsd.chrish.local.cf
bsd# make restart
Restarting: sendmail sendmail-clientmqueue.
bsd#
```

To configure aliases:

Mail aliases let you create a virtual email address that distributes its mail to another alias, a local user, a local file, a command, or another address.

1. Log in as **root** or use **su** to become **root**.

2. `cd /etc`

   The "aliases" file resides in the general configuration directory (although on FreeBSD it's actually in `/etc/mail`, and there's a symbolic link in `/etc`).

3. Use your favorite text editor to edit the aliases file.

4. Each line of the aliases file follows this form:

   `name: addr_1, addr_2, ..., addr_n`

   Where *name* is the alias; messages sent to this virtual email address will be distributed to the address (or addresses) listed on the rest of the line (*addr_1*, *addr_2*, and so on). Only one address is required.

For example, maybe I want mail that is sent to **root** on this system to actually be delivered to the user **chrish**. Adding the following line to the aliases file accomplishes this:

`root: chrish`

Lines starting with a # character are comments.

5. To send the email to a command, use |*command* as the address. You might use this to scan incoming email for viruses or dangerous attachments.

6. You can send the email to a file by specifying a full path (`/path/to/the/file`) as the address.

7. Email can be forwarded to a user on another system by using the user's email address (*spamvictim*@hotmail.com) as the address.

8. Save the aliases file, then exit your editor.

9. `newaliases`

   Run the `newaliases` command (**Code Listing 8.2**) to update the aliases database and restart Sendmail.

Code Listing 8.2 Rebuilding the email-address-alias database with the `newaliases` command.

```
[root@dhcppc1 ~]# cd /etc
[root@dhcppc1 etc]# vi aliases
...
[root@dhcppc1 etc]# newaliases
/etc/aliases: 80 aliases, longest 16 bytes, 845 bytes total
[root@dhcppc1 etc]#
```

Installing Postfix

Postfix is a fast, secure replacement for Sendmail. Although it shares several standard Sendmail configuration files (such as the /etc/aliases file), it was designed for maximum security in a modern email environment (that is, one filled with spam, viruses, attacks against the server software, and so on).

Our goal in this section is to replace Sendmail completely. Consult the Postfix documentation for information about using Postfix for sending mail without touching your existing Sendmail installation, or for using Postfix with a virtual host, also without modifying an existing Sendmail setup.

Postfix is the default Unix mailer on Mac OS X systems, so Mac users can skip this section.

To install Postfix (Fedora Core):

We'll install Postfix (**Code Listing 8.3**) from the source for that freshly brewed flavor.

1. Use your favorite Web browser to visit the Postfix download page (www.postfix.org/download.html).

2. Click the link for a mirror that's close to you. You can't choose wrong on the download page.

3. Download the latest official release ("2.1 patchlevel 5" as of this writing) and save the file.

4. `tar -xzf postfix-2.1.5.tar.gz`
   Unpack the Postfix source code. This creates a `postfix-2.1.5` directory.

5. `cd postfix-2.1.5`
   Change to the Postfix source directory.

6. `make`
   Build Postfix from the source code.

continues on next page

Code Listing 8.3 Installing Postfix on Fedora Core.

```
[chrish@dhcppc1 ~] tar -xzf postfix-2.1.5.tar.gz
[chrish@dhcppc1 ~] cd postfix-2.1.5
[chrish@dhcppc1 postfix-2.1.5] make
...
[chrish@dhcppc1 postfix-2.1.5] su -
Password:
[root@dhcppc1 postfix-2.1.5] groupadd -r postfix
[root@dhcppc1 postfix-2.1.5] groupadd -r postdrop
[root@dhcppc1 postfix-2.1.5] useradd -g postfix -G mail -M -n -r -s /bin/false postfix
[root@dhcppc1 postfix-2.1.5] make install
...
[root@dhcppc1 postfix-2.1.5] echo postfix: root >> /etc/aliases
[root@dhcppc1 postfix-2.1.5] newaliases
[root@dhcppc1 postfix-2.1.5] cd /etc/rc.d/init.d
[root@dhcppc1 init.d] ln -s /usr/sbin/postfix postfix
[root@dhcppc1 init.d] cd /etc/rc.d/rc5.d
[root@dhcppc1 rc5.d] ln -s /etc/rc.d/init.d/postfix S63postfix
[root@dhcppc1 rc5.d] service sendmail stop
Shutting down sendmail:                [OK]
[root@dhcppc1 rc5.d] chkconfig --del sendmail
[root@dhcppc1 rc5.d] postfix start
postfix/postfix-script: starting the Postfix mail system
```

7. `su -`

The rest of the configuration commands need to be done as **root**, so we'll use the **su** command to become **root**.

8. `groupadd -r postfix`

Create a new system group named **postfix** for our Postfix installation.

9. `groupadd -r postdrop`

Create a new system group named **postdrop**.

10. `useradd -g postfix -G mail -M -n -r`
↦ `-s /bin/false postfix`

Use the **useradd** command to create a new user named **postfix**. The **-g** option puts it in the **postfix** group, and the **-G** option puts it in the **mail** groups, too. The **-n** option means this user has no home directory, and the **-s** option specifies `/bin/false` as a shell. (That stops people from being able to log in as this user.)

11. `make install`

Install our fresh new Postfix.

You will be prompted for several Postfix configuration options; press Enter for each one to go with the default.

12. `echo postfix: root >> /etc/aliases`

Add an alias for the **postfix** address to the "aliases" file.

13. `newaliases`

Rebuild the alias database.

14. `cd /etc/rc.d/init.d`

Change to the system-startup-script directory.

15. `ln -s /usr/sbin/postfix postfix`

Create a symbolic link to the **postfix** control program.

16. `cd /etc/rc.d/rc5.d`

Change to the run level 5 startup-script directory.

17. `ln -s /etc/rc.d/init.d/postfix`
↦ `S63postfix`

Create a symbolic link to start Postfix during the boot process.

18. `service sendmail stop`

Stop the Sendmail service.

19. `chkconfig --del sendmail`

Remove Sendmail from the list of services to start at boot time.

20. `postfix start`

Start the Postfix daemon.

✔ Tips

- You can use **up2date** to install Postfix from a binary package:

  `up2date --install postfix`

- If you specifically select Postfix as your mail system while installing Fedora Core, Sendmail won't be installed at all.

Code Listing 8.4 Installing Postfix on FreeBSD.

```
bsd# cd /usr/ports/mail/postfix
bsd# make install clean
...
bsd# vi /etc/rc.conf
...
bsd# cd /usr/local/etc/rc.d
bsd# ln -s /usr/local/sbin/postfix postfix.sh
bsd# vi /etc/periodic.conf
...
bsd# /etc/rc.d/sendmail stop
bsd# /usr/local/etc/rc.d/postfix.sh start
postfix/postfix-script: starting the Postfix
mail system
bsd#
```

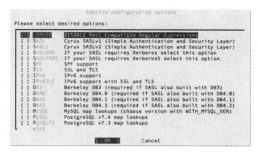

Figure 8.1 The "Postfix configuration options" dialog appears during installion of Postfix on FreeBSD.

To install Postfix (FreeBSD):

We install Postfix (**Code Listing 8.4**) from the ports collection on FreeBSD.

1. Log in as **root** or use **su** to become **root**.

2. `cd /usr/ports/mail/postfix`

   Change to the Postfix directory in the ports collection.

3. `make install clean`

   We're going to build Postfix, install it, and then clean up.

   The ports build process displays the "Postfix configuration options" dialog (**Figure 8.1**).

4. None of the options are required for a basic installation; if you're setting up a more complex authentication scheme, refer to the Postfix documentation.

   Press Tab to move your cursor to the OK button in the "Postfix configuration options" dialog, and then press Enter to continue with the build process.

5. During installation, Postfix will create two new groups (`postfix` and `maildrop`) and a new user (`postfix`). You will also be prompted to add the `postfix` user to the `mail` group.

   Press Y, then press Enter to add the `postfix` user to the `mail` group.

   continues on next page

6. When prompted to activate Postfix in /etc/mail/mailer.conf, press Y, then press Enter to continue. This replaces the existing Sendmail with our new Postfix.

7. Using your favorite text editor, edit /etc/rc.conf and add the following line:

   `sendmail_enable="NO"`

   This prevents Sendmail from starting during the boot process.

8. `cd /usr/local/etc/rc.d`

   Change to the local rc.d directory.

9. `ln -s /usr/local/sbin/postfix postfix.sh`

   Create a symbolic link from the **postfix** command to **postfix.sh** in the local rc.d directory. This lets Postfix start during the boot process.

10. Use your favorite text editor to edit (or create) the /etc/periodic.conf file so that it includes the following lines:

    ```
    daily_clean_hoststat_enable="NO"
    daily_status_mail_rejects_enable
    → ="NO"
    daily_status_include_submit_mailq
    → ="NO"
    daily_submit_queuerun="NO"
    ```

    These are all Sendmail-related daily cleanup tasks that aren't necessary with Postfix.

11. `/etc/rc.d/sendmail stop`

    Stop the running Sendmail daemon.

12. `/usr/local/etc/rc.d/postfix.sh`
    `→ start`

    Start the new Postfix daemon.

Configuring Postfix

Now that we've got Postfix installed and running, we'll need to configure it so that it knows about our domain name and how to transfer mail out to other systems.

To configure Postfix:

1. Log in as `root`, or use `su` to become `root`.

2. `cd /etc/postfix`

   Or, if you're using FreeBSD,

   `cd /usr/local/etc/postfix`

3. Use your favorite text editor to edit the main.cf file. This is Postfix's main configuration file.

   Lines that begin with a # character are comments. Blank lines are ignored.

   You can use $*variablename* to reference another variable configured previously in the file.

   The sections mentioned in the steps below are just headings in comments. Postfix's configuration files aren't organized in specific sections—the configuration lines can appear anywhere in the file.

4. Search for the INTERNET HOST AND DOMAIN NAMES section.

5. Add a `myhostname` line:

   `myhostname = full.hostname`

   Where `full.hostname` is your fully qualified hostname.

6. In the SENDING MAIL section, add a `myorigin` line if you want your email to appear to come from a different domain or host:

   `myorigin = domain`

   For example, you might use your ISP's hostname here, or your company's domain name.

7. In the RECEIVING MAIL section, use the `mydestination` line to indicate which email needs to be delivered locally. By default, only mail addressed specifically for users on this machine have their mail delivered locally (that is, saved to a mail spool file instead of sent over the network to its destination). For example, to keep mail for the entire domain on this machine:

   `mydestination = $myhostname,`
   `→ localhost.$mydomain localhost`
   `→ $mydomain`

8. In the TRUST AND RELAY CONTROL section we need to specify which hosts are allowed to relay mail through this server. The default is to authorize all clients in every subnet the system is attached to. If you're connected to the Internet, this leaves you open to abuse from spammers!

   Add a `mynetworks` line to indicate which IP addresses and networks are allowed to send mail through this system:

   `mynetworks = 127.0.0.0/8`
   `→ 192.168.0.0/24`

   This `mynetworks` line authorizes the local host, plus every host on the 192.168.0.* local network.

9. To send mail through your ISP's SMTP server, add a `relayhost` line in the INTERNET OR INTRANET section specifying the ISP's server name:

   `relayhost = smtp.your.isp.com`

10. Save the file and exit your text editor.

11. `postfix check`

    Check the Postfix configuration files for errors.

12. `postfix reload`

    Tell Postfix to reload its configuration data. You don't need to stop/start the server to make configuration changes active.

continues on next page

CONFIGURING POSTFIX

✔ Tips

- Postfix has hundreds of configuration options; look around in the main.cf file and read the many comments to see some of the most useful options. For full documentation, check the Postfix Web site (www.postfix.org).

- To add email aliases on a Postfix system, use the information in the "Configuring Sendmail" section earlier in this chapter; Postfix's aliases are compatible with Sendmail's.

- You can tell Postfix to immediately reload its email address aliases with the following command, as root:

```
postfix reload
```

- Webmin has a detailed Postfix configuration section at https://*hostname*: 10000/postfix/.

- To distribute email to client systems that can't (or won't) run a traditional Unix mailer like Sendmail or Postfix, you'll need to install an IMAP or POP3 server. Cyrus IMAP (http://asg.web.cmu.edu/ cyrus) and UW IMAP (www.washington .edu/imap) handle these duties.

HOSTING A WEB SERVER

Since its introduction in 1993, the World Wide Web has become a great tool for spreading information, rumors, and entertainment. Nearly 70 percent of the systems hosting the Web are running Apache, according to the Netcraft Web Server Survey, a monthly survey of the Web servers running on systems connected to the Internet.

Not bad for a piece of free, open-source software that many people think was named Apache because it's "a patchy" Web server.

Apache grew out of an older, mostly abandoned Web server (the National Center for Supercomputing Applications' HTTPd) early in 1995 and has become the standard for speed, reliability, and flexibility in Web servers.

In this chapter, we'll look at installing and configuring the latest Apache server to add our own data to the World Wide Web or to a local Intranet.

Installing Apache

Apache is a complex piece of software because of the many features and standards it supports. Most of these features are added through optional modules that can be loaded dynamically and configured through Apache's configuration files.

To install Apache (Fedora Core):

Installing Apache on Fedora Core is as simple as pulling in the prebuilt binary package.

1. Log in as **root**, or use **su** to become **root**.

2. `up2date --install httpd`

   Use the **up2date** command to install the latest version of the Apache HTTP daemon (**Code Listing 9.1**).

   The prebuilt package for Apache is downloaded and installed.

3. `service start httpd`

   Start our new HTTP service. If your machine is visible to the outside world, you should probably start it after Apache has been configured.

4. Launch the Services control panel (from the Applications menu in the top left of your screen choose System Settings > Server Settings > Services).

5. Scroll down the list of services until you find the **httpd** entry (**Figure 9.1**).

   As you can see in the screen shot, the **httpd** service isn't set to start at boot time (it has no check mark). Also, you can see that I've started it by hand (in step 3) because the Status section is listing several process IDs for the **httpd**.

6. Check the box next to **httpd** to make Apache start when the system boots, and then close the Service Configuration window.

Code Listing 9.1 Using up2date to install Apache on Fedora Core.

```
[root@dhcppc1 ~]# up2date --install httpd
...
The following packages were added to your selection to satisfy dependencies:

Name          Version      Release
-------------------------------------
apr           0.9.4        23
apr-util      0.9.4        17
httpd-suexec  2.0.52       3.1


[root@dhcppc1 ~]# service start httpd
Starting httpd: [OK]
```

INSTALLING APACHE

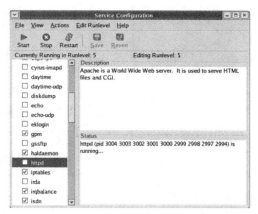

Figure 9.1 Activating the Apache server on Fedora Core.

Code Listing 9.2 Using the ports system to install Apache on FreeBSD.

```
bsd# cd /usr/ports/www/apache2
bsd# make install clean
...
bsd# vi /etc/rc.conf
...
bsd# /usr/local/etc/rc.d/apache2.sh start
Starting apache2.
```

To install Apache (FreeBSD):

Naturally, the FreeBSD ports system has an entry for the latest Apache.

1. `cd /usr/ports/www/apache2`

   Change to the Apache 2.x directory in the ports tree (**Code Listing 9.2**). Apache 1.3.x is also available, which is why there isn't an "apache" directory in the ports tree.

2. `make install clean`

   Download the Apache source code (plus any dependencies), compile it, and install it, then clean up.

3. Edit the `/etc/rc.conf` file with your favorite text editor.

4. Add the following line to start Apache during the boot process:

   `apache2_enable="YES"`

5. Save the rc.conf file and exit your editor.

6. `/usr/local/etc/rc.d/apache2.sh start`

   Start the Apache HTTP server.

To install Apache (Cygwin):

Cygwin has a port of Apache 1.3 but no port of Apache 2, so we're going to break form and install the "native" Windows Apache, and then hook it up with Cygwin's file system.

1. Use your favorite Web browser to visit the Apache Software Foundation site (www.apache.org) (**Figure 9.2**).

2. Click the "HTTP Server" link in the project list on the left-hand side to visit the Apache HTTP Server Project page.

3. Click the "from a mirror" link under Download! in the table of contents along the left-hand side. Your Web browser displays the download page.

4. Scroll down to the "Apache 2.0.52 is the best available version" section, then click the "Win32 Binary (MSI Installer)" link.

5. Save the installer file to your desktop.

6. Double-click the installer file to launch the Apache HTTP Server 2.0 Installation Wizard (**Figure 9.3**).
   Click Next to continue.

7. Read the License Agreement (**Figure 9.4**), then click the "I accept the terms in the license agreement" radio button.
   Click Next to continue.

Figure 9.2 The Apache group's Web site.

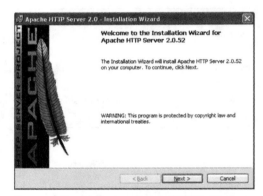

Figure 9.3 The Apache installation wizard on Windows.

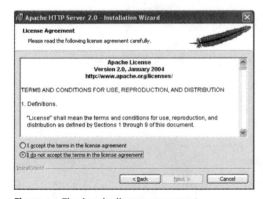

Figure 9.4 The Apache license agreement.

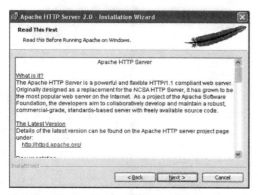

Figure 9.5 The Apache Read This First information.

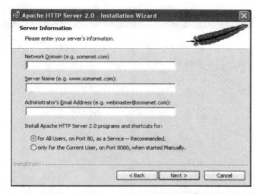

Figure 9.6 Entering server information in the Apache installation wizard.

8. Read the Read This First information (**Figure 9.5**).

Click Next to continue.

9. In the Server Information pane (**Figure 9.6**), enter your Web server's information in the following areas:

▲ Network Domain—This can be a real registered domain or something like "local" for your LAN. The default is to use your computer's domain.

▲ Server Name—The hostname, plus Network Domain. The default is your computer's fully qualified domain name.

▲ Administrator's Email Address—The email address of the owner of this server. You might want to set up a new email address for this; visitors will send you problem reports, but the address will also start to get a lot of spam email.

▲ A choice between having the server run as a service (the default) or manually. You want the default.

Click Next to continue.

continues on next page

10. Choose Typical (the default) in the Setup Type pane (**Figure 9.7**).

Choosing Custom lets you install the headers and libraries needed to compile additional Apache modules, but they won't be compatible with the compiler installed with Cygwin.

11 Click Next to continue.

12. In the Destination Folder pane (**Figure 9.8**), click the Change button.

13. In the Change Current Destination Folder pane, use the file selector to navigate to C:\cygwin\usr\local\ (**Figure 9.9**), then click OK.

Click Next in the installation wizard to continue.

14. Click the Install button in the installation wizard to install Apache.

15. Click the Finish button in the installation wizard to exit the installer.

✔ Tip

■ If your Apache 2 server is causing problems on Windows (corrupted or incomplete file downloads, unexplained error messages, or conflicts with software), add the following directives to Apache's configuration file, and then restart the server:

```
EnableSendfile Off
EnableMMAP Off
Win32DisableAcceptEx
```

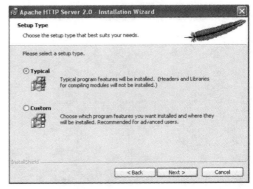

Figure 9.7 Choosing the Typical or Custom installation in the Apache installation wizard.

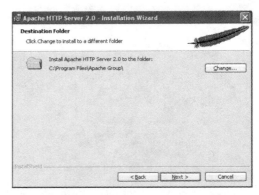

Figure 9.8 Choosing the destination folder in the Apache installation wizard.

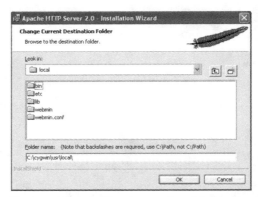

Figure 9.9 Using the file selector to install Apache in our Cygwin directory.

INSTALLING APACHE

To install Apache (Mac OS X):

Although Mac OS X comes with an older version of Apache, we'd like to use the current version, and Fink can help us install it.

1. `sudo fink install apache2`

   Tell Fink to install the latest version of Apache (**Code Listing 9.3**) and any dependencies it might have.

continues on next page

Code Listing 9.3 Using Fink to install Apache on Mac OS X.

```
bender:~ chrish$ sudo fink install apache2
Password:
Information about 1977 packages read in 3 seconds.

fink needs help picking an alternative to satisfy a virtual dependency. The
candidates:

(1)   apache2-mpm-worker: Apache2 Server Binary - [MPM WORKER]
(2)   apache2-mpm-perchild: Apache2 Server Binary - [MPM PERCHILD *EXPERIMENTAL*]
(3)   apache2-mpm-prefork: Apache2 Server Binary - [MPM PREFORK]
(4)   apache2-mpm-leader: Apache2 Server Binary - [MPM LEADER *EXPERIMENTAL*]
(5)   apache2-mpm-threadpool: Apache2 Server Binary - [MPM THREADPOOL *EXPERIMENTAL*]

Pick one: [1]
...
The following package will be installed or updated:
apache2
The following 7 additional packages will be installed:
 apache2-common apache2-mpm-worker apr apr-common apr-shlibs db42 db42-shlibs
Do you want to continue? [Y/n]
...
bender:~ chrish$ cd /Library/StartupItems/
bender:/Library/StartupItems chrish$ sudo mkdir Apache2
bender:/Library/StartupItems chrish$ cd Apache2
bender:/Library/StartupItems/Apache2 chrish$ sudo ln -s /sw/sbin/apachectl Apache2
bender:/Library/StartupItems/Apache2 chrish$ sudo sh -c "sed -e 's/Apache/Apache 2/g' <
/System/Library/StartupItems/Apache/StartupParameters.plist > StartupParameters.plist"
bender:/Library/StartupItems/Apache2 chrish$ sudo ./Apache2 start
```

2. You'll be prompted to satisfy a "virtual dependency" with five different candidates:

▲ `apache2-mpm-worker`—The standard multiprocessing model (MPM), which uses multiple server processes and multiple threads to service large numbers of requests.

▲ `apache2-mpm-perchild`—An experimental MPM, which isn't currently finished. Don't use this.

▲ `apache2-mpm-prefork`—This MPM behaves like Apache 1.3, by creating sub-processes to handle requests without using multiple threads. This is useful only if you need to use libraries that aren't thread-safe for an add-on module. I'd suggest fixing the old library instead, but that's a personal preference.

▲ `apache2-mpm-leader`—An experimental MPM that uses a Leader/Follower design pattern to coordinate work between threads.

▲ `apache2-mpm-threadpool`—An experimental MPM similar to the "worker" MPM, but slower. It uses a pool of idle threads to handle requests.

Press Enter to go with the default (`apache2-mpm-worker`), unless you want to experiment with one of the unfinished MPMs listed above.

3. Fink resolves Apache's dependencies, lists the additional packages required to install Apache, and asks, "Do you want to continue? [Y/n]"

Press Enter to install Apache and its dependencies.

4. `cd /Library/StartupItems`

Change to the local `StartupItems` directory.

5. `sudo mkdir Apache2`

Create a new directory for our Apache startup script and .plist file.

6. `cd Apache2`

Change to our new Apache directory.

7. `sudo ln -s /sw/sbin/apachectl Apache2`

Apache kindly includes a startup script (`apachectl`) that accepts the **start**, **stop**, and **restart** arguments required for a Mac OS X startup script, so all we need to do is put a symbolic link to it here.

8. `sudo sh -c "sed`
   → `-e 's/Apache/Apache 2/' <`
   → `/System/Library/`
   → `StartupItems/Apache/`
   → `StartupParameters.plist >`
   → `StartupParameters.plist"`

Copy the StartupParameters.plist that Mac OS X uses with its version of Apache, change "Apache" to "Apache 2" inside, and create our own StartupParameters.plist file (**Code Listing 9.4**).

You could also use your favorite text editor, but that can be tricky if it happens to be a GUI editor. You'll probably have to save it somewhere and then use a **sudo cp** command to copy it here.

9. `sudo ./Apache2 start`

Launch our new version of Apache. If you've got Apple's Personal Web Sharing active, launching our Apache will fail, because there's already a service (the Personal Web Sharing) running on the default HTTP port.

Code Listing 9.4 The StartupParameters.plist file for Apache on Mac OS X.

```
{
  Description = "Apache 2 web server";
  Provides = ("Web Server");
  Requires = ("DirectoryServices");
  Uses = ("Disks", "NFS");
  OrderPreference = "None";
}
```

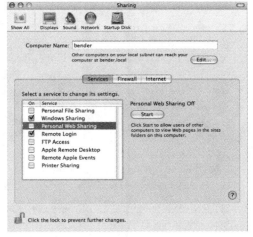

Figure 9.10 Mac OS X's Personal Web Sharing is actually an Apache 1.3 server.

✔ Tip

■ Mac OS X comes with an old version of Apache (1.3.29) installed and configured as Personal Web Sharing in the Sharing pane of System Preferences (**Figure 9.10**). The current version of Apache 1.3 is 1.3.33, which fixes several known security issues present in 1.3.29. If you don't want to install and configure Apache 2, 1.3 is stable and well known, despite these minor security vulnerabilities.

Configuring Apache

The Apache Web server is highly configurable to help you tune and manage your Web site. The list of supported configuration options is quite long (take a look for yourself at the Apache Directive Index—http://httpd .apache.org/docs-2.0/mod/directives.html), but very few of them actually need to be specified.

To read an Apache configuration file:

Apache's configuration directives come in two flavors, which are quite straightforward, even if the httpd.conf file is found in a different location for almost every OS.

1. Do one of the following:
   ▲ `cd /etc/httpd/conf` on Linux
   ▲ `cd /usr/local/etc/apache2` on FreeBSD
   ▲ `cd /usr/local/Apache2/conf` on Cygwin
   ▲ `cd /sw/etc/apache2` on Mac OS X

   Change to the Apache configuration directory.

2. `less httpd.conf`
   View the main configuration file.

3. The first type of directive in an Apache configuration file is a *single-line directive*:

   `DirectiveName value`

   This specifies the given `value` for `DirectiveName`. For example, this directive sets the server's name to www.*example*.com on the default HTTP port:

   `ServerName www.example.com:80`

4. The second type of directive is a *block directive*, which looks a bit like an HTML or XML tag surrounding other single-line or block directives:

   `<DirectiveName value>`
   `    AssociatedDirective value`
   `    ...`
   `</DirectiveName>`

   As you can see, block directives can carry their own `value` and also have additional directives associated with them.

5. Note the many helpful comments in the httpd.conf file. Comments start with the # character and end at the end of the line.

Code Listing 9.5 Apache's basic server settings.

```
# The basic server settings for Apache 2.
ServerAdmin admin@example.com
ServerName chrish.example.com:80
Listen 80
```

To configure basic server settings for Apache:

By default, Apache sets up a Web server at port 80, the standard HTTP port.

1. Using your favorite text editor, edit the httpd.conf file we found in the previous section (**Code Listing 9.5**).

2. Search for the `ServerAdmin` directive, and change its value to the email address of the server administrator (or Webmaster). For example:

   `ServerAdmin admin@example.com`

3. Search for the `ServerName` directive, and change its value to the fully qualified domain name and port of the server. This is used when generating redirection URLs.

   `ServerName chrish.example.com:80`

4. Search for the `Listen` directive and set it to the port or IP address and port (if you have multiple network interfaces) you want the server to use. The default is port 80, the well-known HTTP port. For example, to set it to port 8000, a common personal server or proxy port:

   `Listen 8000`

   This port should match the one you specify in the `ServerName` directive, unless your redirections are handled by a Web server running on a different port.

5. Save the file, then exit your text editor.

6. `apachectl -t`

   Test the configuration for syntax errors. It should respond with "Syntax OK."

7. `apachectl restart`

   Restart the server to pick up the configuration changes.

   If you're not logged in as **root**, you'll need to use **su** to become **root** before running this command, or use **sudo** to run the command as **root**.

To configure Web directories:

The heart of any Web server is the set of files and other resources it provides.

1. Using your favorite text editor, edit the httpd.conf file (**Code Listing 9.6**).

2. Search for the `DocumentRoot` directive. This defines the base directory for all Web requests (although symbolic links and `Alias` directives can bring in resources from other locations). For example, this sets the document root to /www:

```
DocumentRoot "/www"
```

3. Every directory published through your Web server, including the `DocumentRoot`, needs a `Directory` block to specify permissions and directory-related options:

```
<Directory /full/path>
directives
</Directory>
```

The /full/path is the path on the server's file system, not the path that Web browsers use. For example, you'd use /www (the path of the `DocumentRoot`, above) instead of just / (the path a Web browser would use to access the `DocumentRoot`).

The directives apply specifically to this directory and its subdirectories. The most common directives used with `Directory` are `Allow`, `AllowOverride`, `Deny`, `Options`, and `Order`. Here's what they're used for:

▲ `Allow from` hosts—Allow access to the specified hosts. The hosts can be `All`, a partial domain name (such as apache.org), a full IP address, a partial IP address (for example, 10.1 would match all hosts in the 10.1.*.* network), a network/netmask pair (for example, 10.1.0.0/255.255.0.0 for all hosts in the 10.1.*.* network), or a network/CIDR specification (10.1.0.0/16

for all hosts in the 10.1.*.* network). Multiple `hosts` can be specified, separated by spaces.

▲ `AllowOverride`—Indicate which directives in the httpd.conf file can be overridden by an .htaccess file in the directory. Can be set to `All`, `None` (the .htaccess files are completely ignored), `AuthConfig` (override authorization directives), `FileInfo` (directives for controlling document types), `Indexes` (directives for controlling directory indexing), `Limit` (directives for controlling host access), and `Options` (directives for controlling directory features).

▲ `Deny from` hosts—Deny access to the specified hosts. The hosts can be any of the hosts values used with the `Allow` directive.

▲ `Options`—Controls which features are available in the directory. Can be `All` (allow everything except `MultiView`), `ExecCGI` (allow CGI scripts in this directory to run), `FollowSymlinks` (the server will follow symbolic links), `Include` (process server-side include directives), `IncludesNOEXEC` (as `Includes`, but disable the `#exec cmd` and `#exec cgi` directives), `Indexes` (automatically produce directory indexes when the `DirectoryIndex` file, usually index.html, isn't present), `MultiViews` (enable content-negotiated multiviews), and `SymLinksIfOwnerMatch` (follow symbolic links only if the owner of the link matches the owner of the link's target). If you precede the specified `Options` with + (to enable) or - (to disable), they will be merged with any other `Options` that apply to this directory.

▲ `Order`—Set this to `Allow,Deny` or `Deny,Allow` to specify the order in which `Allow` and `Deny` directives are evaluated.

Code Listing 9.6 Apache's directory-configuration directives.

```
# Directory configuration directives
DocumentRoot "/www"


<Directory />
    Options FollowSymlinks
    AllowOverride None
    Order Deny, Allow
    Deny from All
</Directory>


<Directory /www>
    Options +IncludesNOEXEC
    Order Allow, Deny
    Allow from All
</Directory>


Alias /icons/ /usr/local/share/icons/
<Directory /usr/local/share/icons/>
    Options -Indexes
    Order Allow, Deny
    Allow from All
</Directory>


ScriptAlias /cgi-bin/ /www/cgi-bin/
<Directory /www/cgi-bin/>
    AllowOverride None
    Options None
    Order allow,deny
    Allow from all
</Directory>
```

The **Directory** directives are checked in the order in which they appear in the httpd.conf file, and the most specific **Directory** directive that matches the requested file is used to determine the permissions and options that apply to that request.

4. Find the **Directory** directive for /, and add **Order** and **Deny** directives to restrict access to every directory:

```
<Directory />
    Options FollowSymlinks
    AllowOverride None

    # We add these to improve
    # security.
    Order Deny, Allow
    Deny from All
</Directory>
```

5. Find the **Directory** directive for your **DocumentRoot** directory, and add an **Options** directive to modify the **Options** specified in the **Directory** directive for /:

```
<Directory /www>
    # Add this to enable server-side
    # includes on the site.
    Options +IncludesNOEXEC

    # The standard directives for
    # your DocumentRoot directory:
    Order Allow, Deny
    Allow from All
</Directory>
```

In this example, we add **IncludesNOEXEC** to the **Options** so that the HTML documents on this site can use *server-side includes* (*SSI*) without allowing the potentially dangerous **#exec** commands.

continues on next page

CONFIGURING APACHE

6. Add `Alias` directives to bring directories outside of `DirectoryRoot` into the Web server's space:

```
Alias fakepath realpath
```

For example, to bring /home/marketing/company-site into the Web server as /company, use

```
Alias /company /home/marketing/
↪ company-site
```

Note that if the `Alias` ends in a /, it only matches URLs that include the /. For example, making an `Alias` for /icons/ doesn't alias the URL for /icons (that is, http://*myserver*/icons will fail, but http://*myserver*/icons/ will succeed).

7. Add `Directory` directives for each `Alias` to change the default directory access permissions and options. For some aliases, you might want to disable directory indexes:

```
<Directory /www/icons/>
    ...
    Options -Indexes
    ...
</Directory>
```

8. Add `ScriptAlias` directives to add directories that can contain CGI programs. `ScriptAlias` works just like `Alias`:

```
ScriptAlias /cgi-bin/ /www/cgi-bin/
```

`Directory` options should be more restrictive for `ScriptAlias` directories to reduce the potential for security problems:

```
<Directory /www/cgi-bin/>
    ...
    AllowOverride None
    Options None
    Order Allow,Deny
    Allow from All
    ...
</Directory>
```

9. Save the httpd.conf file and exit your text editor.

10. `apachectl -t && apachectl restart`

Check your httpd.conf for errors, then restart the server if no errors are found.

To configure hostname lookups:

By default, Apache's access logs record the IP addresses of visitors to your site, but it's possible to have the logs record their hostnames instead.

1. Use your favorite text editor to edit Apache's httpd.conf file.

2. Find the `HostnameLookups` directive and set it to `On` instead of `Off`.

3. Save the httpd.conf file and exit your editor.

4. `apachectl -t && apachectl restart`

Check your httpd.conf for errors, and then restart the server if no errors are found.

✔ Tip

■ Don't turn on `HostnameLookups` unless you really need it; it's off by default because it increases network traffic and also introduces latency for the visitor during the lookup. That's because the HTTP server needs to ask its DNS server to map your IP address into a hostname before it can log and process your request.

To configure extended status reporting:

By default, Apache's extended status reporting is disabled. This prevents its information from being used to compromise the system unless you activate it yourself.

1. Use your favorite text editor to edit Apache's httpd.conf file.

2. Find the ExtendedStatus directive and set it to On instead of Off.

3. Add a Location directive to attach the server-status handler to /server-status:

   ```
   <Location /server-status>
       SetHandler server-status
   </Location>
   ```

4. Save the httpd.conf file and exit your editor.

5. `apachectl -t && apachectl restart`
   Check your httpd.conf for errors, and then restart the server if no errors are found.

✔ Tip

■ You can limit access to the server-status report by adding the standard Order, Deny, and Allow directives to the Location block (this example only allows connections from members of the foo.com domain):

```
<Location /server-status>
    SetHandler server-status

    Order Deny,Allow
    Deny from All
    Allow from .foo.com
</Location>
```

To add handlers and types:

By adding handlers and types, you can extend the functionality of Apache without needing to rebuild the software.

1. Use your favorite text editor to edit Apache's httpd.conf file.

2. Add an `AddHandler` directive to associate a handler with the given file extension:

   `AddHandler cgi-script .cgi`

   The above `AddHandler` directive tells Apache that any file ending with .cgi is a CGI script and should be handled by the `cgi-script` handler.

   Handlers represent the actions to perform when a file is accessed. By default, all files are simply downloaded to the visitor, but certain types may need to be handled differently. Apache's handlers include the following:

   ▲ `cgi-script`—Treat the file as a CGI script.

   ▲ `default-handler`—The handler used by default to download the requested file to the visitor's Web browser.

   ▲ `imap-file`—Treat the file as a server-side image map. You should use client-side image maps instead unless you need to support ancient Web browsers for some pathological reason.

   ▲ `send-as-is`—Send the file without adding HTTP headers.

   ▲ `server-info`—Provide server information.

   ▲ `server-status`—Provide a server-status report.

   ▲ `type-map`—Parse a type map file for content negotiation.

3. You can also insert `AddType` directives to specify the MIME type for certain files, overriding the standard mime.types file. For example, to tell Apache what an .shtml file (HTML with SSI commands) is:

   ```
   AddType text/html .shtml
   AddOutputFilter INCLUDES .shtml
   ```

   This `AddOutputFilter` directive explicitly activates SSI for this extension.

4. Save the httpd.conf file and exit your editor.

5. `apachectl -t && apachectl restart`

Check your httpd.conf for errors, and then restart the server if no errors are found.

CONFIGURING APACHE

Securing Apache

In addition to properly configuring Apache, you can secure access to directories (or even the entire server) through authentication.

Before you enable authentication in the server, you're going to need to create an authentication database of users and passwords.

To create an Apache password file:

1. Log in as **root**, or use **su** to become **root**.

2. cd */path/to/*apache

   Change to the directory with your Apache httpd.conf file (**Code Listing 9.7**). This isn't a requirement, as you can put the password file anywhere.

   Don't put your password file in a directory that's accessible through the Web server, as this would be a security risk.

3. htpasswd -c
   → */path/*basic-auth-passwords *user*

   Create (the -c option) the basic-auth-passwords file in *path* (you can put this in the same directory as httpd.conf, and you can name it anything). Add *user* to this file after prompting for *user*'s password.

   This password is used only for this Web server, and it should be different from the user's usual passwords.

Code Listing 9.7 Creating a password file for use with Apache's basic authentication.

```
bsd# cd /usr/local/etc/apache2
bsd# htpasswd -c basic-auth-passwords chrish
New password:
Re-type new password:
Adding password for user chrish
bsd# chmod 640 basic-auth-passwords
bsd# htpasswd basic-auth-passwords megatron
New password:
Re-type new password:
Adding password for user megatron
```

4. At the "New password" prompt, enter *user*'s password. Enter the password again at the "Re-type new password" prompt to verify it.

5. chmod 640 */path*/basic-auth-passwords

Make the basic-auth-passwords file readable/writable by **root**, and readable by members of **root**'s primary group (usually **wheel**, but **admin** on Mac OS X).

6. htpasswd */path*/basic-auth-passwords → *user*

Use the htpasswd command without the -c option to add more users to the basic-auth-passwords file.

To enable basic authentication in Apache:

You can specify these authentication directives in .htaccess files or in the httpd.conf file's `Directory` directive.

1. Log in as **root**, or use **su** to become **root**.

2. Use your favorite text editor to edit the httpd.conf file.

3. Find the `Directory` directive you want to restrict to authenticated users. You can add this to the default `Directory` directive if you want to restrict the entire site.

4. Add the following directives to the `Directory` block:

   ```
   AuthType Basic
   AuthName "message"
   AuthUserFile
   → /path/basic-auth-passwords
   Require valid-user
   ```

   The *message* is displayed in visitors' Web browsers when they are prompted for a user name and password to access the site. Replace the *path* with the full path to your basic-auth-passwords file.

5. Save the httpd.conf file and exit your editor.

6. `apachectl -t && apachectl restart`

   Check the httpd.conf for syntax errors and restart the server.

7. Use your favorite Web browser to access an authenticated part of the browser. You should be prompted for a user name and password before being allowed to access the page.

HOSTING A DATABASE SERVER

Databases supporting the industry-standard *Structured Query Language* (*SQL*) have become a mainstay for producing dynamic Web pages, as well as storing, collating, and indexing data. In addition to the expensive high-end database servers like Oracle, a number of powerful, freely usable open-source database-management systems, such as MySQL, have arisen over the past few years.

MySQL is the world's most popular open-source database (although PostgreSQL does seem to be on the rise), claiming to be unmatched in speed, compactness, stability, and ease of development. These claims have been proved on busy Web servers across the Internet, making it ideally suited to even small Web servers hosting e-commerce sites, forums, or even just a listing of your CDs or books.

This chapter focuses on installing MySQL and handling administrative tasks. If you want to learn SQL, check out Larry Ullman's *MySQL: Visual QuickStart Guide* (Peachpit Press, 2002).

Installing MySQL

As with most open-source applications, installing MySQL is straightforward on every popular Unix platform (including Fedora Core, FreeBSD, and Mac OS X). A GUI-based installer makes it easy to install and configure MySQL on your Windows-based Cygwin system.

To install MySQL (Fedora Core):

We'll use the up2date command to install a binary package for MySQL (**Code Listing 10.1**) from the Fedora repositories.

1. Log in as **root**, or use **su** to become **root**.

2. `up2date --install mysql mysql-server`
Download and install the MySQL client applications and the MySQL server.

3. `service mysqld start`
Initialize and start the MySQL database server.

4. `chkconfig mysqld on`
Tell the system to start MySQL when rebooting.

5. `mysqladmin -u root password` → `'new-password'`
Change the MySQL **root** user's password to *new-password*. Note that MySQL users are separate from your operating-system users.

6. `mysqladmin -u root -h $(hostname)` → `password 'new-password'`
MySQL also has a second **root** account for access from the local host's hostname or IP address. Here the **hostname** command is called, and its output is used as the `-h` argument. Again, we set the **root** user's password to *new-password*.

Code Listing 10.1 Installing MySQL with up2date on a Fedora Core system.

```
[root@dhcppc1 ~]# up2date --install mysql mysql-server
. . .
[root@dhcppc1 ~]# service mysqld start
Initializing MySQL database: [OK]
Starting MySQL:              [OK]
[root@dhcppc1 ~]# chkconfig mysqld on
[root@dhcppc1 ~]# mysqladmin -u root password 'new-password'
[root@dhcppc1 ~]# mysqladmin -u root -h $(hostname) password 'new-password'
```

To install MySQL (FreeBSD):

Installing MySQL through the FreeBSD ports system (**Code Listing 10.2**) gives you a choice of MySQL versions; we'll go with the current 4.1 version.

1. Log in as root, or use su to become root.

2. cd /usr/ports/databases/
    → mysql-41-server

    Change to the MySQL 4.1 directory in the ports collection.

continues on next page

Code Listing 10.2 Installing MySQL from the ports collection on FreeBSD.

```
bsd# cd /usr/ports/databases/mysql-41-server
bsd# make WITH_CHARSET=utf8 install clean
. . .
bsd# cd ../mysql-41-client
bsd# make WITH_CHARSET=utf8 install clean
. . .
For more information, and contact details about the security status of this software, see the
following Webpage:
http://www.mysql.com/
===>   Cleaning for mysql-client-5.0.1
===>   Cleaning for libtool-1.5.10
===>   Cleaning for mysql-server-5.0.1
bsd# echo 'mysql_enable="YES"' >> /etc/rc.conf
bsd# /usr/local/etc/rc.d/mysql-server.sh start
Starting mysql.
bsd# mysqladmin -u root password 'new-password'
bsd# mysqladmin -u root -h bsd.chrish.local password 'new-password'
```

INSTALLING MySQL

3. `make WITH_CHARSET=utf8 install clean`

   Install the MySQL server and its dependencies, including the MySQL client applications. The `WITH_CHARSET=utf8` argument tells the ports system to build MySQL with UTF-8 as its default character set. This lets it work with data in any language without introducing much overhead (if any).

4. Use your favorite text editor to edit `/etc/rc.conf`.

5. Add the following line to the rc.conf file:

   `mysql_enable="YES"`

6. Save the rc.conf file and exit your editor.

7. `/usr/local/etc/rc.d/mysql-server.sh`
   `→ start`

   Start the newly installed MySQL server.

8. `mysqladmin -u root password`
   `→ 'new-password'`

   Change the MySQL **root** user's password to *new-password*. Note that MySQL users are separate from your operating-system users.

9. `mysqladmin -u root -h $(hostname)`
   `→ password 'new-password'`

   MySQL also has a second **root** account for access from the local host's hostname or IP address. Here the `hostname` command is called (because it's surrounded by backticks), and its output is used as the -h argument. Again, we set the **root** user's password to *new-password*.

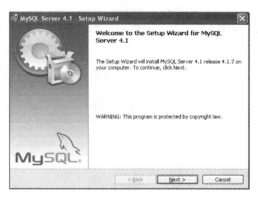

Figure 10.1 The MySQL installation wizard.

Figure 10.2 Choosing a setup type in the MySQL installation wizard.

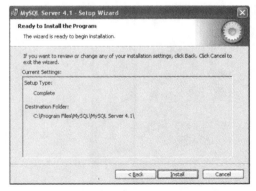

Figure 10.3 Reviewing installation settings in the MySQL installation wizard.

To install MySQL (Cygwin):

We're going to install MySQL as a native Windows service for best performance (and to make the installation easier).

1. Use your favorite Web browser to visit the MySQL 4.1 Downloads page (http://dev.mysql.com/downloads/mysql/4.1.html).

2. On the downloads page, scroll down to the Windows section, then click "Pick a mirror" in the Windows (x86) column.

3. On the mirror-site page, you can fill out the survey or click the "No thanks, just take me to the downloads!" link (or just scroll down the page).

4. Click the "HTTP" or "FTP" link next to a mirror that's close to you; as always, with mirrors you can't choose wrong.

5. Save the file (mysql-4.1.7-win.zip) to disk.

6. Double-click the MySQL archive file to open it.

   If you're not using Windows XP, use your favorite ZIP file extractor, such as Info-ZIP's free Zip and UnZip tools (www.info-zip.org).

7. Double-click the MySQL Setup program icon inside the ZIP file to launch the installer (**Figure 10.1**). Click Next to continue.

8. In the Setup Type pane (**Figure 10.2**), choose Typical (the default) or Complete (which includes a Windows GUI for administering MySQL, as well as development headers and libraries). Click Next to continue.

9. In the Ready to Install the Program pane (**Figure 10.3**), review the installation settings, then click Install to continue.

continues on next page

INSTALLING MySQL

10. In the MySQL.com Sign-Up pane (**Figure 10.4**), you can choose to log in to an existing MySQL.com account, create a new account, or skip signing up.

Having a MySQL.com account lets you subscribe to the monthly MySQL newsletter, add comments to the MySQL online manuals, and report bugs using the bug tracker at MySQL.com.

11. Click Next to continue.

12. In the Wizard Completed pane that appears, leave the "Configure the MySQL Server now" box checked, then click Finish (**Figure 10.5**).

When the installation finishes, the MySQL Server Instance Configuration Wizard appears to lead you through the next task.

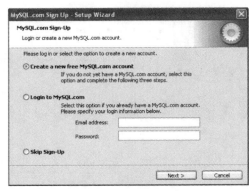

Figure 10.4 The MySQL.com Sign-Up pane in the MySQL installation wizard.

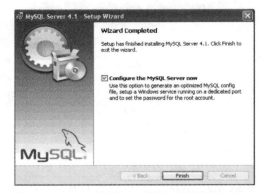

Figure 10.5 Finished with the MySQL installation wizard.

Figure 10.6 The opening pane of the MySQL Server Instance Configuration Wizard.

Figure 10.7 Selecting a configuration type.

Figure 10.8 Choosing a server type.

To configure MySQL (Cygwin):

Now let's move on to the configuration.

1. In the MySQL Server Instance Configuration Wizard (**Figure 10.6**), click Next to continue.

2. In the MySQL Server Instance Configuration pane that appears, select Detailed Configuration (the default configuration type) and click Next to continue (**Figure 10.7**).

3. In the next pane, select a server type and click Next to continue (**Figure 10.8**).

   Choose the default option, Developer Machine, unless your system is a Server Machine or a Dedicated MySQL Server Machine.

   continues on next page

INSTALLING MySQL

4. In the next pane, select the type of database usage and click Next to continue (**Figure 10.9**).

Choose Multifunctional Database (the default), Transactional Database Only, or Non-Transactional Database Only, depending on your needs. If you don't know, go with the default.

5. In the next pane, choose a location for the InnoDB database files, or if you want to place them in the default location, simply click Next to continue (**Figure 10.10**).

6. In the next pane, set the number of concurrent connections and click Next to continue (**Figure 10.11**).

Choose Decision Support (DSS)/OLAP for up to 20 concurrent connections (the default), Online Transaction Processing (OLTP) for up to 500 concurrent connections, or Manual Setting.

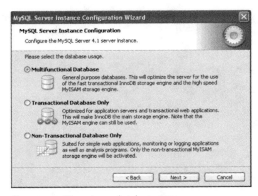

Figure 10.9 Choosing a database type.

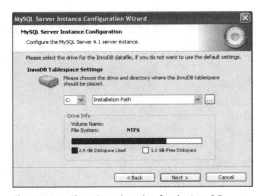

Figure 10.10 Choosing a location for the InnoDB database files.

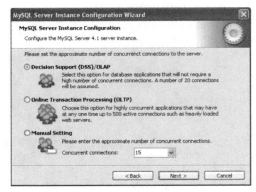

Figure 10.11 Choosing the number of concurrent database connections.

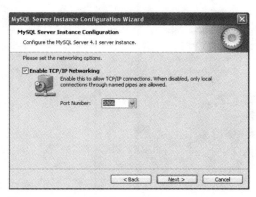

Figure 10.12 Choosing the TCP/IP settings.

Figure 10.13 Choosing a default character set.

Figure 10.14 Choosing whether or not to install MySQL as a service under Windows.

7. In the next pane, you can change the server's TCP/IP settings; click Next to continue (**Figure 10.12**).

   By default, TCP/IP connections to the server are allowed on port 3306. You can disable this by unchecking the box (only local connections are allowed) or changing the port.

8. In the next pane, choose Best Support for Multilingualism (UTF-8) for your default character set, and click Next to continue (**Figure 10.13**).

9. The next pane lets you set the Windows service options, but we want the default options (install as a Windows service named "MySQL"), so click Next to continue (**Figure 10.14**).

   continues on next page

INSTALLING MYSQL

10. In the next pane, enter a password for the **root** account in the "New root password" field, then enter it again in the "Confirm" field to verify the password (**Figure 10.15**).

Note that this database user is specific to MySQL and has no interaction with your operating system.

11. Check the "Root may only connect from localhost" box to prevent **root** from accessing the server remotely, and click Next to continue.

12. In the next pane, click Execute to configure the server with your chosen settings (**Figure 10.16**).

The things that look like radio buttons in this pane are actually progress indicators, so you don't need to choose anything here.

13. In the last pane, click Finish to exit.

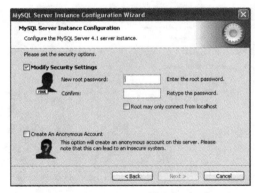

Figure 10.15 Setting a password for the database's **root** account.

Figure 10.16 Applying the configuration changes to the database server.

To install MySQL (Mac OS X):

Use Fink to install MySQL on Mac OS X (**Code Listing 10.3**).

1. `fink install mysql mysql-client`
   Tell Fink to install MySQL and the MySQL client applications.

2. Enter your password at the Password prompt, then press Enter to continue.
   Fink downloads and installs MySQL and its client applications.

3. If Fink prompts you with "Do you want to continue? [Y/n]," press Y, then press Enter to continue.
   Fink downloads and installs MySQL and its client applications.

continues on next page

Code Listing 10.3 Installing MySQL with Fink on Mac OS X.

```
bender:~ chrish$ fink install mysql mysql-client
Password:
Information about 1977 packages read in 1 seconds.


The following 2 packages will be installed or updated:
 mysql mysql-client
The following 3 additional packages will be installed:
 libtool14 libtool14-shlibs mysql12-shlibs
Do you want to continue? [Y/n]
. . .
bender:~ chrish$ cd /Library/StartupItems
bender:~ chrish$ sudo mkdir MySQL
bender:~ chrish$ cd MySQL
bender:~ chrish$ sudo ln -s /sw/share/mysql/mysql.server MySQL
bender:~ chrish$ vi StartupParameters.plist
. . .
bender:~ chrish$ sudo ./MySQL start
bender:~ chrish$ mysqladmin -u root password 'new-password'
bender:~ chrish$ mysqladmin -u root -h $(hostname) password 'new-password'
```

INSTALLING MySQL

4. `cd /Library/StartupItems`

Change to the local startup-items directory.

5. `sudo mkdir MySQL`

Create a directory named MySQL as root.

6. `cd MySQL`

Change to the MySQL directory you just created.

7. `sudo ln -s /sw/share/mysql/`
  `↪ mysql.server MySQL`

Since the `mysql.server` script that gets installed with MySQL works as a startup script, we'll create a symbolic link to it, named "MySQL."

8. Use your favorite text editor to create a StartupParameters.plist file (see **Code Listing 10.4** for its contents). Save the file, then exit your text editor.

Note that you need to do this as root; if you can't start your editor with sudo, you'll need to create the file somewhere else and then use **sudo cp** to copy it here.

9. `sudo ./MySQL start`

Start the MySQL server.

10. `mysqladmin -u root password`
  `↪ 'new-password'`

Change the MySQL **root** user's password to *new-password*. Note that MySQL users are separate from your operating-system users.

11. `mysqladmin -u root -h $(hostname)`
  `↪ password 'new-password'`

MySQL also has a second **root** account for access from the local host's hostname or IP address. Here the **hostname** command is called, and its output is used as the -h argument. Again, we set the **root** user's password to *new-password*.

Code Listing 10.4 The StartupParameters.plist file for MySQL on Mac OS X.

```
{
  Description = "MySQL database server";
  Provides = ("Database Server");
  Requires = ("DirectoryServices");
  Uses = ("Disks", "NFS");
  OrderPreference = "None";
}
```

Administering MySQL

In day-to-day operations, a database server can usually be ignored. The server will be running, handling requests, without intervention.

However, the administrator still needs to create (or delete) users, change their passwords, modify permissions, and make regular backups. (Remember, "users" here are database users, and your database user ID might have no relation to the user ID you use to log in to the system.)

To create a user:

Creating new users for your database can be something you do rarely (maybe all of your users access the database with the same user ID) or whenever you need to give someone else access to the database.

1. `mysql -u user -p`

   Launch the MySQL client, logging in as a *user* who has **GRANT** privileges.

2. Enter *user*'s password at the "Enter password" prompt, then press Enter.

   The MySQL client displays the mysql> prompt.

3. Use the **GRANT** statement (a standard SQL statement) to create the new user and set his or her privileges:

   `GRANT priv ON *.* TO 'user'@'host'`
   `→ IDENTIFIED BY 'password';`

   Create an account for *user* with the specified *password* when logging in from *host* (use % to represent any host other than localhost; to let *user* log in from any system, you need one **GRANT** with *host* set to localhost and one with *host* set to %).

You can use `ALL PRIVILEGES` for *priv* to grant all privileges, or you can specify one or more of the following:

▲ ALTER
▲ CREATE
▲ CREATE TEMPORARY TABLES
▲ DELETE
▲ DROP
▲ EXECUTE
▲ FILE
▲ GRANT
▲ INDEX
▲ INSERT
▲ LOCK TABLES
▲ PROCESS
▲ REFERENCES
▲ RELOAD
▲ REPLICATION CLIENT
▲ REPLICATION SLAVE
▲ SELECT
▲ SHOW DATABASES
▲ SHUTDOWN
▲ SUPER
▲ UPDATE

Please refer to an SQL manual for details.

You can also specify a *database.table* instead of *.* if the user has access only to specific databases and/or tables.

✔ Tip

■ You can also use the **GRANT** statement to give additional privileges to a user. Use the **REVOKE** statement to remove privileges.

To change a user's password:

For as long as we've had passwords, users have been forgetting them. As the administrator, you're responsible for dealing with this problem.

1. `mysql -u user -p`

    Launch the MySQL client, logging in as a *user* who has **GRANT** privileges.

2. Enter *user*'s password at the "Enter password" prompt, then press Enter.

    The MySQL client displays the mysql> prompt.

3. `SET PASSWORD FOR 'user'@'host' =`
   `→ PASSWORD('pass');`

    Set the specified *user*'s password to *pass*.

To delete a user:

Sometimes users need to have their database accounts removed, which is a little more work than creating their accounts.

1. `mysql -u user -p`

    Launch the MySQL client, logging in as a *user* who has **GRANT** privileges.

2. Enter *user*'s password at the "Enter password" prompt, then press Enter.

    The MySQL client displays the mysql> prompt.

3. `SHOW GRANTS FOR 'user'@'host';`

    List the privileges granted to *user* when logged in from *host*. These must be revoked before the user can be removed.

4. `REVOKE priv ON *.* FROM`
   `→ 'user'@'host';`

    Revoke *user*'s privileges; *priv* is the privileges shown in step 3.

5. `DELETE FROM mysql.user WHERE`
   `→ User='user' AND Host='host';`

    Delete *user*'s account.

6. `FLUSH PRIVILEGES;`

    Tell the MySQL server that privileges have been modified.

✔ Tips

- If you have MySQL 4.1.1 or later installed, you can combine steps 5 and 6 into one **DROP USER** command:

    `DROP USER 'user'@'localhost'`

- Although Fedora Core ships with MySQL 3.23.58, you can install newer versions by downloading RPMs from MySQL (www.mysql.com).

Code Listing 10.5 Dropping a database with the mysqladmin command.

```
bender:~ chrish$ mysqladmin -u root -p drop
cd
Enter password:
Dropping the database is potentially a very
bad thing to do.
Any data stored in the database will be
destroyed.

Do you really want to drop the 'cd' database
[y/N] y
Database "cd" dropped
```

To create a database:

You can create databases from the command line or with the standard SQL CREATE statement. Although SQL commands are uppercase, the <code>mysqladmin</code> command uses lowercase arguments.

◆ mysqladmin -u *user* -p create *name*

Create an empty database with the specified *name*. You will be prompted for *user*'s password (because of the -p option), and *user* must have the CREATE privilege.

To drop a database:

You can delete databases from the command line or with the standard SQL DROP statement.

◆ mysqladmin -u *user* -p drop *name*

Drop the database (**Code Listing 10.5**) with the specified *name*. You will be prompted for *user*'s password (because of the -p option), and *user* must have the DROP privilege.

You will also be warned about the dangers of dropping databases, and you'll be asked if you really want to drop the database. Press Y, and then press Enter to continue with the drop.

ADMINISTERING MySQL

To dump a database:

To properly back up MySQL databases, you'll need to dump the data in a format that can be restored later.

◆ `mysqldump -u user -p --all-databases`
`⇥ > backup_file`

Log in to the database as *user*, then dump all of the databases (and all of the tables in each database, and all of the rows in each table) to `backup_file`.

To restore a database:

Because the `mysqldump` command dumps the database as a series of SQL commands, you can use the `mysql` client to restore your database.

◆ `mysql -u 'user' -p < backup_file`

Restore the databases and tables in `backup_file` after logging in as *user*.

To shut down MySQL:

In addition to the usual operating-system techniques for shutting down a service, MySQL's `mysqladmin` program can gracefully shut down the server:

◆ `mysqladmin -u user -p shutdown`

Use the `mysqladmin shutdown` command to shut down the server, using the specified user ID.

The *user* must have the SHUTDOWN privilege on the server. You will be prompted for *user*'s password courtesy of the -p option.

PROGRAMMING FOR THE WEB

PHP (*PHP Hypertext Processor*) is an extremely popular open-source scripting language most often used on the Web. Unlike the ECMAScript (formerly known as JavaScript) that runs in your Web browser after the page loads, PHP runs on the server before (or while) servicing your request. A large library of add-ons lets PHP work with databases, compression schemes, email and news servers, graphics files, XML, and pretty much anything else you'd ever need to write powerful and interesting Web-based applications.

In this chapter, we'll see how to install and configure PHP (including how to hook up the PHP module for Apache), and we'll take a look at a couple of simple PHP scripts to get you started in the wonderful world of Web scripting.

Installing PHP

Because PHP is a mature piece of software, its installation process is fairly smooth on all platforms.

Mac OS X systems come with PHP installed, although Mac users will still need to tell Apache how to handle PHP scripts.

To install PHP (Fedora Core):

Luckily for us, a binary distribution of PHP is available through the up2date command.

1. Log in as **root**, or use the **su** command to become **root**.

2. up2date --install php

   Tell up2date to download and install the php package (**Code Listing 11.1**) and its dependencies.

   PHP is installed with a CGI-capable interpreter, as well as an Apache module.

Code Listing 11.1 Installing PHP with the up2date command on Fedora Core.

```
[root@dhcppc1 ~]# up2date --install php
...
The following packages were added to your
selection to satisfy dependencies:

Name                    Version  Release
------------------------------------------
php-pear                4.3.9       3
```

Code Listing 11.2 Installing PHP with the ports system on FreeBSD.

```
bsd# cd /usr/ports/lang/php4
bsd# make install clean
...
```

Figure 11.1 There are several options while installing PHP on FreeBSD.

To install PHP (FreeBSD):

FreeBSD's ports collection includes three different versions of PHP (good old PHP 3, the current PHP 4, and the experimental PHP 5).

1. Log in as root, or use su to become root.

2. `cd /usr/ports/lang/php4`

   Change to the PHP 4 directory in the ports collection.

3. `make install clean`

   Tell the ports system (**Code Listing 11.2**) to download the PHP 4 source code, compile it and install it, and then clean up.

4. The ports system displays the "Options for php4 4.3.9" dialog (**Figure 11.1**). Press the spacebar to select the APACHE2 option. Press the down arrow key twice, then press the spacebar to disable the IPV6 option (unless you need IPv6 support).

5. Press Tab to move the cursor to OK in the dialog. Press the spacebar to exit the dialog and continue.

6. `cd /usr/local/etc`

   Change to the directory with the PHP configuration file.

7. `cp php.ini-recommended php.ini`

   Copy the recommended PHP configuration file to php.ini; this lets PHP find its settings.

INSTALLING PHP

To install PHP (Cygwin):

To match our native Apache installation, we're going to install the native Windows PHP distribution instead of building our own under Cygwin.

1. Visit the PHP download page (http://ca3 .php.net/downloads.php) using your favorite Web browser.

2. Click the link for the Windows binary Zip package ("PHP 4.3.9 zip package" as of this writing). Although we need to install this distribution "by hand," it comes with the most extensions and the Apache module we'll need later.

    Your browser displays the PHP mirrors page.

3. Click the link for a mirror close to you. Don't worry if you're not sure which mirror to choose; you can't pick a bad one.

4. Save the file to your desktop.

5. Right-click the file, then choose Extract All from the contextual menu.

    If you're not using Windows XP, use your favorite ZIP-archive extractor to unpack the file.

6. Rename the extracted directory as `php` (from `php-4.3.9-Win32` in our case) and move it to the root of your C: drive (giving you `C:\php`).

    Depending on your ZIP extractor, you might have to get the `php-4.3.9-Win32` directory from a `php-4.3.9-Win32` directory created by the extractor. You want to rename and move the directory that contains the PHP directories and files.

INSTALLING PHP

Code Listing 11.3 The final contents of the PHP directory on Cygwin.

```
chrish@vm-taffer ~

$ cd /cygdrive/c/php
chrish@vm-taffer /cygdrive/c/php
$ ls -F
FDFTK.DLL*          pdf-related/
PEAR/               php.exe*
Yaz.dll*            php.gif*
cli/                php.ini-dist*
dlls/               php.ini-recommended*
expat.dll*          php4activescript.dll*
extensions/         php4apache.dll*
fribidi.dll*        php4apache2.dll*
gds32.dll*          php4embed.lib*
go-pear.bat*        php4isapi.dll*
iconv.dll*          php4nsapi.dll*
install.txt*        php4pi3web.dll*
libeay32.dll*       php4ts.dll*
libmhash.dll*       php4ts.lib*
libmySQL.dll*       phpsrvlt.dll*
license.txt*        phpsrvlt.jar*
mSQL.dll*           pws-php4cgi.reg*
magic.mime*         pws-php4isapi.reg*
mibs/               sablot.dll*
news.txt*           sapi/
ntwdblib.dll*       ssleay32.dll*
openssl/
```

7. Open your new C:\php directory, then move all of the files in the dlls and sapi subdirectories into the main C:\php directory.

   The contents of your C:\php directory should look like that shown in **Code Listing 11.3**.

8. Add C:\php to your system PATH environment variable.

9. Add a new system environment variable, PHPRC, and set its value to C:\php.

10. In the C:\php directory, rename the php.ini-recommended file to php.ini.

To activate the PHP module for Apache:

In most cases, you'll want to use PHP as an Apache module. This gives you the best performance and protects you from potential CGI security issues. The only danger is that not all PHP libraries and extensions are thread-safe; you may run into hard-to-reproduce problems when running in the multithreaded Apache 2 server.

If you're using Mac OS X, you can activate PHP as an Apache module for the server installed as Personal Web Sharing. You'll have to use PHP as a CGI application if you're using Apache 2.

1. Log in as **root**, or use **su** to become **root**.

2. **cd /etc/httpd/conf** on Fedora Core, *or*
   cd /usr/local/etc/apache2 on FreeBSD, *or*
   cd /usr/local/Apache2/conf on Cygwin, *or*
   cd /sw/etc/apache2 on Mac OS X.
   Change to the Apache configuration file directory.

3. Using your favorite text editor, open the httpd.conf file (**Code Listing 11.4**).

Code Listing 11.4 Setting up PHP as an Apache module.

```
# Apache 2 httpd.conf entries for using
# PHP as a module.

# See text for a description of path.
LoadModule php4_module path

DirectoryIndex index.html index.php

AddType application/x-httpd-php .php
AddType application/x-httpd-php-source .phps
```

INSTALLING PHP

4. Find the `LoadModule` directives and add the following line to enable the PHP module:

`LoadModule php4_module` *path*

The *path* depends on your OS:

▲ Fedora Core—`modules/libphp4.so`

▲ FreeBSD—`libexec/apache2/libphp4.so`

▲ Cygwin—`C:/php/php4apache2.dll`

▲ Mac OS X—`libexec/httpd/libphp4.so` (Remember, don't try to use this with Apache 2. At best, it will fail immediately; at worst, it will behave erratically.)

5. Find the `DirectoryIndex` directive and add index.php to the list of files there. Your `DirectoryIndex` should have at least index.html and index.php listed:

`DirectoryIndex index.html index.php`

Some Apache distributions include additional filenames here. You can leave them in the list, or delete them if you're not using them.

6. Find the `AddType` directives, and add the following lines to enable .php files as PHP scripts:

`AddType application/x-httpd-php .php`
`AddType`
`→application/x-httpd-php-source .phps`

7. Save your httpd.conf file, then exit your text editor.

8. `apachectl configtest`

Tell the `apachectl` command to check your httpd.conf for errors. If you see any, you'll need to fix them before restarting the server.

9. `apachectl restart`

Restart the server. PHP is now available as an Apache module.

INSTALLING PHP

To configure PHP as a CGI application for Apache:

If you don't want to use PHP as an Apache module (maybe you're concerned about thread-safety issues with Apache 2), or you can't (if you're on Mac OS X using the canned PHP with Apache 2), you can still make use of it as a regular CGI application.

Note that this will be slower than running it as a module (the PHP interpreter is loaded every time someone accesses a .php file instead of once when the server starts up), and it might open up your server to CGI-related exploits.

1. Log in as **root**, or use **su** to become **root**.

2. **cd /etc/httpd/conf** on Fedora Core, *or*
   cd /usr/local/etc/apache2 on FreeBSD, *or*
   cd /usr/local/Apache2/conf on Cygwin, *or*
   cd /sw/etc/apache2 on Mac OS X.
   Change to the Apache configuration file directory.

3. Using your favorite text editor, open the httpd.conf file (**Code Listing 11.5**).

4. Find the **ScriptAlias** directives and add the following line:
   ScriptAlias /php/ *path*
   The *path* depends on your OS:
   - ▲ Fedora Core—**/usr/lib/php4/**
   - ▲ FreeBSD—**/usr/local/lib/php/**
   - ▲ Cygwin—**C:/php/**
   - ▲ Mac OS X—**/usr/lib/php/**

Code Listing 11.5 Setting up PHP as a CGI application.

```
# Apache 2 httpd.conf entries for using
# PHP as a CGI program.

# See text for a description of path.
ScriptAlias /php/ path

DirectoryIndex index.html index.php

AddType application/x-httpd-php .php
AddType application/x-httpd-php-source .phps

# See text for a description of php-path.
Action application/x-httpd-php php-path
```

5. Find the `DirectoryIndex` directive, and add index.php to the list of files there. Your `DirectoryIndex` should have at least index.html and index.php listed:

```
DirectoryIndex index.html index.php
```

Some Apache distributions include additional filenames here. You can leave them in the list, or delete them if you're not using them.

6. Find the `AddType` directives, and add the following lines to enable .php files as PHP scripts:

```
AddType application/x-httpd-php .php
AddType
→ application/x-httpd-php-source
→ .phps
Action application/x-httpd-php
→ php-path
```

The *php-path* depends on your OS:

▲ Fedora Core—`/usr/bin/php`

▲ FreeBSD—`/usr/local/bin/php`

▲ Cygwin—`C:/php/php.exe`

▲ Mac OS X—`/usr/bin/php`

7. Save your httpd.conf file, then exit your text editor.

8. `apachectl configtest`

Tell the `apachectl` command to check your httpd.conf for errors. If you see any, you'll need to fix them before restarting the server.

9. `apachectl restart`

Restart the server. PHP is now available as an Apache module.

Programming with PHP

A powerful and capable scripting language, PHP lets you do almost anything, including

◆ Processing HTML forms

◆ Dynamically generating Web pages based on file or database entries

◆ Sending email notifications to visitors or the system's administrators

◆ Creating an e-commerce site

◆ Generating images, PDFs, or XML files on demand

This isn't a PHP programming book, though, so for more information about actually doing these things with PHP, check out *PHP for the World Wide Web: Visual QuickStart Guide, 2nd Edition (2004),* and *PHP Advanced for the World Wide Web: Visual QuickPro Guide (2001),* both written by Larry Ullman and published by Peachpit Press.

Code Listing 11.6 The world-famous "Hello world" program written in PHP.

```
<!DOCTYPE html
PUBLIC "-//W3C//DTD XHTML 1.0 Strict//EN"
"http://www.w3.org/TR/xhtml1/DTD/xhtml1-
strict.dtd">
<html xmlns="http://www.w3.org/1999/xhtml"
xml:lang="en" lang="en">
<head>
<title>PHP Testing</title>
</head>
<body>
<h1>PHP Test</h1>

<?php
echo "<p>Hello world.</p>\n";
?>
</body>
</html>
```

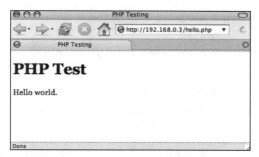

Figure 11.2 The output of the "Hello world" script in a Web browser.

Figure 11.3 The document source for the "Hello world" output. The browser doesn't see any PHP code.

To test your PHP installation:

We'll create a really trivial PHP program to make sure that PHP is functioning properly.

1. Log in as **root**, or use **su** to become **root**. If your **DocumentRoot** directory can be accessed by other users, you might be able to skip this step.

2. **cd** /var/www/html on Fedora Core, *or*
   cd /usr/local/www/data on FreeBSD, *or*
   cd /usr/local/Apache2/htdocs on Cygwin, *or*
   cd /Library/WebServer/Documents on Mac OS X.
   Change to the Apache document directory.

3. Use your favorite text editor to create hello.php (**Code Listing 11.6**).
   Most of Code Listing 11.6 is just the HTML document; only the text between <?php and ?> is actual PHP code.

4. Use your favorite Web browser to access http://*hostname*/hello.php.
   You should see something like what's shown in **Figure 11.2**.
   If you view the document's source in your Web browser, you'll see something like what's shown in **Figure 11.3**. Note how the PHP code is replaced in the document with the arguments of the **echo** statement (Code Listing 11.6).

To use PHP to upload files to the server:

A common, simple application for PHP is to let Web-site visitors upload files to the Web server.

1. Log in as **root**, or use **su** to become **root**. If your **DocumentRoot** directory can be accessed by other users, you might be able to skip this step.

2. cd /var/www/html on Fedora Core, *or*
   cd /usr/local/www/data on FreeBSD, *or*
   cd /usr/local/Apache2/htdocs on Cygwin, *or*
   cd /Library/WebServer/Documents on Mac OS X.
   Change to the Apache document directory.

3. Use your favorite text editor to create upload.html (**Code Listing 11.7**).
   The HTML document in Code Listing 11.7 has no PHP code in it at all, although it does submit the form's contents to validate-upload.php.

Code Listing 11.7 The HTML form used to upload a file from a Web browser to the server.

```
<!DOCTYPE html
    PUBLIC "-//W3C//DTD XHTML 1.0 Strict//EN"
   "http://www.w3.org/TR/xhtml1/DTD/xhtml1-strict.dtd">
<html xmlns="http://www.w3.org/1999/xhtml" xml:lang="en" lang="en">
<head>
<title>PHP Upload</title>
</head>
<body>
<h1>Upload a file</h1>


<p>
Enter a full path to the file, or click Browse&hellip; to select a file. Click the Send File
button to upload the file.
</p>


<!-- The data encoding type, enctype, MUST be specified as below -->
<form enctype="multipart/form-data" action="/validate-upload.php" method="POST">
    <!-- MAX_FILE_SIZE must precede the file input field -->
    <input type="hidden" name="MAX_FILE_SIZE" value="30000" />
    <!-- Name of input element determines name in $_FILES array -->
    Send this file: <input name="userfile" type="file" />
    <input type="submit" value="Send File" />
</form>


</body>
</html>
```

PROGRAMMING WITH PHP

4. Use your favorite text editor to create validate-upload.php (**Code Listing 11.8**).

This is the PHP code that handles the upload and moves the transferred file from PHP's temporary directory to a more permanent storage location.

If the file isn't moved, it will be deleted at the end of the PHP script.

continues on next page

Code Listing 11.8 The PHP script that processes an uploaded file.

```php
<?php
// Change $uploaddir to the directory for storing uploaded files.
$uploaddir = '/tmp/';
$uploadfile = $uploaddir . basename($_FILES['userfile']['name']);

// HTML document preamble.
echo '<!DOCTYPE html PUBLIC "-//W3C//DTD XHTML 1.0 Strict//EN"';
echo '  "http://w3.org/TR/xhtml1/DTD/xhtml1-strict.dtd">';
echo '<html xmlns="http://www.w3.org/1999/xhtml" xml:lang="en" lang="en">';
echo '<head>';
echo '<title>PHP Upload Complete!</title>';
echo '</head>';
echo '<body>';
echo '<h1>Upload a file</h1>';

echo '<pre>';
if (move_uploaded_file($_FILES['userfile']['tmp_name'], $uploadfile)) {
    echo "File is valid, and was successfully uploaded.\n";
} else {
    echo "Possible file upload attack!\n";
}

echo 'Here is some more debugging info:';
print_r($_FILES);

print "</pre>";

echo '</body>';
echo '</html>';

?>
```

5. Use your favorite Web browser to access http://*hostname*/upload.html.

You should see something like what's shown in **Figure 11.4**.

6. Enter the full path to a file in the "Send this file" field, or click the Browse button on the PHP Upload page to select a file using your system's file selector. Click the Send File button to complete the transaction and send the file.

You should see something like what's shown in **Figure 11.5**.

Figure 11.4 The upload form in action.

Figure 11.5 The results of a successful upload.

ADVANCED SERVICES

Now that we've covered the basics of administering a small Unix server and installing and configuring various helpful services, we'll talk about a couple of advanced services that might be useful for you.

In this chapter, we'll look at setting up our own domain-name server; configuring the built-in firewalls supported by Fedora Core 3, FreeBSD 5.3, and Mac OS X; and setting up the Squid caching Internet proxy server.

Resolving Network Names

One of the fundamental applications that make the Internet work is the *Domain Name Service* (*DNS*). The tireless DNS servers translate human-readable hostnames (such as "www.peachpit.com") into the numerical IP addresses needed by applications (such as "63.240.93.140"), and back from IP addresses to hostnames.

Under normal circumstances, a small network has no need for a DNS server. The ISP's DNS servers can handle requests for hosts in the outside world, and a simple "hosts" file can handle your LAN's hostnames.

It can be quite useful to have a local caching DNS server, especially if you're unlucky enough to have an ISP with slow or unreliable DNS servers. If you've got several people sharing an Internet connection through your LAN, the cached DNS lookups will speed up access and can also reduce Internet traffic.

We're going to use the de facto standard DNS server, *Berkeley Internet Name Daemon* (*BIND*). If it's good enough for most of the Internet's root name servers, it's probably good enough for a LAN.

BIND is already installed with the base operating system on FreeBSD and Mac OS X.

To install BIND (Fedora Core):

Fedora Core's binary package archives include an up-to-date version of BIND.

1. Log in as root, or use su to become root.

2. `up2date --install bind`
   `→ system-config-bind`

   Install BIND (**Code Listing 12.1**), which we'll refer to as named from now on (you'll see why in a minute), and the graphical configuration tool for DNS.

3. `chkconfig named on`

   Enable named during the boot process.

That's it for now; we won't actually start named until we've had a chance to configure it.

✔ Tip

- Use the Domain Name Service application (Applications menu > System Settings > Server Settings > Domain Name System) if you want a graphical interface for configuring named. If you go this route, don't edit /etc/named.conf by hand, because the Domain Name Service application will overwrite this file when you apply your changes.

Code Listing 12.1 Installing BIND on Fedora Core.

```
[root@dhcppc1 ~]# up2date --install bind system-config-bind
http://fedora.redhat.com/download/up2date-mirrors/fedora-core-3
using mirror: http://mirror.stanford.edu/fedora/linux/core/3/i386/os/
http://fedora.redhat.com/download/up2date-mirrors/updates-released-fc3
using mirror: http://www.las.ic.unicamp.br/pub/fedora/linux/core/updates/3/i386
...
[root@dhcppc1 ~]# chkconfig named on
```

RESOLVING NETWORK NAMES

To install BIND (Cygwin):

BIND isn't available as part of Cygwin, but you can find an official binary distribution on the Web site for the Internet Systems Consortium.

1. Using your favorite Web browser, visit www.isc.org/index.pl?/sw/bind (the BIND homepage).

2. Scroll down the page until you find the Downloads list (**Figure 12.1**).

3. Click the link for the latest BIND release (9.3.0 as of this writing); this takes you to the ISC BIND 9.3.0 page.

4. Scroll down to find the "Windows NT 4.0 and Windows 2000 (binary)" link, "BIND9.3.0."

   Note that this build will run on Windows NT 4.0, Windows 2000, Windows XP, and Windows Server 2003.

5. Click the "BIND9.3.0" link, and save the archive (BIND9.3.0.zip) to your hard drive.

6. Right-click the BIND9.3.0.zip file, then choose Extract All to unpack the archive.

   If you're not using Windows XP, you can use any archive utility, such as Info-ZIP's free tools (www.info-zip.org), to unpack the file.

7. Run the BINDInstall program (**Figure 12.2**) to install BIND.

8. Change the Target Directory to C:\cygwin \etc\named; this is the directory in which the BIND files will be installed.

   Note that we'll refer to the DNS server as named from now on.

9. The named needs to run as a very restricted user for security reasons; the installer creates a named user (unless you change the Service Account Name field)

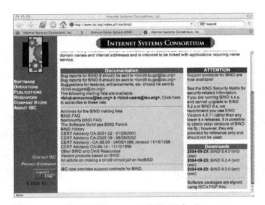

Figure 12.1 The BIND page at ISC's Web site.

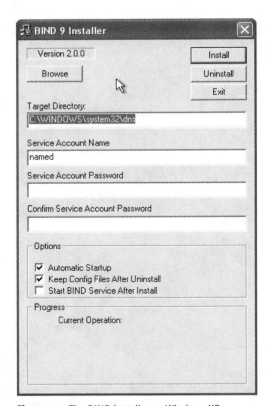

Figure 12.2 The BIND installer on Windows XP.

Code Listing 12.2 Creating the rndc.key file on Cygwin.

```
chrish@vm-taffer ~
$ cd /etc/named

chrish@vm-taffer /etc/named
$ ./bin/rndc-confgen -a
wrote key file
"C:\cygwin\etc\named\etc\rndc.key"
```

with the appropriate permissions and the password specified in the Service Account Password field.

Enter the password again in the Confirm Service Account Password field to validate it.

The rest of the settings can be left at their default values.

10. Click the Install button to install named and create the named user.

When prompted to create the Target Directory, click Yes.

11. When the installation is complete, click the Exit button to close the BINDInstall program.

12. Open a Cygwin window.

13. `cd /etc/named`

Switch to the named installation directory (**Code Listing 12.2**).

14. `./bin/rndc-confgen -a`

Create the rndc.key file, required to allow DNS configuration (through the rndc command) from the local system.

To enable BIND (Mac OS X):

Although BIND is already installed on Mac OS X, it's not turned on by default.

1. `sudo vi /etc/hostconfig`

Use your favorite text editor to edit /etc/hostconfig; you need to do this as the super user.

2. Find the DNSSERVER=-NO- line and change it to DNSSERVER=-YES-.

3. Save the file and exit your text editor.

To configure rndc:

The rndc command lets you control the running named, but it needs to have a trust relationship set up (through the use of a shared key).

1. Log in as **root**, or use **su** to become **root**.
   If you're using Cygwin, open a Cygwin window.

2. **cd /etc** on Fedora Core or Mac OS X, *or*
   cd /etc/namedb on FreeBSD, *or*
   cd /etc/named/etc on Cygwin.
   Switch to the named configuration file directory.

3. **rndc-confgen -a**, or
   /etc/named/bin/rndc-confgen -a on Cygwin.
   Create the rndc.key file containing the shared key that lets **rndc** control **named**.

4. Use your favorite text editor to edit (or create) the rndc.conf file (**Code Listing 12.3**).
   The rndc.conf file in Code Listing 12.3 lets you control **named** from the local host only, as long as **rndc** and **named** agree on the same key.
   Note that you'll have to replace the **/etc** directory in the **include** statement with the directory you used in step 2. For example, on FreeBSD you would use **"/etc/namedb/rndc.key"** instead.

5. Save the rndc.conf file and exit your editor.

Code Listing 12.3 A basic rndc.conf file.

```
/* rndc configuration file */

options {
    default-server  localhost;
    default-key     "rndckey";
};

server localhost {
    key      "rndckey";
};

/* Change this directory to match your
 * named configuration directory.
 */
include "/etc/rndc.key";
```

Code Listing 12.4 A basic named.conf file.

```
// named configuration file

options {
    directory "/path";

    forwarders {
        192.168.0.1;
    };

    // Use this if you're behind a
    // firewall, otherwise named will use
    // random ports for its queries.
    query-source address * port 53;
};

include "/etc/rndc.key";

// Zones for a caching name server:
zone "." IN {
    type hint;

    // Change if you have an existing
    // root zone file under a different
    // name.
    file "named.root";
};

zone "localhost" IN {
    type master;

    // Change if you have an existing
    // localhost zone file under a
    // different name.
    file "localhost.zone";

    allow-update { none; };
};

zone "0.0.127.in-addr.arpa" IN {
    type master;

    // Change if you have an existing
    // reverse-lookup localhost zone file
    // under a different name.
    file "localhost.rev ";

    allow-update { none; };
};
```

To configure named as a caching DNS server:

The named distributed in the BIND packages is configured through its named.conf file.

1. Log in as root, or use su to become root.

2. cd /etc on Fedora Core or Mac OS X, *or*
   cd /etc/namedb on FreeBSD, *or*
   cd /etc/named/etc on Cygwin.
   Switch to the named configuration file directory.

3. Use your favorite text editor to edit (or create) named.conf (**Code Listing 12.4**). The settings in Code Listing 12.4 configure named as a caching name server.

4. Change *path* to the named path:
   /var/named, *or*
   /etc/namedb on FreeBSD, *or*
   C:/cygwin/etc/named/etc on Cygwin.

5. Change 192.168.0.1 in the forwarders section to be your ISP's DNS server. This lets your server query their server, reducing Internet traffic by preventing requests to the root DNS servers.

6. Change "/etc/rndc.key" in the include statement to the path to the rndc.key file you created in the "To configure rndc" section, above.

continues on next page

RESOLVING NETWORK NAMES

7. If you have existing zone files (an existing named.conf file will list them already), change the `file` commands in the zone blocks to use these existing files.

   If you don't have an existing root zone file (named.root in Code Listing 12.4), download the named.root file from ftp://rs.internic.net/domain/named.root.

   If you don't have an existing local-host zone file (localhost.zone in Code Listing 12.4), you can use the one in **Code Listing 12.5**.

   If you don't have an existing reverse local-host zone file (localhost.rev in Code Listing 12.4), you can use the one in **Code Listing 12.6**.

8. Save the named.conf file and exit your editor.

9. `named-checkconf`

   Use the `named-checkconf` command to check your named.conf changes. If all is well, it produces no output.

10. `service named start` on Fedora Core, *or* `/etc/rc.d/named start` on FreeBSD, *or* `net start named` on Cygwin, *or* `sudo /System/Library/StartupItems/` → `BIND/BIND start` on Mac OS X. Start the name server.

✔ Tips

- If you plan on using the graphical Domain Name Service configuration tool on Fedora Core, put the configuration options from Code Listing 12.4 in the named.custom file instead of named.conf. Otherwise, the configuration tool will overwrite them.

- On Fedora Core, you can also install the caching-nameserver package, which includes everything you need for a caching DNS server.

Code Listing 12.5 A basic local-host zone file.

```
$TTL     86400
$ORIGIN localhost.
@                 1D IN SOA       @ root (
                  42   ; serial (d. adams)
                  3H   ; refresh
                  15M  ; retry
                  1W   ; expiry
                  1D ) ; minimum

                  1D IN NS        @
                  1D IN A         127.0.0.1
```

Code Listing 12.6 A basic reverse local-host zone file.

```
$TTL     86400
@  IN  SOA  localhost. root.localhost.  (
               1997022700 ; Serial
               28800      ; Refresh
               14400      ; Retry
               3600000    ; Expire
               86400 )    ; Minimum
   IN  NS  localhost.

1  IN  PTR  localhost.
```

RESOLVING NETWORK NAMES

Figure 12.3 The Security Level Configuration application.

Blocking Access

Even home users can afford a packet-inspecting firewall that's stateful (meaning that it keeps track of a connection's state, instead of just inspecting the port and IP addresses); in fact, it's probably built into your cable or DSL router for free! But if you're unwilling (or unable) to invest in a hardware firewall, the "real" Unix operating systems all have built-in software firewalls.

Why did I say "real" Unix systems? Cygwin doesn't have a firewall, but Windows XP does, as of Service Pack 2. Check your Windows XP documentation for details. Users of older Windows systems can look into other software firewalls, such as Zone Alarm.

Fedora Core 3's firewall is `iptables`.

FreeBSD and Mac OS X both include the very powerful, and potentially complex, IP Firewall (`ipfw`).

To enable the firewall (Fedora Core):

Fedora Core provides a GUI for controlling the basic firewall functions.

1. Log in as `root`.

   This step is optional; if you're not logged in as `root`, you will be prompted for `root`'s password after the next step.

2. Launch the Security Level Configuration application (**Figure 12.3**) by choosing Applications menu > System Settings > Security Level.

3. Click the "Security level" pop-up menu and choose "Enable firewall" to activate the `iptables` firewall.

   By default, the firewall denies all incoming packets. This is very secure, but also rather inconvenient because nothing can contact your system.

continues on next page

4. Check the boxes for any services you need to trust in the "Trusted services" list. For example, if you're running the OpenSSH server, check SSH.

Remember that if you check only that box, data sent over any of the listed services, *except SSH*, is sent in the clear, without encryption.

5. If your system has more than one network connection (maybe it's acting as a gateway for your LAN), you can also choose to allow any packets coming from a specific network interface by checking the box for that interface in the "Trusted devices" list.

Note that specifying this "Trusted device" for the interface you use to connect to the Internet will effectively disable your firewall.

6. If you know of other ports that need to make it through the firewall, enter them in the "Other ports" field, separated by spaces. The format is *port/connection*, where *port* is the port number and *connection* is either tcp or udp.

7. Click OK to enable the firewall and apply rules to let your specified services, devices, and other ports through unmolested.

The Security Level Configuration application displays a warning (**Figure 12.4**).

8. Click the Yes button in the warning dialog to apply your firewall changes, or the No button to discard them.

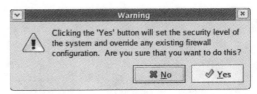

Figure 12.4 The Security Level Configuration application warns you about overwriting the existing firewall rules.

To enable the firewall (FreeBSD):

Enabling `ipfw` on FreeBSD is fairly straightforward.

1. Log in as **root**, or use **su** to become **root**.

2. `cd /etc`

   Switch to the configuration directory.

3. Use your favorite text editor to edit the rc.conf file.

4. Add the following lines anywhere in the rc.conf file:

   ```
   firewall_enable="YES"
   firewall_script="/etc/ipfw.rules"
   firewall_logging="YES"
   ```

5. Save the rc.conf file and exit your editor.

6. Use your favorite text editor to create (or edit) `/etc/ipfw.rules` (**Code Listing 12.7**) with the rules for your firewall.

   Things to change for your firewall (they've been marked with "CHANGE THIS" in the listing):

   ▲ Change `interface` in the `pif=` line to be the name of your network interface (such as `lnc0`; use the `ifconfig` command to find this).

   ▲ In the OUTBOUND CONNECTIONS section, change `x.x.x.x` to the IP address of your ISP's DNS server. If the ISP has more than one, duplicate both lines for each DNS IP address.

   ▲ Enter your ISP's DHCP server (if you're connected directly to a cable or DSL modem) in the DHCP rules. This lets you make DNS requests through your ISP's server.

   ▲ In the INCOMING CONNECTIONS section, you may need to comment out one of the non-routable reserved address spaces if your system is connected to a LAN instead of the Internet.

   ▲ Comment out the NetBIOS rules if you want to allow connections to a Samba server running on this system.

   ▲ Enter your ISP's DHCP server (if you're connected to a cable or DSL modem) in the incoming DHCP rule. This lets your ISP's DNS server return request results to your DNS server.

   ▲ Uncomment the Web server rule if you're running a Web server (change the `80` to the server's port if it's not running on the default port).

   ▲ Uncomment the OpenSSH rule if you're running OpenSSH.

7. Save your ipfw.rules file and exit your editor.

8. `/etc/rc.d/ipfw start`

   Start the firewall.

BLOCKING ACCESS

Code Listing 12.7 A good `ipfw` rules file blocks everything, then allows specific services to have access.

```
# ipfw rules file
#
# Based on the ipfw rules file in the
# FreeBSD Handbook
# (www.freebsd.org/doc/).

# Delete the existing rules.
ipfw -q -f flush

# Shorthand.
cmd="ipfw -q add"

# CHANGE THIS:
#
# The interface you're applying these
# rules to, facing the public Internet.
pif="interface"

# Loopback has no restrictions.
$cmd 00010 allow all from any to any via lo0

# Allow packets through if they've been
# added to the dynamic rules table by an
# allow keep-state statement.
$cmd 00015 check-state

# OUTBOUND CONNECTIONS

# CHANGE THIS:
#
# Allow out access to your ISP's domain
# name server.
# x.x.x.x must be changed to the IP
# address of your ISP's DNS.
# Copy these lines if your ISP has more
# than one DNS server.
# You can get the IP addresses from the
# /etc/resolv.conf file.
$cmd 00110 allow tcp from any to x.x.x.x 53 out via $pif setup keep-state
$cmd 00111 allow udp from any to x.x.x.x 53 out via $pif keep-state

# CHANGE THIS:
#
# Allow out access to my ISP's DHCP
# server for cable/DSL configurations.
#
# Use the following rule and check the
# log for the server's IP address,
# then put the server's IP address in the
# commented out rule and delete the
# first rule.
$cmd 00120 allow log udp from any to any 67 out via $pif keep-state
#$cmd 00120 allow udp from any to x.x.x.x 67 out via $pif keep-state

# Allow out non-secure standard WWW HTTP
# and secure HTTPS connections.
```

(code continues on next page)

Code Listing 12.7 *continued*

```
$cmd 00200 allow tcp from any to any 80 out via $pif setup keep-state
$cmd 00220 allow tcp from any to any 443 out via $pif setup keep-state

# Allow out send and get email functions
# (SMTP and POP3).
$cmd 00230 allow tcp from any to any 25 out via $pif setup keep-state
$cmd 00231 allow tcp from any to any 110 out via $pif setup keep-state

# Allow out FreeBSD (make install and
# CVSUP) functions.
# Note that this basically gives the root
# user "GOD" privileges.
$cmd 00240 allow tcp from me to any out via $pif setup keep-state uid root

# Allow out ping, Time, NNTP news, SSH,
# and whois connections.
$cmd 00250 allow icmp from any to any out via $pif keep-state
$cmd 00260 allow tcp from any to any 37 out via $pif setup keep-state
$cmd 00270 allow tcp from any to any 119 out via $pif setup keep-state
$cmd 00280 allow tcp from any to any 22 out via $pif setup keep-state
$cmd 00290 allow tcp from any to any 43 out via $pif setup keep-state

# Deny and log everything else trying to
# get out.
# This rule enforces the "deny everything
# by default" logic.
$cmd 00299 deny log all from any to any out via $pif

# INCOMING CONNECTIONS

# CHANGE THIS:
#
# Deny all inbound traffic from non-
# routable reserved address spaces.
#
# You'll want to comment out the line
# that corresponds to your LAN if
# this system isn't directly connected to
# the Internet.
$cmd 00300 deny all from 192.168.0.0/16 to any in via $pif  #RFC 1918 private IP
$cmd 00301 deny all from 172.16.0.0/12 to any in via $pif   #RFC 1918 private IP
$cmd 00302 deny all from 10.0.0.0/8 to any in via $pif       #RFC 1918 private IP
$cmd 00303 deny all from 127.0.0.0/8 to any in via $pif       #loopback
$cmd 00304 deny all from 0.0.0.0/8 to any in via $pif          #loopback
$cmd 00305 deny all from 169.254.0.0/16 to any in via $pif  #DHCP auto-config
$cmd 00306 deny all from 192.0.2.0/24 to any in via $pif      #reserved for docs
$cmd 00307 deny all from 204.152.64.0/23 to any in via $pif #Sun cluster interconnect
$cmd 00308 deny all from 224.0.0.0/3 to any in via $pif        #Class D & E multicast

# Deny public pings and ident requests.
$cmd 00310 deny icmp from any to any in via $pif
$cmd 00315 deny tcp from any to any 113 in via $pif

# CHANGE THIS:
#
# Deny all NetBIOS service. 137=name, 138=datagram, 139=session
```

(code continues on next page)

Code Listing 12.7 *continued*

```
# NetBIOS is MS/Windows sharing services.
# Block MS/Windows hosts2 name server
# requests 81
#
# You'll want to comment these out if
# you're serving directories with Samba.
$cmd 00320 deny tcp from any to any 137 in via $pif
$cmd 00321 deny tcp from any to any 138 in via $pif
$cmd 00322 deny tcp from any to any 139 in via $pif
$cmd 00323 deny tcp from any to any 81 in via $pif

# Deny any late arriving packets
$cmd 00330 deny all from any to any frag in via $pif

# Deny ACK packets that did not match the
# dynamic rule table
$cmd 00332 deny tcp from any to any established in via $pif

# CHANGE THIS:
#
# Allow traffic in from ISP's DHCP
# server. This rule must contain
# the IP address of your ISP.s DHCP
# server as it's the only
# authorized source to send this packet
# type.
# Only necessary for cable or DSL
# configurations.
# This rule is not needed for .user ppp.
# type connection to
# the public Internet. This is the same
# IP address you captured
# and used in the OUTBOUND CONNECTIONS
# section.
#$cmd 00360 allow udp from any to x.x.x.x 67 in via $pif keep-state

# CHANGE THIS:
#
# Uncomment this if you're running a web
# server.
#$cmd 00400 allow tcp from any to me 80 in via $pif setup limit src-addr 2

# CHANGE THIS:
#
# Uncomment this if you're running
# OpenSSH.
$cmd 00410 allow tcp from any to me 22 in via $pif setup limit src-addr 2

# Reject & Log all incoming connections
# from the outside
$cmd 00499 deny log all from any to any in via $pif

# Everything else is denied by default
# Deny and log all packets that fell
# through to see what they are.
$cmd 00999 deny log all from any to any

# End of ipfw rules.
```

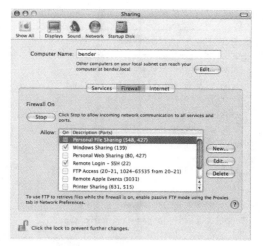

Figure 12.5 Mac OS X's firewall-configuration pane.

To enable the firewall (Mac OS X):

Naturally, Mac OS X comes with a nice graphical user interface for configuring the firewall.

1. Open System Preferences, then click the Sharing icon to display the Sharing pane.

2. Click the Firewall tab (**Figure 12.5**).

3. If the firewall is currently off, click the Start/Stop button to start the firewall.

4. Check the boxes for the services that you want to allow in the list.

5. To allow a service that isn't listed, click the New button and enter the port details in the New Port dialog.

6. Close the Sharing preferences pane to apply your firewall changes.

BLOCKING ACCESS

Speeding Up the Web

One thing everyone wants is faster access to their Web sites. Popular sites can slow down to a crawl during high-traffic times, and nothing is more frustrating than having people on your LAN telling you they pulled the site up without problems a few minutes earlier.

One way to reduce traffic to popular sites but still give access to the information is to run a cache, like Squid. Then people can configure their Web browsers to use the cache as a proxy, and it stores the pages they visit. The next person who requests a cached page gets it right away from the cache, instead of having to download it across the Internet.

Although Cygwin has a Squid package, it doesn't work with the current versions of the Cygwin core shared libraries.

To install Squid (Fedora Core):

The up2date command will provide us with a binary distribution of Squid.

1. Log in as root, or use su to become root.

2. up2date --install squid

   Install Squid (**Code Listing 12.8**) from the binary repository.

3. chkconfig squid on

   Add Squid to the list of services to start at boot time.

4. service squid start

   Start the Squid server.

Code Listing 12.8 Installing Squid on Fedora Core.

```
[root@dhcppc1 ~]# up2date --install squid

http://fedora.redhat.com/download/
up2date-mirrors/fedora-core-3

using mirror: http://fr.rpmfind.net/
linux/fedora/core/3/i386/os

http://fedora.redhat.com/download/up2date-
mirrors/updates-released-fc3

using mirror: http://sunsite.informatik.
rwth-aachen.de/ftp/pub/linux/fedora-core/
updates/3/i386/

...

[root@dhcppc1 ~]# chkconfig squid on
[root@dhcppc1 ~]# service squid start
```

Code Listing 12.9 Installing Squid on FreeBSD.

```
bsd# cd /usr/ports/www/squid
bsd# make install clean
...
===>  Vulnerability check disabled,
database not found
===>  Found saved configuration for
squid-2.5.7_3
>> squid-2.5.STABLE7.tar.bz2 doesn't seem to
exist in /usr/ports/distfiles/squid2.5.
>> Attempting to fetch from ftp://
ftp.squid-cache.org/pub/squid-2/STABLE/.
...
bsd# rehash
bsd# squid -z
```

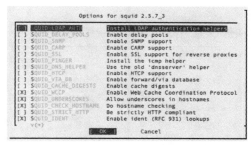

Figure 12.6 Squid options on FreeBSD.

To install Squid (FreeBSD):

FreeBSD's excellent ports system includes Squid, so we'll have no trouble installing it on this OS.

1. Log in as **root**, or use **su** to become **root**.

2. `cd /usr/ports/www/squid`
   Change to the Squid directory in the ports system (**Code Listing 12.9**).

3. `make install clean`
   Tell the ports system to build and install Squid, and then clean up after itself.
   The ports system displays the "Options for squid 2.5.7_3" dialog (**Figure 12.6**).

4. Press the up and down arrow keys to move the cursor, then press the spacebar to select (or deselect) the highlighted item.
   Unless you know you need one of these options, go with the defaults.

5. Press Tab and then Enter to exit the "Options for squid 2.5.7_3" dialog and continue.

6. `squid -z`
   Initialize the Squid cache directories.

7. Use your favorite text editor to add the following line to /etc/rc.conf:
   `squid_enable="YES"`

8. `/usr/local/etc/rc.d/squid.sh start`
   Start the Squid server.

To install Squid (Mac OS X):

On Mac OS X, Fink includes a Squid port.

1. Open a Terminal.

2. `fink install squid`

   Tell Fink to install Squid (**Code Listing 12.10**).

3. Enter your password at the Password prompt, then press Enter to continue. Fink downloads and installs Squid.

4. `cd /Library/StartupItems`

   Change to the startup-items directory so that we can create a startup script for Squid.

5. `sudo mkdir Squid`

   Create a directory for Squid's startup files.

6. `cd Squid`

   Change to the Squid startup directory.

7. Use your favorite text editor to create the Squid startup script (**Code Listing 12.11**).

   If you use a GUI editor, you'll need to create this file somewhere else, and then use `sudo cp` to copy it here.

8. Use your favorite text editor to create the StartupParameters.plist file (**Code Listing 12.12**).

   Again, you may need to create it somewhere else and `sudo cp` it here.

9. `./Squid start`

   Start the Squid cache.

Code Listing 12.10 Installing Squid on Mac OS X.

```
bender:~ chrish$ fink install squid
Password:
Information about 4201 packages read in 5
seconds.
...
Setting up squid (2.5.stable5-1) ...
2004/12/09 23:14:01| Creating Swap
Directories
bender:~ chrish$ cd /Library/StartupItems
bender:~ chrish$ sudo mkdir Squid
bender:~ chrish$ cd Squid
bender:~ chrish$ sudo vi Squid
...
bender:~ chrish$ sudo chmod +x Squid
bender:~ chrish$ sudo vi
StartupParameters.plist
...
bender:~ chrish$ ./Squid start
```

Code Listing 12.11 A Squid startup script for Mac OS X.

```
#!/bin/sh

. /etc/rc.common

case $1 in
    start)
        /sw/sbin/squid
        ;;

    restart)
        /sw/sbin/squid -k reconfigure
        ;;

    stop)
        /sw/sbin/squid -k shutdown
        ;;

    *)
        # Unknown command.
        ;;
esac
```

Code Listing 12.12 A StartupParameters.list file for Squid on Mac OS X.

```
{
    Description = "Squid web cache";
    Provides = ("Web Cache");
    Requires = ("DirectoryServices");
    Uses = ("Disks", "NFS");
    OrderPreference = "None";
}
```

Code Listing 12.13 A basic Squid configuration file.

```
# squid.conf file for a web cache

# Define an access control list that
# includes all IP addresses.
acl all src 0.0.0.0/0.0.0.0

# Allow all attempts to access the cache.
http_access allow  all

# Run Squid as nobody in the group
# nogroup for improved security.
cache_effective_user nobody nogroup
```

To configure Squid as a Web cache:

Despite Squid's many options, a basic Web cache configuration requires only a few settings.

1. Log in as **root**, or use **su** to become **root**.

2. `cd /etc/squid` on Fedora Core, *or*
   `cd /usr/local/etc/squid` on FreeBSD, *or*
   `cd /sw/etc` on Mac OS X.
   Switch to the Squid configuration directory.

3. Use your favorite text editor to create the squid.conf file (**Code Listing 12.13**).

4. `service squid restart` on Fedora Core, *or*
   `/usr/local/etc/rc.d/squid.sh` → `restart` on FreeBSD, or
   `/Library/StartupItems/Squid/Squid` → `restart` on Mac OS X.
   Restart Squid to apply your configuration changes.

SPEEDING UP THE WEB

ADDITIONAL RESOURCES

This appendix teaches you how to find out more about everything we've covered so far. Because of the huge scope of all things Unix, it's impossible to cover everything in one place, let alone go into exhaustive detail. But here you'll find a compendium of the Web sites mentioned throughout this book, as well as a laundry list of additional online resources presented in the same order as the topics in this book.

Learning More

To be accepted among hard-core Unix users, you need to be able to learn about the system and its programs on your own, using whatever resources are available. These days, there's a wealth of information installed with every Unix system, so learning how to do something usually means reading and putting your new information to use.

The Internet makes available even more information, in the form of FAQ (lists of frequently asked questions, with answers), how-to documents, and mailing lists and Web forums for more interactive help.

To find out what command to use:

Sometimes you know what you need to do, but you aren't sure how to do it, or you know that there's a command you want to use, but you can't remember its name.

apropos *keyword*

or

whatis *keyword*

Search the online list of command keywords for *keyword*. The whatis command usually displays better results (**Code Listing A.1**), because it limits its output to complete word matches.

Code Listing A.1 The whatis output only matches complete words, which focuses your search. The apropos output includes partial matches.

```
bender:~ chrish$ whatis mount
amd(8)                     - automatically mount file systems
automount(8)               - automatic NFS mount / unmount daemon
exports(5)                 - define remote mount points for NFS mount requests
fixmount(8)                - fix remote mount entries
mount(2), unmount(2)       - mount or dismount a filesystem
mount(8)                   - mount file systems
mount.cifs(8)              - mount using the Common Internet File System (CIFS)
mount_afp(8)               - mount an afp (AppleShare) filesystem
mount_cd9660(8)            - mount an ISO-9660 filesystem
mount_cddafs(8)            - mount an Audio CD
mount_fdesc(8)             - mount the file-descriptor file system
mount_ftp(8)               - mount a FTP filesystem
mount_hfs(8)               - mount an HFS/HFS+ file system
mount_msdos(8)             - mount an MS-DOS file system
mount_nfs(8)               - mount nfs file systems
mount_ntfs(8)              - mount an NTFS file system
mount_udf(8)               - mount a UDF filesystem
mount_webdav(8)            - mount a WebDAV filesystem
mountd(8)                  - service remote NFS mount requests


bender:~ chrish$ apropos mount
Tcl_FSRegister(3), ... Tcl_AllocStatBuf(3) - procedures to interact with any filesystem
amd(8)                     - automatically mount file systems
amq(8)                     - automounter query tool
automount(8)               - automatic NFS mount / unmount daemon
exports(5)                 - define remote mount points for NFS mount requests
fixmount(8)                - fix remote mount entries
getfsstat(2)               - get list of all mounted file systems
getmntinfo(3)              - get information about mounted file systems
hdik(8)                    - lightweight in-kernel disk image mounting tool
mount(2), unmount(2)       - mount or dismount a filesystem
mount(8)                   - mount file systems
mount.cifs(8)              - mount using the Common Internet File System (CIFS)
```

LEARNING MORE

To find out more about commands or configuration files:

Once you know which command or configuration file you're interested in, you can consult the online manual, or *man pages,* for more information.

◆ man *name*

Display the online manual for *name,* which can be a command or configuration file, among other things.

Remember that this is piped into more or less (depending on your OS), so you can search, move forward and backward, and so on, while viewing the information.

✔ Tips

■ info *name*

If you're using GNU software (such as EMACS), online manuals are installed using the GNU info system, which is a bit like a hypertext version of the traditional man pages. You invoke info the same way as with man, but it brings up an interactive display (**Figure A.1**). Press Q to quit.

■ pinfo *name*

There's an excellent combined man and info viewer called pinfo (http://freshmeat.net/projects/pinfo) that automatically searches the info pages, and then the man pages, for *name.* Press Q to quit.

Figure A.1 The GNU info program gives you access to hypertext online manuals.

Figure A.2 Google's main Web page. You've probably seen this before! (Shown is the Canadian version.)

Googling Info on the Web

Google does a fantastic job of indexing the vast amounts of data out on the World Wide Web, turning that huge pile of information into something useful—if you can find what you're looking for.

Google's pages really do work with any Web browser, even though the W3C's HTML validation service (http://validator.w3.org) does point out some problems with Google's markup.

Google's main page (www.google.com) might redirect you to a local server; in my case, I get redirected to www.google.ca (**Figure A.2**) because I'm located in Canada.

Type your search keywords in the entry field on the Google page. Choosing good keywords is the key to using Google (and other search engines) effectively. Entire books have been written about using Google, but here are a few tips that will make those unnecessary:

◆ Use the most specific terms you can think of. For example, if you're looking for information about FreeBSD, search for *FreeBSD*, not *BSD*. A search for *BSD* returns a lot of irrelevant (to you) matches for the many other BSD flavors (OpenBSD, NetBSD, and so on).

◆ Use quotes around keywords to make Google search for them as a phrase instead of as individual words. For example, search for *"Mac OS X"* instead of just *Mac OS X* to find information about Apple's current operating system.

◆ If you think you've entered keywords that are specific enough to find exactly what you want, click the I'm Feeling Lucky button instead of pressing Enter or clicking the Google Search button. This will take your browser directly to the first search result.

◆ You can enter search keywords directly in the URL you use to access Google if you want to skip its front page and get to the matches right away:

http://www.google.com/search?q= *keywords*

The *keywords* can be a single item, or multiple keywords separated by + characters (for example, *q=magical+trevor*). To quote keywords (such as *"Mac OS X"*), use the URL encoding for a quote (*%22*) around the keywords (*q=%22Mac+OS+X%22*).

After you've typed your search words, press Enter to see a list of matching Web pages. Google defines *matching* as pages that are the most relevant to your search keywords. Then just click the link(s) that appear to most closely match what you are looking for.

LEARNING MORE

Online Resources

There is a wealth of information available on the Internet for every topic covered in this book. In addition to Web sites, there are email discussion lists you can subscribe to and Web-based forums where you can discuss almost any topic.

Apache

One of the cornerstones of the World Wide Web, the Apache Web server is famous for stability and performance.

The Apache Software Foundation

(www.apache.org)

The Apache homepage, with links to its Web server and many other related projects. Extensive online documentation, references to mailing lists (http://httpd.apache.org/lists.html), and more.

ClamAV

Information about the ClamAV antivirus program is mostly centralized on the main Web site.

ClamAV: Project News

(www.clamav.net)

The main ClamAV Web site, featuring documentation, downloads, and information about mailing lists (www.clamav.net/ml.html). You can also submit new virus reports here.

ClamAV: Third-party software

(www.clamav.net/3rdparty.html)

A listing of third-party software that supports ClamAV, including filters for integrating ClamAV with your email server.

Project: Clam AntiVirus: Summary

(http://sourceforge.net/projects/clamav)

The SourceForge project page; this is where ClamAV development takes place.

CUPS

CUPS is rapidly becoming the standard for Unix printing to a wide variety of devices.

Common UNIX Printing System

(www.cups.org)

The CUPS homepage, featuring documentation, newsgroups, and a variety of free and commercial support options.

Cygwin

The Cygwin project is fairly specialized (it tries to provide a Red Hat Linux environment on top of Windows), but there is a lot of good information available.

Cygwin

(www.cygwin.com)

The main Cygwin site includes documentation, FAQ, mailing lists (http://cygwin.com/lists.html), unofficial newsgroups, and a package search engine that can help you decide which packages to install when you're looking for a specific application.

Cyrus

Project Cyrus produces a free IMAP mail server.

Project Cyrus

(http://asg.web.cmu.edu/cyrus)

The Cyrus Project homepage. Plenty of documentation and related IMAP links.

DHCP

This is a fairly standard part of most operating systems, so check your OS documentation too.

DNS, BIND, DHCP, LDAP and Directory Services

(www.bind9.net/dhcp)

Links to lots of articles about DHCP on a variety of subjects.

Internet Systems Consortium

(www.isc.org)

The homepage of the Internet Systems Consortium, which develops several free implementations of core Internet protocols, including DHCP. Its DHCP server is the one that most free operating systems include.

Disk Quotas

Limiting the amount of storage that individual users can consume is a good way of making your system safer; many applications don't behave well when they run out of disk space.

FreeBSD Handbook—File System Quotas

(www.freebsd.org/doc/en_US.ISO8859-1/books/handbook/quotas.html)

Detailed information about activating and administering disk quotas under FreeBSD.

How to Enable Disk Quotas in Windows 2000

(http://support.microsoft.com/kb/183322/EN-US)

An article on enabling and administering disk quotas under Windows 2000 (which also applies to Windows XP).

Quota support on Mac OS X

(http://sial.org/howto/osx/quota/)

Details on how to set up and administer disk quotas under Mac OS X.

Red Hat Linux—Specific Information

(www.redhat.com/docs/manuals/linux/RHL-9-Manual/admin-primer/s1-storage-rhlspec.html#S2-STORAGE-QUOTAS)

Detailed information about activating and administering disk quotas under Red Hat (and Fedora Core) Linux.

DNS

DNS is a backbone Internet service, with vast amounts of written and online information available.

DNS Resources Directory

(www.dns.net/dnsrd)

Provides a large number of documents about DNS and DNS-related topics.

DNS Stuff

(www.dnsstuff.com)

A page filled with DNS-related tools that you can use from your Web browser.

DynDNS.org

(www.dyndns.org)

A domain-registration service that also offers a free dynamic DNS service for people on DHCP networks, such as those provided by most DSL and cable ISPs.

Fedora Core Linux

Despite the fact that Fedora is a relatively new project, there are a number of good sources for information on it.

DAG: Apt/Yum RPM Repository

(http://dag.wieers.com/home-made/apt)

Features binary packages (and instructions on integrating them with the standard yum/up2date system in Fedora Core) of many useful applications.

Fedora Project

(http://fedora.redhat.com)

Red Hat's Fedora Project pages include online documentation, sign-up information for the Fedora mailing lists (http://fedora.redhat.com/participate/communicate/), and much more.

Fedora Project

(http://fedoraproject.org)

As of this writing, the future home of all things Fedora; contains links to other information.

Linuxlinks.com

(www.linuxlinks.com)

A massive index of Linux-related Web sites, organized by category.

The Unofficial Fedora FAQ

(www.fedorafaq.org)

A repository of FAQs maintained by people who aren't directly associated with the Fedora project.

Fink/Mac OS X

Fink's documentation isn't as good as the general Mac OS X documentation provided by Apple, but it's still more than adequate to help you out.

Apple Computer

(www.apple.com)

Detailed information about every aspect of Mac OS X, including the BSD-flavored Darwin core of the operating system.

Apple Developer Connection

(http://developer.apple.com)

Apple's software-development Web site, including its free Mac OS X development tools (which you'll need for Fink).

Darwin—Open Source

(http://developer.apple.com/darwin)

Apple also makes Darwin, the open-source kernel used with Mac OS X, available.

Fink

(http://fink.sourceforge.net)

Fink's homepage features FAQ and documentation in addition to the download links you need when installing Fink.

Mac OS X—Open Source

(www.apple.com/opensource)

A list of the open-source applications used in Mac OS X, including the technologies that Apple has made open source.

netatalk.sourceforge.net

(http://netatalk.sourceforge.net)

The Netatalk server lets Unix systems (such as Linux and FreeBSD) share directories on an AppleTalk network. This is the fastest network file system for networks made up of Mac clients.

FreeBSD

The FreeBSD project is mature and includes detailed and well-tested documentation.

BSDForums.org

(www.freebsdforums.org)

Web-based discussion forums focusing on FreeBSD, its software, and more.

FreeBSD

(www.freebsd.org)

The mother ship, with mailing-list information (www.freebsd.org/support.html# mailing-list), online documentation galore (including the full text of *The FreeBSD Handbook*), FAQ, man pages, and almost anything else you can think of.

MySQL

A very capable open-source database engine, MySQL is being used all over the Internet for a wide variety of projects and sites.

MySQL

(www.mysql.org)

The MySQL homepage, filled with developer information, technical resources, and information about books.

Netatalk

The Netatalk project provides AppleTalk-compatible file (and printer) sharing for Unix servers. In fact, it provides better AppleTalk performance than that of similar Macintosh-based servers.

netatalk.sourceforge.net

(http://netatalk.sourceforge.net)

The SourceForge project page, which includes online versions of the documentation.

NFS

Since NFS is an old standard for networked file systems, plenty of books and other information about it is available.

FreeBSD Handbook—Network File System

(www.freebsd.org/doc/en_US.ISO8859-1/books/handbook/network-nfs.html)

The FreeBSD Handbook's NFS section.

Linux NFS Overview, FAQ, and HOWTO Documents

(http://nfs.sourceforge.net)

The Linux NFS project's homepage on SourceForge includes many links to additional information and mailing lists (http://lists .sourceforge.net/mailman/listinfo/nfs).

OpenSSH

OpenSSH is an implementation of the SSH protocol suite (SSH1 and SSH2) and runs on almost every operating system.

OpenSSH

(www.openssh.com)

The OpenSSH homepage, with links to man pages, FAQ, bug-report forms, mailing lists (www.openssh.com/list.html), downloads, and more.

LFTP

(http://lftp.yar.ru)

lftp is an excellent text-based FTP/HTTP/ SSH client that makes a great replacement for sftp.

PHP

The ubiquitous Web-page scripting language.

PHP

(www.php.net)

PHP's homepage has links to tutorials, documentation, FAQ, bug-report forms, and a wide variety of other PHP sites.

ONLINE RESOURCES

phpbb

phpbb is a Web forum system written entirely in PHP.

phpBB

(www.phpbb.com)

The phpBB homepage, where you can try a forum demo, get support, interact with the phpbb community, and download styles and add-ons for phpbb.

Postfix

Postfix is a fast, easy-to-administer, secure Sendmail replacement.

The Postfix Home Page

(www.postfix.org)

You can download the source code; subscribe to mailing lists (www.postfix.org/lists.html); read the online documentation, how-to articles, and FAQ; and find out about third-party add-ons.

Samba

The standard for high-performance network file (and printer) sharing. You can also find a number of Samba books at your local bookstore.

Samba.org

(www.samba.org)

The Samba homepage, with complete documentation, mailing lists (http://lists.samba.org/), IRC channels, and more.

Samba Resources

(www.plainjoe.org/samba)

Links to various supplementary Samba information sites and books, maintained by a member of the Samba development team.

Security

Being aware of new security issues is a great way to avoid being hacked by nefarious individuals.

Computer Security Information

(www.alw.nih.gov/Security/security.html)

Links to computer-security advisories, documentation, electronic magazines, FAQ, groups, organizations, and more, from the Center for Information Technology, National Institutes of Health.

The Risks Digest

(http://catless.ncl.ac.uk/Risks)

The Association for Computing Machinery's RISKS Forum ("Risks to the public in computers and related systems"), which often has information about new security problems before any other venue.

US-CERT

(www.us-cert.gov)

The most up-to-date computer-security site, featuring information about security issues and solutions.

Sendmail

The old workhorse of Unix mail transports, Sendmail has been written about extensively in books and online.

Sendmail Consortium

(www.sendmail.org)

The Sendmail Consortium's homepage, with FAQ, documentation, and news.

Squid

You can speed up access to the World Wide Web for users on your network by caching commonly visited pages using Squid.

Squid Web Proxy Cache

(www.squid-cache.org)

The Squid homepage, with FAQ, online documentation, support information, and related projects.

Webmin

Lots of information about Webmin (and the Perl programming language it's written in) is available.

ActivePerl

(www.activestate.com/Products/ActivePerl)

The ActiveState port of Perl for Windows has better performance (and fewer memory leaks) than the Cygwin port. You'll probably want this if you're going to run Webmin for any length of time under Cygwin.

CPAN

(www.cpan.org)

The Comprehensive Perl Archive Network is a huge, distributed database of Perl modules and source code. If you need to do something with Perl, this is going to be one of your favorite sites.

Webmin

(www.webmin.com)

Webmin's homepage includes an array of links to detailed documentation, FAQ, third-party extension modules, and articles about Webmin.

Miscellaneous

These interesting links don't really fit into any of the above categories, but they're still useful.

freshmeat.net

(http://freshmeat.net)

The Web's largest index of Unix and cross-platform software, updated constantly.

ISO Recorder Power Toy

(http://isorecorder.alexfeinman.com)

ISO Recorder is a Windows XP add-on that lets you burn CD-ROM images to disc directly from the Windows desktop.

Kuro5hin

(www.kuro5hin.org)

Another high-tech news portal, similar to Slashdot but covering a wider variety of topics.

Peachpit Press

(www.peachpit.com)

Publisher of fine computer books of all kinds.

rsnapshot

(www.rsnapshot.org)

The homepage for `rsnapshot`, a backup utility written in Perl that works over the `rsync` protocol.

Slashdot

(http://slashdot.org)

"News for Nerds. Stuff that matters." Slashdot is a news portal focusing on high-tech and computer-related articles and discussion.

Wikipedia

(http://en.wikipedia.org/wiki/Main_Page)

Not strictly a computing resource, Wikipedia is a fantastic free online encyclopedia. Everyone should know about this.

INSTALLING FEDORA CORE LINUX

B

Red Hat began its spin-off Fedora Project (http://fedora.redhat.com) to work with the Linux community to produce a complete, robust general-purpose operating system. The idea was to create an outstanding Linux distribution with the latest software, to let any developer contribute to the evolution of the operating system, and to speed up the OS-development process.

The Fedora Project's own Web site (http://fedoraproject.org) is filled with information about the various parts of the Fedora Project, and it has links to downloads, documentation, and FAQ.

Fedora Core Linux is a direct descendant of Red Hat Linux and a sibling of Red Hat Enterprise. It's shaping up to be one of the best user-friendly Linux distributions, which is why we're covering it in this book.

This appendix will show you how to get Fedora Core Linux, how to install it, and how to keep it up-to-date.

Getting Fedora Core 3 Linux

Red Hat started the Fedora Project when Red Hat announced that it would be dropping support for its retail Linux distributions to focus on its enterprise offerings.

Fedora Core is what Red Hat's workstation product would have been if the company hadn't "dropped" it. I say "dropped" because the Fedora Project is hosted on Red Hat's servers, even though it doesn't receive support or certification from Red Hat.

Fedora Core 3 is the third major release of this excellent distribution.

To get Fedora Core 3:

1. Visit the Fedora download page (http://fedora.redhat.com/download).

2. Read the information there, and then choose a download method.

   FTP and HTTP downloads are available from a large number of mirrors. Choose one close to you.

   If you've got a BitTorrent client installed, such as Azureus, there are also torrents you can use that include all of the required disc images as well as an MD5SUM file for authenticating the image.

   DVD images are also available if you happen to have a DVD burner.

3. Use your favorite CD- or DVD-burning software to transfer the disc images onto CDs or a DVD.

✔ Tip

- Write your Fedora Core 3 images to CD-RW discs so that you can reuse them when a new version becomes available (roughly every six months).

Now that you've got Fedora Core 3, do whatever you need to clean up your system before installation. Backing up your data is always a very good idea!

Burning Disc Images in Windows XP

Although it's possible to burn CDs in Windows XP, it's not possible to burn an ISO image (.iso file) to a CD using the built-in tools.

Luckily, you can grab Alex Feinman's excellent ISO Recorder Power Toy (http://isorecorder.alexfeinman.com), which adds the ability to write ISO images to blank CDs directly from Windows Explorer.

Installing Fedora Core 3

These days, installing one of the major Linux distributions from CD-ROMs or a DVD is a fairly easy and straightforward process. Open-source developers around the world have worked tirelessly over the last ten years to simplify installations.

Booting

One of the things that make it easier to install Linux (and any other operating system, for that matter) is the fact that almost every PC built in the past five or so years can boot from a CD-ROM.

When you boot your computer, press the magic key (usually the Delete key or one of the function keys) that brings up your BIOS configuration screen.

Hidden somewhere among the many arcane settings will be a "Boot order" or "Boot device" setting. This will be a list of three or four devices that the computer will try to boot from, in order.

Most systems default to Floppy, First Hard Drive, CD/DVD, and Other (usually SCSI or Network). You want to change this order so that CD or DVD is first, then Hard Drive, then the others.

If your system BIOS doesn't support booting from CD-ROMs, check the OS installation CDs for floppy disk images and a tool to write them. You can boot from these until the installation process is able to start using the CD-ROM drive.

To install Fedora Core 3:

1. Insert the first Fedora Core 3 CD after turning on your computer's power.

   After a few moments, Fedora Core 3 will start up and display its boot menu (**Figure B.1**).

2. You want to install in graphical mode, so press Enter.

   Before Fedora starts up in its graphical mode, the installer gives you a chance to check the validity of your install discs (**Figure B.2**). This helps guard against bad CD copies and incorrect downloads.

3. Press Return to follow the onscreen instructions for testing the installation CDs (**Figure B.3**), or press Tab to move the cursor to the Skip button if you've already tested these CDs.

   Once you've tested your installation CDs, the graphical installer starts (**Figure B.4**).

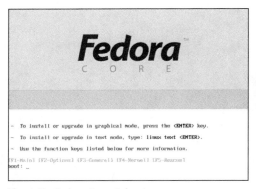

Figure B.1 Fedora Core 3's boot menu.

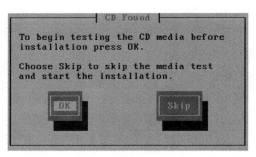

Figure B.2 To validate the installation CDs, choose OK.

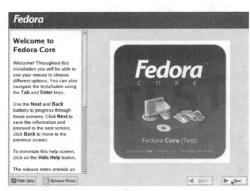

Figure B.3 Validating your installation CDs.

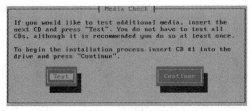

Figure B.4 Fedora Core's graphical installer.

Figure B.5 Choosing an installation language.

Figure B.6 Choosing a keyboard type.

4. Read the information onscreen, and then click Next to continue.

The installer displays the Language Selection screen (**Figure B.5**).

5. Select a language, and then click Next to continue.

The installer displays the Keyboard Configuration screen (**Figure B.6**).

continues on next page

The Custom Option

Linux is all about freedom, and the Fedora Core 3 installer certainly gives you freedom in the form of the Custom installation type.

Custom lets you pick and choose from any of the hundreds of packages on the installation CDs. This is a great way to make sure you've only got what you need installed on your system, assuming you already know what you need.

On the other hand, disk space is cheaper than your time, and you can always install "missing" packages yourself later when you realize you need them.

6. Select your keyboard layout, and then click Next to continue.

The installer displays the Installation Type screen (**Figure B.7**).

7. This is where you can choose from different preconfigured package sets suitable for personal desktop, workstation, or server use. Since we're going to need a reasonably useful system with a development environment, we're going to choose Workstation and then click Next to continue.

The installer displays the Disk Partitioning Setup screen (**Figure B.8**).

8. If you're putting Fedora Core 3 on a disk by itself, choose "Automatically partition" and click Next to continue. You'll still be able to review the changes to your disk before they happen.

If you need to partition your disk by hand, choose "Manually partition with Disk Druid."

Disk Druid is a straightforward disk-partitioning application that shouldn't hold any surprises. If it does, go back and let the installer partition the disk for you.

The installer displays the Automatic Partitioning screen (**Figure B.9**).

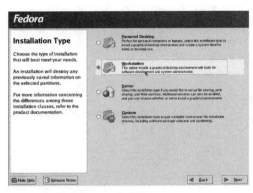

Figure B.7 Choosing the installation type.

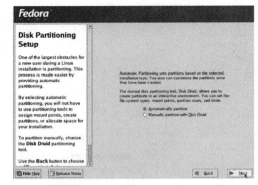

Figure B.8 Partitioning your disk.

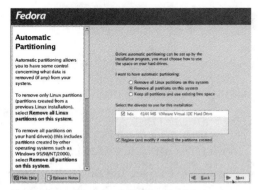

Figure B.9 Letting the installer handle disk partitioning.

INSTALLING FEDORA CORE 3

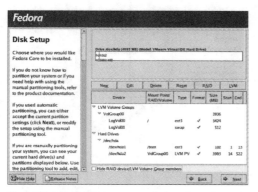

Figure B.10 Reviewing your new Fedora Core partitions.

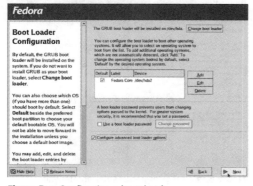

Figure B.11 Configuring a boot loader.

9. The Automatic Partitioning screen lets you control how the installer partitions your disk:

▲ "Remove all Linux partitions on this system" will delete any existing Linux partitions (from a previous installation) and use that space for the new Fedora partitions.

▲ "Remove all partitions on this system" will delete any existing partitions (no matter what OS created them) and use that space for the new Fedora partitions.

▲ "Keep all partitions and use existing space" is the safest option if you have an existing operating system on the disk. It will create the new Fedora partitions in the disk's free space. Note that this "free space" is *unpartitioned* space, not any extra space you might have on a Windows XP disk (for example).

Check the drives you want to use for the Fedora partitions.

We want to see what changes the installer is going to make to our hard drive, so check the Review box, and then click Next to continue.

The installer displays the Disk Setup screen (**Figure B.10**).

10. Now you can check (and modify) the disk layout created by the installer.

If you want to change the partition layout, use the New button to create partitions, the Edit button to change partitions, and the Delete button to delete a partition.

Click Next to continue.

The installer displays the Boot Loader Configuration screen (**Figure B.11**).

continues on next page

INSTALLING FEDORA CORE 3

11. The Boot Loader Configuration screen lets you change the boot loader (between GRUB and LILO if your platform is supported by LILO; unless you know what you're doing, stick with GRUB) and the list of operating systems shown at boot time.

To add an installed operating system to the list, click the Add button. You can edit or delete existing entries by selecting them and clicking the appropriate button.

To add a boot password, check the "Use a boot loader password" box and click the "Change password" button.

If you need to tweak advanced boot loader options, check the "Configure advanced boot loader options" box. You probably don't need to do this, and it's beyond the scope of this book.

Click Next to continue.

The installer displays the Network Configuration screen (**Figure B.12**).

12. If you're using DHCP on your network, click Next to continue.

If you're not using DHCP, select the "manually" option and enter your network information, and then click Next to continue.

The installer displays the Firewall Configuration screen (**Figure B.13**).

13. Unless you know what you're doing, leave the defaults on this screen and click Next to continue. We're going to cover enabling services and firewalls later in the book.

The installer displays the Additional Language Support screen (**Figure B.14**).

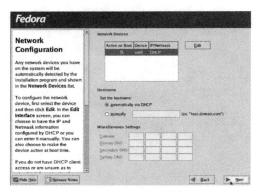

Figure B.12 Configuring your network.

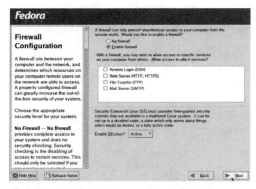

Figure B.13 Configuring your software firewall.

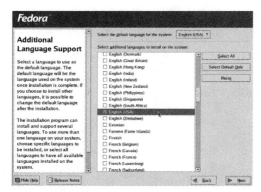

Figure B.14 Adding support for other languages.

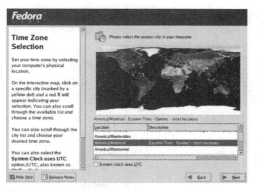

Figure B.15 Choosing your time zone.

Figure B.16 Setting the password for the root account.

Figure B.17 Installing your packages.

14. If you want to add support for additional languages to your system, choose from the languages here.

Click Next to continue.

The installer displays the Time Zone Selection screen (**Figure B.15**).

15. Select a city in your time zone on the map. You can also click the Description column to find your time zone in the list.

If your system clock is set to UTC (universal time), check the "System clock uses UTC" box. If you don't know what this is, leave it unchecked.

Click Next to continue.

The installer displays the Set Root Password screen (**Figure B.16**).

16. Enter a password for the **root** account on this screen. It's important for **root** to have a password because the **root** account can do literally anything to the system.

Click Next to continue.

The installer displays the Package Installation Defaults screen (**Figure B.17**).

continues on next page

INSTALLING FEDORA CORE 3

17. This is another chance for you to add (or remove) packages from the installation. Select the Customize option to add/remove packages, or just click Next to continue.

The installer displays the About to Install screen (**Figure B.18**).

18. If you need to change anything, click the Back button and tweak the installation settings.

Click Next to continue.

The installer displays a dialog telling you which installation CDs will be required to complete the installation (**Figure B.19**).

19. Make sure you have the required Fedora Core installation CDs handy, and then click Continue.

The installer changes your partitions, formats your filesystems, and starts installing packages (**Figure B.20**).

20. Swap CDs if you're prompted to, and when the installer is finished (**Figure B.21**), remove the installation CDs and click Reboot.

Once your machine reboots, you're up and running Fedora Core 3!

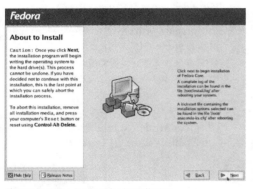

Figure B.18 Reviewing the installation.

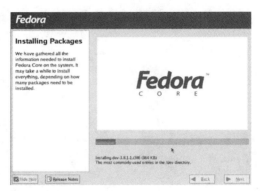

Figure B.20 Installing Fedora Core.

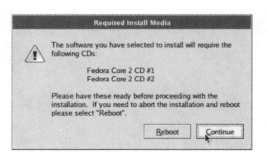

Figure B.19 The CDs you need to complete your installation.

Figure B.21 Finally, the end!

Updating Fedora Core 3 with yum

The yum tool (*Yellow Dog updater, modified*) is used to keep Fedora Core 3 up-to-date and to install new software. Use it to check the Fedora site, looking for updates to any of the packages you have installed, as well as for core OS updates and security patches. One of the best features of yum is that it automatically determines (and, better yet, installs) any dependencies for the packages you're installing.

✔ Tips

■ Before you start using yum, you might want to grab the improved configuration file from the Fedora FAQ Web site (www.fedorafaq.org/samples/yum.conf).

■ Move your current /etc/yum.conf file to yum.conf.orig, and then install the new yum.conf. The yum.conf from fedorafaq.org tells yum to use various Fedora mirror sites, which might speed up your yum operations.

Note that this new yum.conf file does add a few extra repositories that aren't normally checked by yum for updates.

■ The first time you run yum it will download package information for every known package. Depending on how fast your network is, this could take some time.

■ You might prefer to use up2date, a front end to yum.

To update the system with yum:

1. Open a Terminal window by clicking the Red Hat logo icon in the bottom left of the screen, then System Tools, then Terminal.

2. `yum check-update`

   Use the `yum check-update` command to see if there are updated packages to install (**Code Listing B.1**).

   If no updated packages are listed, you're already up-to-date.

3. `yum update`

   Use the `yum update` command to update the packages already installed on your system (**Code Listing B.2**).

   The `yum` command downloads updated package information (if necessary), checks for dependencies, and asks you to verify the operation it's about to perform.

4. Press Y, and then press Enter to continue. The `yum` command downloads and installs the changed packages, bringing your system up-to-date.

✔ Tips

- Use yum's -y option to automatically answer yes to any prompts. Be careful!

- Specify one or more package names in the `yum update` command to update only those packages:

  ```
  [chrish@fedora ~] sudo yum update
  → bash
  ```

- Use `up2date -v -u` if you're having trouble getting connections to the yum repository; it randomly chooses from a list of known mirrors and updates the installed packages in your system.

Code Listing B.1 Checking for updates to Fedora Core.

```
[chrish@fedora ~] sudo yum check-update
Password:
Gathering header information files(s) from
server(s)
Server: Fedora Core 2.90 - Development Tree
Finding updated packages
Downloading needed headers
. . .
```

Code Listing B.2 Updating the installed packages.

```
[chrish@fedora ~] sudo yum update
Password:
Gathering header information file(s) from
server(s)
Server: Fedora Core 2.90 - Development Tree
Finding updated packages
Downloading needed headers
Resolving dependencies
Dependencies resolved
I will do the following:
[update: zlib-devel 1.2.1.2-1.i386]
[update: zlib 1.2.1.2-1.i386]
Is this ok [y/N]:
```

INSTALLING FREEBSD

The FreeBSD project (www.freebsd.org) provides software (the FreeBSD operating system) that can be used by anyone for any purpose. There are no strings attached and no strange licensing issues to worry about. FreeBSD is a "true" Unix (unlike Linux, which is a Unix clone), directly descended from the original AT&T Unix systems.

FreeBSD's reputation as an excellent network operating system and a stable server has left it quietly humming away on a huge number of Internet hosts throughout the world. That said, it only requires a little more work (and quite a bit more reading, sometimes!) than Linux to use on a home network or even as a desktop system.

Getting FreeBSD 5.3

As with all free software, you can get FreeBSD by downloading it. But before you start downloading large CD-ROM files, make sure you have a PS/2 port handy for your keyboard. Unfortunately, at the time of this writing, you can't install FreeBSD on a system with a USB keyboard.

To get FreeBSD:

1. Visit the FreeBSD Web site (www.freebsd.org).

2. Click the "Getting FreeBSD" link under Software.

3. Click the "FTP Sites" link.

4. Choose a mirror close to you.

5. When you open a connection to your chosen mirror, change to the `ISO-IMAGES-i386` directory.

6. Change to the 5.3 directory and download the ISO images (.iso files). You can skip the CHECKSUM.MD5 file if you don't have an `md5sum` program handy. The `md5sum` program will verify that you've downloaded the files as they were released (and that they haven't been tampered with).

7. Use your favorite CD-burning software to copy the ISO images to CDs.

The brave new world of FreeBSD awaits!

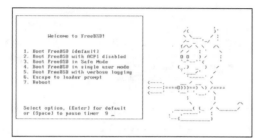

Figure C.1 The FreeBSD boot menu, featuring FreeBSD's daemon mascot.

Figure C.2 The sysinstall tool's main menu.

Figure C.3 How to use the partitioning tool.

Figure C.4 The FDISK Partition Editor.

Installing FreeBSD 5.3

FreeBSD has a reputation for being difficult to install. While this was true in the past, today's FreeBSD installation CDs lead you through the install without causing brain hemorrhages.

To install FreeBSD 5.3:

1. Insert the FreeBSD 5.3 boot disc while booting.

   After a few moments, FreeBSD 5.3 starts up and displays its boot menu (**Figure C.1**).

2. Unless you've been having trouble booting FreeBSD, press 1 or wait for the timer to run out.

   After a few moments, the sysinstall main menu is displayed (**Figure C.2**). The sysinstall application is FreeBSD's system-installation tool.

3. Use the arrow keys to choose Standard from the main menu, and press Enter.

   sysinstall displays a message telling you how to use the partitioning tool (**Figure C.3**).

4. Read the message, then press Enter to continue.

   The installer displays the FDISK Partition Editor (**Figure C.4**).

   continues on next page

5. To use the entire disk for FreeBSD, press the A key to automatically allocate a FreeBSD partition.

Press Q to exit the partition editor. The installer displays the boot-manager installation screen (**Figure C.5**).

6. Choose BootMgr if FreeBSD is the only operating system installed on this system.

Choose None if you've already got a boot manager installed (such as LILO or GRUB from Linux). You'll need to add your FreeBSD installation to the existing boot manager yourself.

You now need to create BSD partitions (or *slices,* in BSD parlance) inside the partition you just created (**Figure C.6**).

7. Read the message, then press Enter to continue.

The installer displays the FreeBSD Disklabel Editor (**Figure C.7**).

8. Press A to let the installer choose some sensible defaults, then press Q to exit.

The installer displays the Choose Distributions screen (**Figure C.8**).

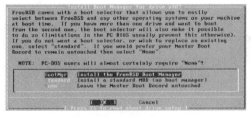

Figure C.5 Installing a boot manager.

Figure C.6 Creating slices in your FreeBSD partition.

Figure C.7 The FreeBSD Disklabel Editor.

Figure C.8 Choosing a distribution set.

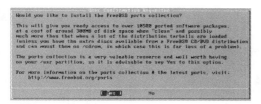

Figure C.9 Confirming your choice.

Figure C.10 Configuring your X.Org distribution.

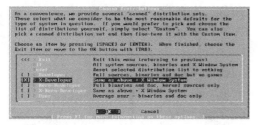

Figure C.11 Returning to the Choose Distributions screen.

Figure C.12 Choosing your installation media.

9. We'll need a developer distribution so that we can compile programs later, and it's always good to have a graphical user interface available. Use the arrow keys to select X-Developer, then press Enter.

   The installer displays a confirmation dialog (**Figure C.9**).

10. The ports collection is one of FreeBSD's great strengths—more than 10,000 programs that can be easily installed from the network whenever you need them. Select Yes with your arrow keys, then press Enter.

    The installer displays the X.Org Distribution screen (**Figure C.10**).

11. Luckily, the installer has already chosen the most useful parts of X. Select Exit, then press Enter to continue.

    The installer returns you to the Choose Distributions screen (**Figure C.11**).

12. We're done here, so select Exit, then press Enter to continue.

    The installer displays the Choose Installation Media screen (**Figure C.12**).

To install the FreeBSD packages:

1. Remove the FreeBSD boot CD and insert the first FreeBSD installation CD.

2. Select CD/DVD in the Choose Installation Media screen, and press Enter to continue the installation from the CD.

   You could also install directly over the network using FTP, HTTP, or NFS, as well as several other kinds of media (such as tapes).

   The installer displays the Last Chance! confirmation dialog (**Figure C.13**). Up until this point, the installer has not touched your system. No changes have been made to your hard drive, and nothing has been installed. This really is your last chance to back out of the install.

3. If you're ready to install, make sure that Yes is selected and then press Enter to continue.

   The installer creates your FreeBSD partition, formats the slices using the appropriate filesystems, and installs FreeBSD on your system (**Figure C.14**).

   When the installer is finished, it displays a congratulations message (**Figure C.15**).

To configure FreeBSD:

1. Press Enter to begin configuring FreeBSD.

   The installer displays a dialog asking if you need to install any Ethernet or PPP devices.

2. Select Yes and press Enter to configure your Ethernet card.

   The installer displays the "Network interface information required" screen (**Figure C.16**).

3. Select your Ethernet card from the list and press Enter.

Figure C.13 It's your last chance!

Figure C.14 Installing FreeBSD.

Figure C.15 Congratulations!

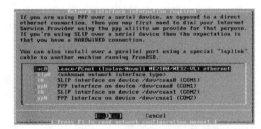

Figure C.16 Gathering network-configuration information.

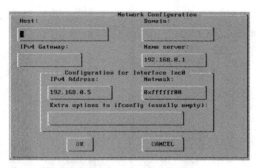

Figure C.17 Configuring your network.

4. Select No in the user confirmation dialog unless you know you need IPv6 support, then press Enter.

If you do need IPv6 support, the configuration is very similar to the IPv4 networking described here, but with the longer IP addresses.

5. Select Yes to use DHCP to configure your network. If you're not using DHCP, select No.

6. Press Enter to continue.

The installer displays the Network Configuration screen (**Figure C.17**).

7. *Do all of the following:*

▲ Enter your system's fully qualified host name (such as chrish.peachpit.com) in the Host field. If you don't have a host name, ask your network administrator (or if you're on your home LAN, make one up). Press Tab to move to the next field (or press Shift-Tab to move to the previous field).

▲ Enter your system's domain name in the Domain field. This is usually the host name, minus the computer's name (such as peachpit.com).

▲ Enter your gateway and DNS server in the IPv4 Gateway and "Name server" fields.

▲ Select OK, then press Enter to continue.

8. Select No in the confirmation dialog that appears because you're not configuring this machine to act as a gateway, then press Enter.

9. Select Yes to enable inetd and its services, then press Enter.

continues on next page

10. Select Yes to enable `inetd` even after being warned about the potential for security problems, then press Enter.

11. Select No when asked if you want to edit inetd.conf now, then press Enter. We looked at this in Chapter 5.

12. Select No when asked if you want to enable `ssh` login, then press Enter. We also looked at this in Chapter 5.

13. Select No for anonymous FTP, then press Enter.

14. Select No for acting as an NFS server, then press Enter.

15. Select Yes for acting as an NFS client if you have NFS servers on your network; otherwise, select No. Press Enter to continue.

16. Select No to customizing your console settings, then press Enter.

17. Select Yes to set the machine's time zone, then press Enter.

18. Select Yes if your machine's internal clock is set to GMT; otherwise, select No. If you don't know, select No. Press Enter to continue.

19. Use the Time Zone Selector's series of dialogs (**Figure C.18**) to find your current time zone. Select your region, country, and time zone, then press Enter.

20. Select No to Linux binary compatibility, then press Enter. If we wanted to run Linux programs, we'd go back a few pages and install Fedora Core!

21. If you have a PS/2 or serial mouse, choose to configure your mouse, then press Enter.

The installer displays the "Please configure your mouse" screen (**Figure C.19**).

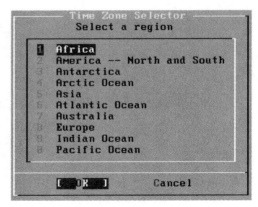

Figure C.18 Selecting a time zone.

Figure C.19 Configuring your mouse.

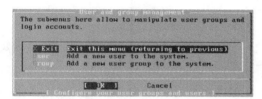

Figure C.20 Managing users and groups.

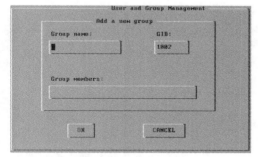

Figure C.21 Adding a new group.

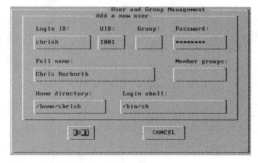

Figure C.22 Adding a new user.

22. Choose Disable, then choose Exit, and press Enter to continue.

23. Select No to browsing the ports collection, then press Enter.

24. Select Yes to adding a user account, then press Enter.

The installer displays the "User and group management" screen (**Figure C.20**).

25. Select Group, then press Enter.

26. The installer displays the "Add a new group" screen (**Figure C.21**).

27. Enter the new group's information:

Group name—We're making a group for users, so enter *users*.

GID—Group ID; you can leave the default alone.

Group members—A list of users that belong to this new group; leave this blank.

Select OK and press Enter to return to the "User and group management" screen (Figure C.20).

28. Select User, then press Enter.

The installer displays the "Add a new user" screen (**Figure C.22**).

29. Enter the new user's information:

Login ID—The account's login name.

UID—User ID; you can leave the default alone.

Group—Group ID; enter 1001 here, for the users group we just created.

Password—The user's initial password.

continues on next page

Full name—The user's full name; you can include other useful information (phone extension, and so on) here as well, if there's room (63 characters will fit).

Member groups—Other groups this user will belong to; you can leave this blank.

Home directory—The user's home directory; you can use the default unless you need the user's home to be somewhere else.

Login shell—The shell this user will use by default; use the default.

Select OK and press Enter to return to the "User and group management" screen (Figure C.20).

30. Select Exit, then press Enter.

31. Press Enter to set the root password.

32. Type the root password at the New Password prompt, then press Enter. Type it again at the Retype New Password prompt, then press Enter.

33. Select No, then press Enter when asked if you want to return to the configuration menu.

The installer returns you to the sysinstall Main Menu (Figure C.2)

34. Select Exit Install, then press Enter.

35. Remove your installation CD, select Yes, and press Enter to reboot the system.

Done! Finally!

Updating FreeBSD 5.3 with CVSup and portupgrade

CVSup is a tool that updates your ports tree from the FreeBSD mirrors so that you don't have to. Then you'll use the portupgrade package's commands to collect and install any updates to the packages installed on your system.

Installing CVSup and portupgrade

CVSup and portupgrade are part of the ports collection, so we'll need to build and install them (**Code Listing C.1**) before we can update our system.

Code Listing C.1 Installing CVSup and portupgrade.

```
bsd# cd /usr/ports/net/cvsup-without-gui

bsd# make install clean
===>  Vulnerability check disabled, database not found
>> cvsup-snap-16.1h.tar.gz doesn't seem to exist in /usr/ports/distfiles/.
>> Attempting to fetch from ftp://ftp.FreeBSD.org/pub/FreeBSD/development/CVSup/snapshots/.
. . .


bsd# /usr/local/bin/cvsup -g -L 2 -h cvsup.freebsd.org /usr/share/examples/cvsup/ports-supfile
Parsing supfile "/usr/share/examples/cvsup/ports-supfile"
Connecting to cvsup.freebsd.org
Connected to cvsup.freebsd.org
Server software version: SNAP_16_1e
Negotiating file attribute support
Exchanging collection information
Establishing multiplexed-mode data connection
Running
Updating collection ports-all/cvs
 Edit ports/INDEX-5
  Add delta 1.21 2004.10.14.22.17.33
Kris
. . .


bsd# cd /usr/ports/sysutils/portupgrade

bsd# make install clean
===>  Vulnerability check disabled, database not found
>> pkgtools-20040701.tar.bz2 doesn't seem to exist in /usr/ports/distfiles/.
>> Attempting to fetch from ftp://ftp.iDaemons.org/pub/distfiles/.
. . .


bsd# /usr/local/sbin/portsdb -Uu
Updating the ports index ... Generating INDEX.tmp - please wait... Done.
Done
[Updating the portsdb <format:bdb1_btree> in /usr/ports ... - 11846 port entries found
.........1000.........2000.........3000.........4000.........5000.........6000.........7000......
...8000.........9000.........10000.........11000........ ..... done]
```

To build and install CVSup and portupgrade:

1. `cd /usr/ports/net/cvsup-without-gui`

This is the directory in the ports tree where CVSup resides. You can use `/usr/ports/net/cvsup` if you want to build a version with a GUI.

2. `make install clean`

Download the CVSup source code and any dependencies, compile it, install it, and then clean up.

3. `cvsup -g -L 2 -h cvsup.freebsd.org`
  → `/usr/share/examples/cvsup`
  → `/ports-supfile`

This synchronizes your ports collection with the versions found on the FreeBSD mirrors. Depending on your connection speed, this could take a while.

If http://cvsup.freebsd.org is busy, pick a local mirror from the list of CVSup servers at www.freebsd.org/doc/en_US.ISO8859-1/books/handbook/cvsup.html#CVSUP-MIRRORS.

4. `cd /usr/ports/sysutils/portupgrade`

Next, change to the portupgrade directory in the ports tree.

5. `make install clean`

Download the portupgrade code and any dependencies, compile it, install it, and then clean up.

6. `/usr/local/sbin/portsdb -Uu`

Update the local ports database. Depending on your CPU and disk speed, this could take a *long* time. Be patient.

Using CVSup

After CVSup and portupgrade have been installed, you can use them to update the packages installed on your system (**Code Listing C.2**).

Code Listing C.2 Updating the installed packages in the system.

```
bsd# /usr/local/bin/cvsup -g -L 2 -h cvsup.freebsd.org /usr/share/examples/cvsup/ports-supfile
Parsing supfile "/usr/share/examples/cvsup/ports-supfile"
Connecting to cvsup.freebsd.org
Connected to cvsup.freebsd.org
Server software version: SNAP_16_1e
Negotiating file attribute support
Exchanging collection information
Establishing multiplexed-mode data connection
Running
Updating collection ports-all/cvs
 Edit ports/INDEX-5
  Add delta 1.21 2004.10.14.22.17.33
Kris
. . .


bsd# /usr/local/sbin/portsdb –Uu
Updating the ports index ... Generating INDEX.tmp - please wait... Done.
Done
[Updating the portsdb <format:bdb1_btree> in /usr/ports ... - 11846 port entries found
.........1000.........2000.........3000.........4000.........5000.........6000.........7000......
...8000.........9000.........10000.........11000........ ..... done]


bsd# /usr/local/sbin/portversion -l "<"
[Rebuilding the pkgdb
<format:bdb1_btree> in /var/db/pkg ... - 22 packages found (-0 +22)
..................... done]
libtool                 <


bsd# /usr/local/sbin/portupgrade –arR
-->  Upgrading 'libtool-1.5.8' to 'libtool-1.5.10' (devel/libtool15)
-->  Building '/usr/ports/devel/libtool15'
===>  Cleaning for libtool-1.5.10
===>  Vulnerability check disabled, database not found
>> libtool-1.5.10.tar.gz doesn't seem to exist in /usr/ports/distfiles/.
>> Attempting to fetch from http://ftp.gnu.org/gnu/libtool/.
```

UPDATING FREEBSD 5.3

To update installed packages with CVSup and portupgrade:

1. `/usr/local/bin/cvsup -g -L 2`
   → `-h cvsup2.freebsd.org /usr/share`
   → `/examples/cvsup/ports-supfile`

   Synchronize your local ports collection with the FreeBSD mirrors.

2. `/usr/local/sbin/portsdb -Uu`

   Update your ports database. Note that this step can take a long time to complete.

3. `/usr/local/sbin/portversion -l "<"`

   List the installed ports that need to be updated.

4. `/usr/local/sbin/portupgrade -arR`

   Finally, update the installed ports.

That's all there is to it! Your FreeBSD system is now up-to-date.

Installing Cygwin

Cygwin is a Linux-like environment that runs on top of recent versions of Microsoft Windows, such as 2000 and XP. The Cygwin DLL provides a rich emulation layer, and the Cygwin project provides a large number of ported Linux and Unix applications.

Cygwin is maintained by Cygnus, which is owned by Red Hat. Like all of Red Hat's software, Cygwin is available under several free software licenses, such as the GNU General Public License and the X11 license.

Getting Cygwin

To get Cygwin:

1. Visit the Cygwin Web site at www
   .cygwin.com.

2. Click the "Install Cygwin now or update
   now!" link in the middle of the page
   (or near any of the stylized C logos on
   the page).

3. Save Cygwin's setup.exe file to your
   desktop.

   What, done already? Well, given that the
   Cygwin setup program is under 300 Kbytes,
   you might guess that it doesn't include
   any of the actual applications. Good
   guess, because you're right.

Figure D.1 The Cygwin installer.

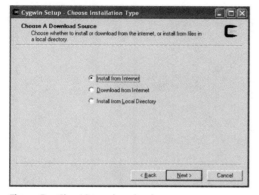

Figure D.2 Choosing a download source.

Installing Cygwin

After downloading the Cygwin setup application, you need to set up and install Cygwin and the applications you're interested in.

To install Cygwin:

1. Run the Cygwin setup application.

   The Cygwin installer (**Figure D.1**) starts up.

2. Click Next to continue.

   The installer displays the Choose A Download Source pane (**Figure D.2**).

continues on next page

3. Choose Install from Internet (the default), and then click Next to continue.

The Download from Internet option will let you download the Cygwin installer packages to use later with the Install from Local Directory option. These options let you grab the Cygwin packages, store them on a server (for example), and then do several installations without having to download the files each time.

When you click Next, the installer displays the Select Root Install Directory pane (**Figure D.3**).

4. You can go with the defaults (I always do), or you can configure things to your liking.

To change the installation directory, enter a full path in the Root Directory field, or click the Browse button to choose a directory.

To install Cygwin for the current user instead of all users, click the Just Me radio button in the Install For box.

To use DOS end-of-line characters instead of the default Unix end-of-line character, choose DOS in the Default Text File Type box. This controls how Cygwin treats text files.

When the configuration is the way you want it, click Next to continue.

The installer displays the Select Local Package Directory pane (**Figure D.4**).

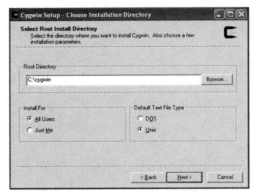

Figure D.3 Choosing an installation directory.

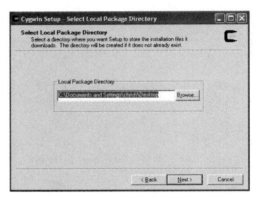

Figure D.4 Choosing a local package directory.

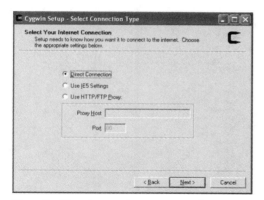

Figure D.5 Choosing your Internet connection settings.

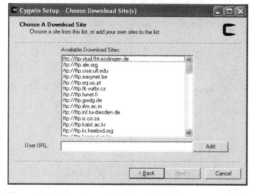

Figure D.6 Choosing a download site.

5. Enter a full path in the Local Package Directory field, or click Browse to select a different directory.

   This directory is used to store downloaded Cygwin package archives during installation. The files aren't automatically deleted afterward, so this should be a temporary file directory. Another option would be to keep the files around in case you needed to reinstall things later.

   Click Next to continue.

   The installer displays the Select Your Internet Connection pane (**Figure D.5**).

6. Select an appropriate option for your Internet connection. The default is probably fine for your home network; at work you can use your Microsoft Internet Explorer settings or specify a proxy (ask your network administrator if you're not sure). Click Next.

   The installer displays the Choose A Download Site pane (**Figure D.6**).

continues on next page

7. Select a nearby mirror site. If you're not sure which ones are close to you, guess.

If you get it wrong, you'll have slower downloads but you'll still get the goods; it's not really a big deal. You can always click Cancel during the download and go back to pick a different mirror.

Click Next to continue.

Cygwin downloads the list of packages from the selected mirror and displays the Select Packages pane (**Figure D.7**).

8. By default, the Select Packages pane displays the packages in collapsed categories. Click the plus sign next to a category name to expand it; the plus sign changes to a minus sign, which can be clicked to collapse the category.

If you want to select some additional packages, scroll through the list and click the circle arrows (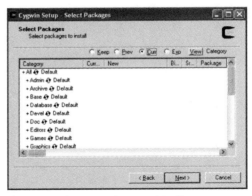) to install one or all of the packages in a category. The Skip action will switch to the version number that will be installed. If you're clicking a package that's already installed, you can install older versions, uninstall, or reinstall, as well.

A fairly useful basic setup is selected by default, so you can just click Next to continue.

The installer downloads and installs the selected applications (**Figure D.8**).

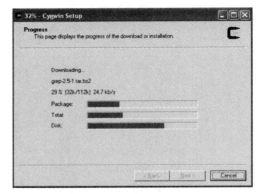

Figure D.7 Selecting packages to install.

Figure D.8 Downloading and installing packages.

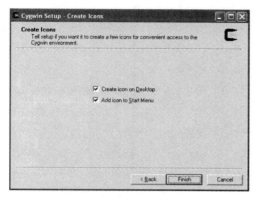

Figure D.9 Creating Cygwin icons.

9. After the Cygwin installer has finished, it displays the Create Icons pane (**Figure D.9**).

Leave both options selected, and click Finish to exit the installer.

You're done! Now you've got a nice Cygwin icon on your desktop (and in your Start menu) that'll launch the **bash** shell in a terminal window.

✔ Tips

■ Click the View button in the Select Packages pane to cycle through different views of the package list. I find the Full view to be most useful, even though it's just a straight listing without categories.

■ You can drag the corners or sides of the Cygwin installer window to make it larger. This feature was a very popular request, since the package descriptions tend to be longer than the window is wide.

Updating Cygwin

After installing Cygwin and some applications, you'll want to make sure your software is up-to-date. You can do this every month or so, unless you know that a specific, important application has been updated or added recently.

To update Cygwin:

◆ Follow the directions in the "Getting Cygwin" and "Installing Cygwin" sections.

You use the same setup.exe file for installing Cygwin as you do for updating it. Any time you run the installer, it'll look for updated versions of any package you have installed and will install them unless you specifically tell it not to.

You can also take this opportunity to uninstall programs you're not using, or to add something interesting that you don't already have installed.

INSTALLING FINK

The Fink project, hosted on SourceForge (http://fink.sourceforge.net), was created to port open-source Unix software to Mac OS X. Even though Mac OS X has a BSD layer underneath, it isn't always easy (or possible!) to port useful Unix applications. If you need something, chances are that it's already covered by Fink, which takes care of installing, compiling, and updating the software for you.

You'll need to install the Apple developer tools (a free download at www.apple.com /macosx/developertools) and the BSD subsystem (my iBook came with the BSD layer preinstalled) before you can install, configure, and use Fink.

Getting Fink for Mac OS X

Fink is a great tool for building and installing almost any Unix program you'll need, but what can you do to get it running? You certainly can't use Fink to install itself if it's not installed yet (although, as you'll see later, you can use it to update itself). Luckily, Fink binary packages are available for download.

To get Fink:

1. Visit the Fink download page at http://fink.sourceforge.net/download.

2. Click the Fink Binary Installer link (version 0.7.1 as of this writing).

   This takes you to the list of SourceForge mirrors.

3. Click one of the icons in the Download column.

   The mirror page lists all of the known SourceForge mirrors for this Fink Binary Installer. Try to pick one physically close to you, but don't worry about it too much.

   After a few seconds, your download begins.

4. Save the Fink installer file (Fink-0.7.1-Installer.dmg) to your Desktop.

   That's it—you've got Fink!

Who's a What Now?

Unlike many open-source projects, *Fink* is just a name, not an acronym. It's the German word for *finch*. The project's originator was thinking about the name for the BSD core of Mac OS X, Darwin, and Charles Darwin, and remembered learning about Darwin finches in school.

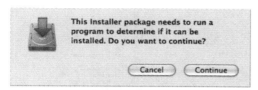

Figure E.1 Starting the Fink installer.

Figure E.2 The Fink installer.

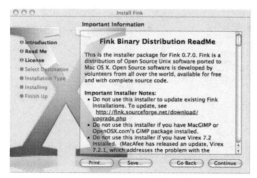

Figure E.3 The Fink Binary Distribution ReadMe file.

Installing Fink

Now that you've got the Fink disk image, it's time to install and configure this handy bit of software.

Before you do this, you should be logged on to your Mac with an administrator account. The first user account created on a Mac OS X system is automatically an administrator account.

To install Fink:

1. Double-click the Fink installer disk image (Fink-0.7.0-Installer.dmg) on your Desktop.

   Mac OS X validates the disk image, mounts it as a virtual disk, and opens it.

2. Double-click the Fink installer package (Fink 0.7.0 Installer.pkg).

   The Fink installer starts up and displays a dialog (**Figure E.1**) asking for permission to run a program to determine if the installer can run.

3. Click the Continue button.

   The dialog goes away, and you can continue the installation (**Figure E.2**).

4. Click the Continue button.

   The installer displays the Fink Binary Distribution ReadMe file (**Figure E.3**).

continues on next page

5. Read the information, and then click the Continue button.

The installer displays the Software License Agreement. Click the selection box at the top (showing English in **Figure E.4**) to select a different language for the license agreement. This won't affect the Fink software, just the displayed license agreement.

6. Read the license agreement, and then click the Continue button.

The installer displays a dialog (**Figure E.5**) asking you to agree or disagree with the license agreement.

7. Click the Agree button. If you don't agree to the terms of the license, you're not allowed to use Fink.

The installer displays the Select a Destination pane (**Figure E.6**).

8. Click the destination volume and then the Continue button. The Fink installer displays a summary telling you what is about to happen.

9. Click the Install button in the summary panel to install Fink.

The installer displays the Authenticate dialog (**Figure E.7**).

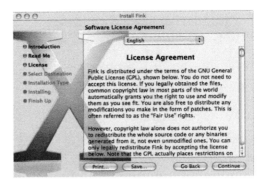

Figure E.4 The Fink License Agreement.

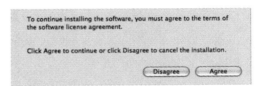

Figure E.5 Agreeing to the License Agreement.

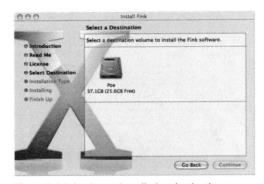

Figure E.6 Selecting an installation destination.

Figure E.7 Authenticating the Fink installer.

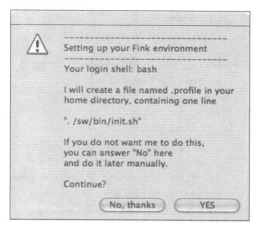

Figure E.8 This dialog adds the Fink software to your path.

10. Enter your account name in the Name field and your password in the Password field. Click OK to continue.

    The installer installs Fink's files and displays the "Setting up your Fink environment" dialog (**Figure E.8**).

11. Click the YES button to let the "Setting up your Fink environment" dialog add the following line to the .profile file in your home directory:

    `. /sw/bin/init.sh`

    This line adds the Fink configuration to your shell environment. Without it, you're still just using the Mac OS X versions of everything and getting no benefit from Fink.

    Click the "No, thanks" button to modify the .profile yourself later.

12. Click OK to exit the Path Setup dialog.

13. Click Close to exit the installer.

✔ Tips

■ If you need to run Path Setup again, enter this in a Terminal window:

   `/sw/bin/pathsetup.sh`

■ All users on your computer need to run Path Setup if they want to use applications installed with Fink.

Fink configuration

After installing Fink, we need to configure it so that we'll be able to install and update software.

To configure Fink:

1. Open a new Terminal window.

   If you type *echo $PATH*, you should see /sw/bin in the result, like this:

   bender:~ chrish$ **echo $PATH**

   /sw/bin:/sw/sbin:/bin:/sbin:
   → /usr/bin:/usr/sbin

2. Type *fink scanpackages ; fink index* and press Enter:

   iBook:~ chrish$ **fink scanpackages;**
   → **fink index**

   /usr/bin/sudo /sw/bin/fink
   → scanpackages

   Password:

   These commands invoke **sudo**, which runs a single command as the administrator (aka **root**). The system wouldn't be very secure if just anyone could use **sudo** all the time, so you're going to be asked for your password.

3. At the Password prompt, type your password, and then press Enter. Various cryptic commands scroll by, looking something like this:

   Information about 1495 packages read
   → in 2 seconds.

   dpkg-scanpackages
   → dists/local/main/binary-darwin-
   → powerpc override | gzip
   → >dists/local/main/binary-darwin-
   → powerpc/Packages.gz

   Wrote 0 entries to output Packages
   → file.

   dpkg-scanpackages
   → dists/stable/main/binary-darwin-
   → powerpc override | gzip
   → >dists/stable/main/binary-darwin-
   → powerpc/Packages.gz

   Wrote 0 entries to output Packages
   → file.

   dpkg-scanpackages
   → dists/stable/crypto/binary-darwin-
   → powerpc override | gzip
   → >dists/stable/crypto/binary-darwin-
   → powerpc/Packages.gz

   Wrote 0 entries to output Packages
   → file.

   dpkg-scanpackages
   → dists/local/bootstrap/binary-
   → darwin-powerpc override | gzip
   → >dists/local/bootstrap/binary-
   → darwin-powerpc/Packages.gz

   Wrote 0 entries to output Packages
   → file.

   /usr/bin/sudo /sw/bin/fink index

   Reading package info...

   Updating package index... done.

4. Enter the following command to make sure the latest version of Fink is installed, and to complete the configuration:

   fink selfupdate

   This command requires administrator privileges, so the **sudo** command asks for your password.

5. Enter your password at the Password prompt, and then press Enter.

   Fink tells you that it needs to choose a SelfUpdateMethod and lists three choices:

   ▲ rsync

   ▲ cvs

   ▲ Stick to point releases

6. The default (`rsync`) is a good choice, although you can certainly use `cvs` if your firewall blocks `rsync` access to the Fink servers. Either way, you'll be getting the same Fink software.

Lots of commands scroll by in the Terminal as the latest version of Fink is downloaded, compiled, and installed. A fresh version of Fink's master package index is also installed.

Next, you must configure the mirror that Fink will use to download packages.

7. Enter *4* and press Enter to select "Search closest mirrors first." since it's always a good idea to use local mirrors if you can.

Fink lists the continents to start figuring out where your local mirrors are:

(1)   `Africa`

(2)   `Asia`

(3)   `Australia`

(4)   `Europe`

(5)   `North America`

(6)   `South America, Middle` → `America and Caribbean`

8. Enter the appropriate number for your continent and then press Enter. I'm in North America, so I can choose the default, 5.

Fink displays the countries that have mirrors in your continent. In my case:

(1)   `No selection - display all` → `mirrors on the continent`

(2)   `Canada`

(3)   `Mexico`

(4)   `United States`

9. Continue selecting appropriate choices and pressing Enter. You'll be prompted for several mirrors:

▲ Master Fink mirrors

▲ RSync SelfUpdate

▲ Apt-Get Repository

▲ GNU Software

▲ GNOME

▲ The GIMP

▲ Comprehensive TeX Archive Network

▲ Comprehensive Perl Archive Network

▲ Debian

▲ KDE

▲ SourceForge

Don't worry if you don't know what these mean; you can't pick any wrong entries in this configuration process. If you're not sure, just go with the default.

More messages scroll past, and eventually Fink finishes updating itself. It lets you know by displaying this message:

`The core packages have been updated. You should now update the other packages using commands like 'fink update-all'.`

10. If the `sudo` command displays the `Password` prompt again, type your password and press Enter.

`sudo` remembers that you've successfully entered your password, but only for the next 5 minutes. In our case, if the `selfupdate` command took more than 5 minutes, you've got to enter your password again.

The `update-all` command updates all of your installed packages, or it tells you that there are no new packages to install.

At this point, Fink is installed, configured, and ready to go!

✔ Tip

■ Instead of updating the individual files in a package, the `Stick to point releases` option will only update something when it has been packaged. Your software might get out of date with this method because "official" packages are rarely built.

Fink quick reference

Fink is a pretty straightforward utility, with a few commands that you'll use all the time. I've listed these helpful commands in alphabetical order in **Table E.1**.

✔ Tip

■ If you're having trouble updating through rsync, you can switch to CVS by using the selfupdate-cvs command. If you need to switch back to rsync updates, use selfupdate-rsync.

Table E.1

Fink Commands	
COMMAND	DESCRIPTION
fink describe *name*	Gives you a long description for the named package or packages. Use the fink list command to find package names.
fink --help	Lists all of the common Fink commands, with brief descriptions. Those are two hyphens before help in the command.
fink install *name*	Download, compile, and install the named package or packages.
fink list	Lists all of the packages that Fink knows about. The first column is the name of the package; this is what you'll use when you install the package. The other two columns are current version and a brief description of the package. If there's an *i* at the start of a row, that package is already installed. You're going to want to combine this with less, grep, head, and so on, to help you find what you're looking for.
fink selfupdate	Update Fink itself, and its database of known packages.
fink update-all	Update all of the software installed with Fink. This automatically downloads, builds, and installs the latest version of every package that has already been installed.

Linking Commands

You probably already know that you can link two or more shell commands in sequence using a semicolon (;) between the commands. For example, the sequence

```
echo Your files: ; ls
```

will print Your files: and then the output of the ls command.

You can also link commands with || or && (two pipe symbols or two ampersands).

Commands linked with || are executed until one of them succeeds. Commands linked with && are executed until one of them fails.

For example, the sequence

```
echo hello || true || echo there
```

will print hello and stop, because there's no need to continue. If echo was able to print something, it succeeds.

With this sequence,

```
echo hello && true && echo there
```

you will see hello on one line, and then there on the next line. The true command always succeeds, so the shell continues to execute the commands in the sequence.

Use || in a command sequence when you only need one of the commands to succeed.

Use && in a command sequence when you want to stop executing commands as soon as something fails.

Updating Fink

With Fink (and possibly some packages) installed, you'll want to stay up-to-date. Security problems and other bugs get fixed, features get added, and software evolves, after all.

The selfupdate and update-all commands keep Fink and its packages (respectively) up-to-date. They'll download, compile, and install everything; you just need to enter the commands once in a while.

Unless you know that a specific package you use has been updated, using selfupdate and update-all once a month is probably enough.

To update Fink and all of the installed packages:

1. In a Terminal window, enter the following command:

   ```
   fink selfupdate && fink update-all
   ```

   This command will update Fink itself, and then, if that was successful, update all of the installed packages.

   These commands require an administrator account, so the sudo command will prompt you for your password.

2. Enter your password at the Password prompt, and then press Enter.

   Fink searches for an updated version of itself and installs it (if one exists). Then it searches for updated versions of the installed packages and installs those as well.

Yes, only one command to update Fink and all of your installed packages. OK, technically it's two commands, but it's only one line in the shell.

Finding useful bits in Fink

If this is your first time installing Fink, and your Mac OS X system is still fairly fresh, you probably want to install a bunch of your favorite Unix applications.

To list Fink's packages:

◆ Use this command to list all of the available Fink packages so that you can find the ones you want:

`fink list | less`

The list is quite long (almost 2000 packages as of this writing!) and growing all the time.

Installing Fink packages

After you've gone through Fink's extensive package list, you can install the packages you can't live without.

To install Fink packages:

1. Use the `fink install` command to install one or more packages. For example,

    `fink install file wtf zip`

    installs the useful `file`, `wtf`, and `zip` packages.

    `sudo` displays the `Password` prompt.

2. Type your password, then press Enter.

3. If the listed packages require any additional packages, such as libraries, Fink will list them and ask if you want to continue. Press Enter to continue.

    Fink downloads, compiles, and installs the specified packages.

INSTALLING WEBMIN

Webmin is a Web-based tool for doing system administration on a Unix system from a Web browser. It supports a huge number of different Unix systems, including Fedora Core, FreeBSD, Cygwin, and Mac OS X.

Using nearly any Web browser (ones that don't support tables and forms are rare these days), you can set up user accounts, control system services, and view logs, among other things. A wide selection of third-party modules enables even more remote administration.

While Webmin doesn't remove the need to know at least a bit about what you're doing, it does make things easier and provides a nice graphical interface for administering a system remotely.

Getting Webmin

Before downloading Webmin, you should make sure that your system has the Perl programming language installed. This is Webmin's only requirement; you don't need to install a Web server, for example, because Webmin provides one.

Fedora Core, FreeBSD, and Mac OS X all include Perl by default. Cygwin is the odd man out, and needs Perl installed before you can continue.

Please note that Fedora Core users might want to avoid using Webmin, at least until it supports Fedora better. Red Hat isn't willing to support installations of Red Hat Enterprise that have been administered through Webmin. Our apologies for sounding vague on this, but check the Fedora and Webmin forums for more information.

To install Perl on Cygwin:

As with any supported Cygwin package, installing Perl is quite easy.

1. Launch the Cygwin installer (setup.exe); if you didn't keep this handy, refer to Appendix D for download instructions.

2. In the installer, click the Next button in the screens that appear until you reach the package list.

3. Expand the Interpreters category by clicking the + sign next to the category name.

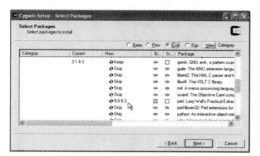

Figure F.1 Finding the Perl packages in the Cygwin installer.

4. Drag the Cygwin Setup window's lower-right corner to expand the window, and scroll down the alphabetical list of programming-language interpreters to the `perl` entry.

5. Click the circle-arrow icon in the `perl` row so that Skip changes to a version number (**Figure F.1**).

This is the version that will be installed.

6. Click the installer's Next button.

Cygwin Setup downloads and installs `perl`, its prerequisites, and any updated versions of packages you've already installed.

7. Click Finish to exit the installer.

✔ Tip

- Please note that Cygwin's Perl seems to have some performance and memory-leaking problems; you don't want to leave a Perl-based service running for very long using the Cygwin version of Perl. An alternative Perl port is ActiveState's ActivePerl (www.activestate.com/Products/ActivePerl), a native port to the Windows environment.

To check for Perl on your system:

If you want to make sure that Perl has installed properly on your system, you can easily check.

◆ `perl -version`

This command loads the Perl interpreter and prints version information (**Figure F.2**), as well as some information about how the interpreter was built, such as whether it was built with thread support.

To download Webmin:

1. Visit the Webmin Web site with your favorite browser:

   www.webmin.com

2. Click the "Downloading and Installing" link.

3. Click the link to the current Webmin archive (`webmin-1.170.tar.gz` at the time of this writing) to see a list of mirror sites.

4. Click in the Download column for a local mirror (don't worry if you're not sure which one to use—they will all work) and save it to your home directory.

✔ Tips

■ Lots of Webmin documentation can be found online. The Webmin Web site (www.webmin.com) features a well-stocked Documentation section that includes links to mailing lists, FAQ, and an entire online book about Webmin.

■ Usermin is a Webmin add-on that provides a graphical interface for tasks that your users might be interested in, such as reading their email, setting up SSH, or forwarding mail. You can find out more about Usermin by visiting www.webmin.com/uintro.html.

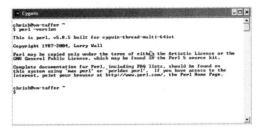

Figure F.2 Printing Perl's version information.

Code Listing F.1 Using the `which` command to find the Perl program.

```
bender:~ chrish$ which perl
/usr/bin/perl
```

Code Listing F.2 Using the `hostname` command to find your system's hostname.

```
bender:~ chrish$ hostname
bender.local
```

Installing Webmin

Now that you've got the Webmin source code, you're ready to install, right? Well, not quite. It's good to collect a bit of helpful information before we start so that we can breeze through the installation without any fuss.

Before you begin installing Webmin, collect the following information:

- The full path to Perl. You can use the `which` command to find it (**Code Listing F.1**). It's usually found in `/usr/bin/perl` or `/usr/local/bin/perl`.

- The directory where you want to install Webmin. `/usr/local/etc/webmin` is a good choice, but it can run from anywhere.

- The directory where you want Webmin to store its configuration files; this lets you preserve your configuration while upgrading Webmin. A good choice is `/usr/local/etc/webmin.conf`, but you can put it anywhere.

- The directory for Webmin logs. A good choice is `/var/log/webmin`.

- Your operating-system type; Webmin's installer will only ask you what OS you're using if you have an unsupported system, which isn't the case here.

- The TCP/IP port to use for Webmin's Web server. Anything over 1024 and under 65536 is valid, but 8080 or 8088 is often used for things like this. If you can't pick one, the default (10000) is fine.

- A login name and password to use while connecting to Webmin. These are specific to Webmin, although you can certainly make them match your own user ID and password, but it's a better idea to make these a "strong" user ID and password combination that won't be guessed. Crackers will try `admin`, `Administrator`, and `root` for the user ID right away, for example, so choose something else. Refer to Chapter 4, "Safety and Security," for some helpful password-selection hints.

- The system's hostname; you can find this by using the `hostname` command (**Code Listing F.2**).

To install Webmin:

Now that we've collected the information we need for a smooth install, we can go ahead and do it (**Code Listing F.3**).

1. Log in as root, or use su or sudo to get a root shell.

2. cd *downloaddir*

   Change to the directory where you downloaded the Webmin source code.

3. tar -xzf webmin-1.160.tar.gz

   Unpack the archive; this creates a webmin-1.160 directory containing the source code.

4. cd webmin-1.160

   Change to the Webmin source directory.

5. ./setup.sh *installdir*

   Launch the Webmin setup script, and install it to *installdir*.

6. At the "Config file directory" prompt, enter the directory you want to use for Webmin configuration files (/usr/local/etc/webmin.conf).

7. At the "Log file directory" prompt, enter the directory you want to use for Webmin's log files (/var/log/webmin).

8. At the "Full path to perl" prompt, enter the full path to your Perl program. The installer will test Perl, so you'll know if you get this wrong.

9. At the "Web server port" prompt, enter the TCP/IP port to use for Webmin's Web server.

Code Listing F.3 Installing Webmin from its source code.

```
bender:~ chrish$ tar -xzf webmin-1.160.tar.gz
bender:~ chrish$ cd webmin-1.160
bender:~/webmin-1.160 chrish$ ./setup.sh
→ /usr/local/etc/webmin
Password:
. . .
Config file directory [/etc/webmin]:
→ /usr/local/etc/webmin.conf
Log file directory [/var/webmin]:
→ /var/log/webmin
. . .
Full path to perl (default /usr/bin/perl):
. . .
Web server port (default 10000):
Login name (default admin):
Login password:
Password again:
The Perl SSLeay library is not installed. SSL
not available.
Start Webmin at boot time (y/n): y
. . .
Webmin has been installed and started
successfully. Use your web
browser to go to

  http://bender.local:10000/


and login with the name and password you
entered previously.
```

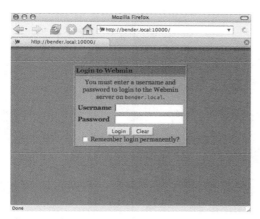

Figure F.3 The Webmin login page.

Figure F.4 The main Webmin interface.

10. At the "Login name" prompt, enter the user ID to use for Webmin logins.

11. At the "Login password" prompt, enter the password to use for Webmin logins. Enter it again at the "Password again" prompt to verify the password.

12. At the "Start Webmin at boot time" prompt, enter *Y* to automatically launch Webmin when the system boots, or *N* to start it manually when necessary.

The setup script copies the Webmin scripts to your installation directory and configures it based on your answers.

To see if Webmin is running:

After installing Webmin, make sure it's running properly.

1. Use your favorite Web browser to visit the Webmin login page (**Figure F.3**).

http://*hostname*:10000/

hostname must match the hostname you used while installing Webmin.

2. Enter your Webmin user ID and password in the form, then click the Login button to reach the main Webmin interface (**Figure F.4**).

Keep in mind that having your Web browser remember the user ID and password, or having Webmin remember your login information (if you check the "Remember login permanently?" box), is a security risk.

Securing Webmin

Because Webmin runs as the **root** user and has full control over important system-configuration files, it's important to keep it as secure as possible.

There are several things we can do to make Webmin safer to run.

To change Webmin's authentication settings:

The authentication settings control the way Webmin reacts to invalid passwords and frequent login attempts, two of the "signatures" of someone trying to crack the Webmin password.

1. Log in to Webmin by visiting it with your favorite Web browser (Figure F.3):

   http://*hostname*:10000/

2. Enter your Webmin user ID and password, then click the Login button. Webmin transfers you to the main page (Figure F.4).

3. Click the "Webmin Configuration" link to get to the Webmin Configuration page (**Figure F.5**).

4. Scroll down if necessary, then click the "Authentication" link to show the authentication settings (**Figure F.6**).

5. Click the "Enable password timeouts" button; this will cause a delay between login attempts if an invalid password is entered.

Figure F.5 Webmin's configuration interface.

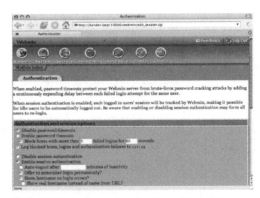

Figure F.6 Webmin's authentication settings let you change the way Webmin treats failed login attempts.

SECURING WEBMIN

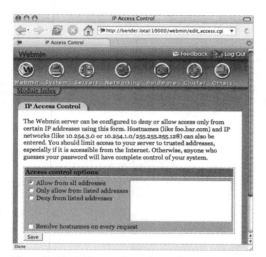

Figure F.7 The IP Access Control page lets you allow access from specific computers or deny access to specific computers.

6. Check the "Auto-logout after *x* minutes of inactivity" box, and enter a number of minutes in the *x* text field. Use whatever you feel comfortable with; this is the length of time your Web browser could be sitting at Webmin unguarded while you're off getting a cup of coffee.

7. Click the Save button at the bottom of the page to save your changes and return to the Webmin Configuration page.

To limit access to certain IP addresses:

Another way of making Webmin safer is to allow access only from specific IP addresses. You can also deny access to specific IP addresses.

1. On the Webmin Configuration page, click IP Access Control to display the IP Access Control page (**Figure F.7**).

2. To allow access for specific IP addresses, host names, or networks, click the "Only allow from listed addresses" button.

3. To deny access from specific IP addresses, hostnames, or networks, click the "Deny from listed addresses" button.

4. Enter the IP addresses, hostnames, or networks in the text field, one per line.

5. Click the Save button to apply your changes and return to the Webmin Configuration page.

✔ Tip

■ You can allow access to Webmin from any system by returning here and clicking the "Allow from all addresses" button.

To encrypt your Webmin connection with SSL:

By default, Webmin uses normal HTTP connections. These aren't encrypted, and if someone were eavesdropping on your network, he or she could discover your Webmin user ID and password. Switching to HTTPS connections removes this problem.

1. Before we can add SSL support to Webmin, we need to have the OpenSSL libraries installed. If you're using Fedora Core or FreeBSD, OpenSSL is already installed.

    If you're using Cygwin, use the Cygwin setup program to install `openssl-devel` from the Devel category. Also, if you haven't already installed a compiler, install `binutils` and `gcc` from the Devel category (these will also install all of their prerequisites).

    If you're using Mac OS X, use Fink to install OpenSSL:

    ```
    sudo fink install openssl097-dev
    ```

2. Use your favorite Web browser to download the Net::SSLeay module for Perl:

    http://search.cpan.org/~sampo/
    Net_SSLeay.pm-1.25/

    Click the Download link and save the Net_SSLeay.pm-1.25.tar.gz file to your home directory.

Securing Webmin

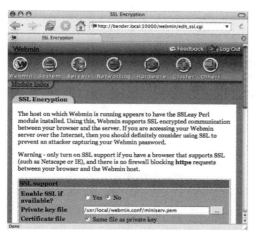

Figure F.8 The SSL Encryption page lets you switch Webmin to encrypted mode.

Figure F.9 Your Web browser will warn you about Webmin's self-signed certificate; this is normal!

3. `tar -xzf Net_SSLeay.pm-1.25.tar.gz`

Unpack the Net::SSLeay code archive.

4. `cd Net_SSLeay.pm-1.25`

Change to the source directory.

5. `./Makefile.PL`

Generate the Makefile, which controls the build process.

6. `make install`

Build and install Net::SSLeay.

7. On the Webmin Configuration page in your browser, click the SSL Encryption link to display the SSL Encryption page (**Figure F.8**).

8. Click the Yes buttons next to "Enable SSL if available?" and "Redirect non-SSL requests to SSL mode?" and then click the Save button.

9. Webmin switches to SSL mode and redirects you to the Webmin Configuration page. On your way, you'll see a warning (**Figure F.9**) about Webmin's certificate.

This certificate warning is normal; unless you install a real certificate (see the Webmin site for details), it uses a self-signed certificate, and this is what your browser is warning you about.

Tell your browser to accept the certificate (temporarily, or permanently if you won't be installing a real certificate).

continues on next page

SECURING WEBMIN

✔ Tips

■ You can also install Net::SSLeay through the Perl CPAN module. Please refer to the CPAN Web site (www.cpan.org) for details.

■ Remember to use https://*hostname*:10000/ to access Webmin if you've switched to SSL mode!

■ To stop Webmin, log in as **root** (or use su to get a **root** shell) and run the **stop** script in the Webmin installation directory (/usr/local/etc/webmin/start in our example).

■ To start Webmin, log in as **root** (or use su) and run the **start** script in the Webmin installation directory (/usr/local/etc/webmin/stop in our example).

■ Restart Webmin by combining the **stop** and **start** scripts in the Webmin installation directory. You need to do this if you've changed Webmin's configuration files (such as miniserv.conf) with a text editor instead of using Webmin itself.

INDEX

INDEX